A Model of Divine Empowerment

A Socio-rhetorical Analysis of the Relationship Between the Ascension of Christ and Leadership Empowerment in Ephesians 4:1-16

Jimmy D. Bayes, Ph.D.

A Model of Divine Empowerment: A Socio-rhetorical Analysis of the Relationship Between the Ascension of Christ and Leadership Empowerment in Ephesians 4:1-16

Copyright © 2018 *Dunamis* Publications
A Service of *Dunamis* Empowerment Foundation
Bryan, TX 77808

ISBN: 0-9965824-5-2
ISBN-13:   978-0-9965824-5-2

Printed in the United States

Unless otherwise noted, scriptures are taken from the Holy Bible, *New International Version®, NIV®*. Copyright © 1973, 1978, 1984, by Biblica, Inc.™ Used by permission of Zondervan. All rights reserved worldwide.

No part of this publication may be reproduced, stored in a retrieval system or transmitted in any form or by any means, electronic, mechanical, photocopying, recording, scanning or otherwise, except as permitted by the U.S. Copyright Act, without either the prior written or electronic permission of the author or the controlling authorities of *Dunamis* Publications.

Communication or requests to the author should be addressed electronically to director@*dunamis*empowerment.org c/o *Dunamis* Empowerment Foundation.

This publication is designed to provide accurate and authoritative information in regard to the subject matter covered. It is provided with the understanding that the author is not responsible for the results that may occur in applying the following information.

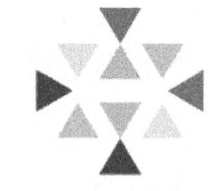

Dunamis Publications
Copyright © 2018
All rights reserved.

Dedication

I would like to dedicate this dissertation to the people whom I owe the most. First, is my Lord and Healer, Jesus Christ, who literally took me off of my death bed and strengthened me to pursue this dream.

To my wife, Michelle, who gave me this gift and has carried our family on her back while I studied and wrote. I love you.

To daughter, Sierra, she is my heart.

To daughter, Amy, she completes our family.

To Luis and Jessie Bayes, my mom and dad, to whom I owe my life in every way. Thank you for your sacrifices.

To Starla Akers, my sister; thank you for being there.

Table of Contents

A Model of Divine Empowerment i

Dedication iv

Table of Contents v

Figures ix

Tables x

Acknowledgements xi

Preface xii

Chapter 1 – Introduction 1

    Section 1.01   Power and Empowerment 3

    Section 1.02   Statement of Problem 5

    Section 1.03   Purpose of this Research 8

    Section 1.04   Research Question 13

    Section 1.05   Significance of This Study 13

    Section 1.06   Scope and Limitations 15

    Section 1.07   Definition of Terms 16

        (a)   Power and Authority 17

        (b)   Empowerment 18

        (c)   Spiritual/Divine Empowerment 18

        (d)   Theology 18

        (e)   Ascension Ministry of Christ 19

    Section 1.08   Organization of Study 19

    Section 1.09   Summary 21

Chapter 2 – Literature Review 24

    Section 1.10   Ephesians 4:1-16 24

        (a)   General Issues 25

        (b)   Specific Issues 28

Section 1.11   Power 32
    (a)   Theoretical Roots of Power 32
    (b)   Modern Conceptualization of Power 35
    (c)   Bases of Power 42
    (d)   Power in Organizational Leadership 44
    (e)   Concepts Related to Power 47

Section 1.12   Empowerment in Leadership 48
    (a)   Critical Social Empowerment 49
    (b)   Structural Empowerment 51
    (c)   Psychological Empowerment 53
    (d)   Concepts Related to Empowerment 57
    (e)   Spiritual Empowerment 58

Section 1.13   Theology and Leadership 61
    (a)   Theology Proper 63
    (b)   Christology 70
    (c)   Pneumatology 74

Section 1.14   Summary 78

Chapter 3 – Method 80

Section 1.15   Research Design 82

Section 1.16   Socio-rhetorical Analysis 82
    (a)   Inner Texture 83
    (b)   Social and Cultural Texture 84
    (c)   Sacred Texture 87

Section 1.17   Data Analysis 87

Section 1.18   Limitations of Study 88

Section 1.19   Summary 89

Chapter 4 - Results 90

Section 1.20		Socio-rhetorical Analysis of Ephesians 4:1-16	93
Section 1.21		Inner Texture Analysis	93
	(a)	Repetitive–Progressive	94
	(b)	Opening–Middle–Closing	98
	(c)	Argumentative	99
	(d)	Summary of Inner Texture Analysis	101
Section 1.22		Cultural and Social Textural Analysis	101
	(a)	Specific Categories	102
	(b)	Common Categories	107
	(c)	Final Categories	116
	(d)	Summary of Cultural and Social Texture Analysis	120
Section 1.23		Sacred Texture Analysis	120
	(a)	Deity	121
	(b)	Holy Persons	123
	(c)	Religious Community	125
	(d)	Ethics	129
	(e)	Summary of Sacred Texture	130
Section 1.24		Summary of Relevant Findings	130
Chapter 5 – Discussion			132
Section 1.25		Summary of Findings	133
Section 1.26		Toward an Integrated Theory of Empowerment	137
	(a)	Divine Empowerment	139
	(b)	Social Empowerment	141
	(c)	Structural Empowerment	143
	(d)	Psychological Empowerment	143
	(e)	Concatenated Empowerment Model	144
Section 1.27		Implications for Leadership Theory	147
	(a)	Transformational Leadership	147

	(b)	Servant Leadership	150
	(c)	Authentic Leadership	153
	(d)	Spiritual Leadership	156
	(e)	Summary	158

Section 1.28　Implications for Ecclesial Leadership 159

Section 1.29　Limitations of This Study 159

Section 1.30　Future Research 160

References 162

Appendix A 192

Appendix B 194

ABOUT THE AUTHOR 197

Figures

Figure 1: Ascension and empowerment—the relationship between the ascension of Christ and empowerment. 12

Figure 2: Multilevel (integrated) empowerment model. Reprinted from "Taking Empowerment to the Next Level: A Multiple-Level Model of Empowerment, Performance, and Satisfaction," by S. E. Seibert, S. R. Silver, and W. A. Randolph, 2004, *Academy of Management Journal, 47*(3), p. 333. Copyright by S. Seibert, S. Silver, and W. A. Randolph. 57

Figure 3: Christological events. Reprinted from *Renewal Theology: Systematic Theology from a Charismatic Perspective* (p. 381), by J. R. Williams, 1996, Grand Rapids, MI: Zondervan. Copyright 1996 by Zondervan. 71

Figure 4: Mediatorial roles (leadership). 110

Figure 5: Ephesians 4:12 (functions of the leaders). 128

Figure 6: Ephesians 4:12 (functions of the saints). 128

Figure 7: Components of divine empowerment. 137

Figure 8: Relationships of empowerment theories. 138

Figure 9: Suggested concatenated empowerment model. 146

Figure 10: Patterson's (2003) servant leader model. Reprinted from *Servant Leadership: A Theoretical Model* (p. 7), by K. Patterson, 2003, paper presented at the Servant Leadership Research Roundtable, Regent University, Virginia Beach, VA. Retrieved from www.regent.edu/acad/global/publications/sl_proceedings/2003/patterson_servant_leadership.pdf 152

Tables

TABLE 1: DETAILS OF POWER DIMENSIONS 40
TABLE 2: COMPONENTS OF STRUCTURAL EMPOWERMENT 52
TABLE 3: COMPONENTS OF PSYCHOLOGICAL EMPOWERMENT (SPREITZER, 1995). 55
TABLE 4: CATEGORIES OF ATTRIBUTES OF GOD 64
TABLE 5: LISTS OF SPIRITUAL GIFTS 75
TABLE 6: SIX KINDS OF INNER TEXTURE (V. K. ROBBINS, 1996A) 83
TABLE 7: SOCIAL RESPONSES (SPECIFIC SOCIAL TOPICS; V. K. ROBBINS, 1996A) . 85
TABLE 8: FINAL CULTURAL CATEGORIES (V. K. ROBBINS, N.D.) 86
TABLE 9: SACRED TEXTURE SUBTEXTURES (V. K. ROBBINS, 1996A) 87
TABLE 10: REPETITIVE WORDS, PHRASES, AND CONCEPTS 95
TABLE 11: DEITY 121
TABLE 12: PAUL'S EXAMPLE (*MIMESIS*) 124
TABLE 13: REFERENCES TO BODY IN EPHESIANS 126
TABLE 14: FAMILY RESEMBLANCE EMPOWERMENT THEORIES 145
TABLE 15: DIFFERENCES BETWEEN LEADERSHIP THEORIES 158
TABLE 16: OPENING–MIDDLE–CLOSING INNER TEXTURE 191

Acknowledgements

I express sincere appreciation to all the faculty and staff of Regent University who made this dissertation possible. In particular, I would like to express truthful gratitude and respect to Dr. Corné Bekker for his excellent comments and thoughtful suggestions to complete this work. Through the doctoral program, he has helped me to improve with his academic leadership and deep consideration. I also express sincere thanks to my committee members, Dr. Kathlene Patterson and Dr. Doris Gomez, for their valuable comments and suggestions. There are also others to whom I am grateful. To all of the professors in the doctoral program, Dr. Fields, Dr. Bocarnea, Dr. Carr and especially Dr. Bruce Winston, for the knowledge, wisdom, and professionalism they are always willing to share.

Preface

I began doctoral studies in Organizational Leadership (Ecclesial Leadership concentration) at Regent University in 2009. The first major project assigned was a literature review of a leadership topic. I randomly chose empowerment as the topic of my literature review. Having accumulated many good books and articles on empowerment (and a fair amount of knowledge), empowerment found its way into almost every subsequent assignment in some form. When it came time to choose a topic for my research, empowerment was an easy choice.

Empowerment is an important leadership topic because it can be argued that empowerment is the essence of leadership and empowerment will continue to be important as we continue into the Twenty-first Century. If a leaders does not do extensive study into empowerment, they are missing one of the primary aspects of being a leader. As a church leader, I am interested in empowerment from a Biblical view.

Church leaders often talk about empowerment. I have heard countless sermons on empowerment and have even preached a few myself. In the church context, empowerment is usually seen as a work of the Holy Spirit—and it is. However, I wanted to do a larger study on empowerment from a Biblical perspective for two reasons. In the first place, I had gained much knowledge about empowerment from a leadership within an organization perspective and wanted to see how it applies in the church context.

Secondly, I read "The Gospel of the Ascension" (Guynes, 1986) years ago that asserted that the ascension of Christ is more integrally linked to the activities of the Church than most Christians realize (Guynes). While the Holy Spirit empowerment is important, it would not be possible if Christ had not ascended to heaven.

I had lofty plans for researching the ascension and exaltation of Jesus in relation to Church Leadership. At first, I wanted to examine every scriptural text which related the work and the ascension of Christ directly to church leadership. My wise dissertation chairman had me narrow the scope of my research, so I decided to limit it to the New Testament. It needed to be narrower still. I considered exploring the gospels, or the book of Acts, or the epistles. I remembered that Paul's letter to Ephesus explicitly links the ascended Christ to the Leadership of the Church in the epistle to the Ephesians. This book is the finished product of my research into Ephesians 4:1-16, Leadership Empowerment, and the Ascension ministry of Christ.

Future plans include putting this material into a book with a more readable and useful format. Those interested in a scholarly treatment of Biblical leadership will appreciate the thoroughness and the research methodology of this project.

May the Ascended Lord and the Blessed Holy Spirit speak to your hearts!

Chapter 1 – Introduction

Empowerment has been an important and popular topic in organizations since the 1980s (Bass, 2008; Bass & Riggio, 2006; A. Howard, 1998; Thomas & Velthouse, 1990). Organizational specialists have believed that empowering employees contributes to positive organizational attributes and goals. Many quantitative studies have shown a positive relationship between empowering concepts (such as empowering practices, psychological empowerment, perceptions of empowerment, structural empowerment, team empowerment) and job satisfaction (Casey, Saunders, & O'Hara, 2010; Chang, Shih, & Lin, 2009; K. J. Harris, Wheeler, & Kacmar, 2009; Hocutt & Stone, 1998; Hui, Au, & Fock, 2004; Humborstad & Perry, 2011; Kirkman & Rosen, 1999; Koberg, Boss, Senjem, & Goodman, 1999; Laschinger, Finegan, Shamian, & Wilk, 2004; Laschinger, Leiter, Day, & Gilin, 2009; Ning, Zhong, Wo, & Qiujie, 2009; Pelit, Öztürk, & Arslantürk, 2011; Seibert, Silver, & Randolph, 2004; Wilkinson, 1998). Aamodt (2010) wrote that many organizations are empowering employees because they are more satisfied with their jobs if they feel they have some control over what they do. In one study, Ostroff (1992) found at the organizational level that organizations with higher average levels of job satisfaction outperformed other organizations.

Research data have also shown that the empowerment of employees positively relates to organizational commitment. Organizational commitment has been defined as an attitude or an orientation that links the identity of a person to the organization, a process by which the goals of the organization and those of the individual become congruent, involvement with a particular organization, and the perceived rewards associated with continued participation in an organization and the costs associated with leaving (Fields, 2002). Kanter (1993) theorized that people are empowered when equipped with the structure and resources leading to positive organizational outcomes such as work effectiveness and organizational commitment. Fairholm (1998) suggested that empowered employees respond to work and to crises at work with commitment because of the motivational aspect of empowerment. At least two studies have found a significant positive relationship between the perception of empowerment by nurses and their reported commitment to the organization (McDermot, Laschinger, & Shamain, 1996; B. Wilson & Laschinger, 1994). Avolio, Zhu, Koh, and Bhatia (2004) and Bartram and Casimir (2006) revealed that empowerment mediated the relationship between transformational leadership and organizational commitment and in-role performance (i.e., completes work on time, works hard, work production is of high standard, and makes good use of working time). These findings may indicate that empowerment is the most important variable in the effectiveness of transformational leadership. Avolio et al. concluded, "Empowered employees appear to be more likely to reciprocate with higher levels of commitment to their organization" (p. 962). Bartram and Casimir wrote, "It appears that in order to improve in-role performance and satisfaction with the leader, followers need to be empowered and to trust their leaders" (p. 14). If empowered employees are more satisfied with their jobs and this satisfaction translates into higher performance, it is no wonder that organizations are interested in empowerment as a concept and as a practice.

In recent years, several theories and definitions of empowerment have been formulated. In spite of the interest in empowerment, it is a daunting task to find an exact definition for empowerment (Honold, 1997). Current conceptualizations of empowerment come from three theoretical perspectives: the structural, the psychological, and the critical social (Casey et al., 2010). According to the structural theory of empowerment, followers are empowered when they are equipped with resources, information, and support necessary to accomplish an organizational goal (Kanter, 1979). Psychological empowerment is not thought to be an enduring trait but is shaped by the work environment thus is unique to the work domain. Independently, researchers in separate studies have identified four dimensions of psychological empowerment: meaning of the work, competence, self-determination, and impact on the outcomes of work (Casey et al., 2010; Spreitzer, 1995; Thomas & Velthouse, 1990). Psychological empowerment is a motivational construct that allows leaders to empower their followers by positively encouraging and influencing the meaning of their work, their competence, their self-determination, and their impact on work outcomes. The social view of empowerment considers the distribution of institutional power in an organization and is in the early stages of development (Casey et al., 2010). People are thought to be empowered as they are given more social power. "Empowerment refers to individuals, families, organizations, and communities gaining control and mastery, within the social, economic, and political contexts of their lives, in order to improve equity and quality of life" (Jennings, Parra-Medina, Messias, & McLoughlin, 2006, p. 32). Social empowerment is generally associated with people groups; thus, terms such as youth empowerment, female empowerment, minority empowerment, and gay and lesbian empowerment have appeared in literature and society. Regardless of the theoretical base of empowerment, the use and distribution of power and authority is its core.

Section 1.01   *Power and Empowerment*

An understanding of power is the key to understanding empowerment (Kuokkanen & Leino-Kilpi, 2000; Sadan, 2004). Power, as an organizational concept, has generated lively interest, debate, and occasionally confusion throughout the evolution of management thought (Hersey, Blanchard, & Natemeyer, 2001). Interest in the acquisition and use of power is as old as history. Traditional paradigms of the use of power were predominately based on strong control, originated by the Greek philosopher Plato about 2,400 years ago (Baruch, 1998). Modern thinking about power traces back to the writings of Niccollò Machiavelli (2012; i.e., *The Prince*, early 16th century) and to Thomas Hobbes (1651; i.e., *Leviathan*, middle 17th century). Both *The Prince* and *Leviathan* are considered classics of political writing and represent divergent thinking about power that continues today (Sadan, 2004). Power for Machiavelli is decentralized, is a means instead of a resource, seeks strategic advantage, and total power is the desired ends. For Hobbes, on the other hand, power is hegemonic. According to Hobbes' basic premise, there exists a total political community, the embodiment of which is the state, community, or society ordered according to a uniform principle, possessing a continuity of time and place from which the power stems (Sadan, 2004). In practice, the American government was an exercise in decentralizing power with Madison's vision of a government with separation of powers, checks and balances, and dispersion of powers across independent governing bodies (Weissberg, 1999). Key elements of Frederick Taylor's scientific management, in the 1920s, was to standardize work procedures, reduce unit costs, and disempower craft labor (Babson, 1995; F. W. Taylor, 2011). In the mid-20th century, Max Weber continued the Hobbesian approach, connecting power with concepts of authority and rule. He defined power as the probability that an actor within a social relationship (community or government) would be in a position to carry out his will despite resistance to it. This activation of power is dependent on a person's will, even in opposition to another's will (Sadan, 2004).

Seminal works about power by French and Raven (2001), Kanter (1993), and Burns (1978) have made great contributions to contemporary organizational and leadership theory, especially pertaining to the use of power and empowerment. In their article, *The Bases of Social Power* (first published in 1959), French and Raven (2001) explicated the use of power in a social context and defined five bases of social power: reward power, coercive power, legitimate power, referent power, and expert power. These power bases have formed the foundation of many leadership theories since it was first published. In *Men and Women of the Corporation* (first printed in 1977), Kanter (1993) defined power as the ability to get things done, to mobilize resources, and to get and use whatever it is that a person needs for the goal he or she is attempting to meet. This definition forms the basis for structural empowerment theory.

James MacGregor Burns' book, *Leadership*, published in 1978, is about power as much as it about leadership. Burns used Weber's definition of power, then addressed the psychological aspect of power that makes three assumptions: (a) power is a relationship and not an entity to be passed around like a baton or hand grenade and (b) power involves intention or purpose of both the power holder and the power recipient; therefore, (c) it is collective, not merely the behavior of one person. Burns' ideas regarding power and leadership are the basis of the theory of transformational leadership. These works have provided the theoretical understanding about the use of power in modern leadership and organizational theory and empowerment as a leadership construct.

Drawing from these sources, in general terms, power is having the ability and/or resources to accomplish desired outcomes and to control one's environment (Kanter, 1993; Salancik & Pfeffer, 2001; Weissberg, 1999); and possessing power means the ability to get others to do something or to change their behavior (Burns, 1978; Hersey et al., 2001; Ivancevich, Konopaske, & Matteson, 2008). Empowerment is much harder to synthesize and there is no universally accepted integrated theory of empowerment. However, a reductionist view can be stated that empowerment is when organizations give their members the ability to accomplish organizational goals or when an individual gives another individual the ability to accomplish tasks.

Section 1.02   Statement of Problem

The term *empowerment* has been extensively used in Christian leadership literature but often has been ill defined and conceptualized. Many books on Christian leadership use the term *empower* or empowerment but often do not offer a definition or explanation of the term, assuming that the reader understands how the concept is used. Some Christian writers have used the term empowerment in the same vein as writers in organizational development. Herrington, Bonen, and Furr (2000) applied Kotter's (1996) change process in church contexts. Stage 6 of the change process is to empower the key leaders. Kotter stated that communicating a sensible vision to employees, making structures compatible with the vision, providing needed training, aligning information and personal systems to the vision, and confronting forces that undercut the change process are empowering elements. Herrington et al. used Kotter's empowering process but specifically defined empowerment structurally with two components: (a) to establish a new model for leadership within the congregation and (b) to remove obstacles that would prevent leaders from serving effectively. They gave participation in decisions as an example of empowerment. Although they wrote in a Christian context, their definition was based more upon organizational theory, such as force field analysis, than upon Christian ideology or biblical principles.

In his book about leadership in a Christian context, Ford (1991) used Bennis and Nanus' (2003) four strategies for taking charge: vision, communication, trust, and empowerment (they referred to empowerment as deployment of self). Bennis and Nanus did not define empowerment as such but indicated that a key to effective leadership is empowerment or power reciprocal. This gives the impression of allowing the involvement of subordinates in planning and decision making, but later they listed significance, competence, community, and enjoyment as components of empowering people (Ford adhered to Bennis and Nanus' concepts closely). These components are elements of psychological empowerment—not structural empowerment. In both cases, a more specific definition of empowerment would better serve their purposes.

Some writers have attempted to address the divine aspect of leadership and leadership empowerment. Elliston (1992) conceptualized empowerment in terms of authority. He stated that the Holy Spirit "empowers, that is, delegates the right to use His power to influence in a variety of ways which are described in Scripture as spiritual gifts" (p. 124). When leaders develop new leaders, Elliston wrote that existing leaders mirror the work of the Holy Spirit empowering the new leaders by delegating authority to them to lead— to influence toward God's purposes. He defined empowerment as the process of enabling, equipping, and allowing (emerging leaders) to make a significant contribution in a situation and then recognizing that contribution. Thus, the established leader acts as moderating influence between God and the emerging leader until the emerging leader reaches maturity.

In a doctoral dissertation, Campbell (2005) attempted to develop a model of leadership development based on a theological and organizational process of empowerment viewed from a theological perspective emphasizing the Holy Spirit's role in the empowerment process. Building from the Greek words for power (*dunamis*) and authority (*exousia*) and understanding that *power* is the strength, ability, or authority to exercise control over a situation, environment, or person, Campbell posited that to empower someone is to give that person the authority, ability, or strength to control or influence surrounding circumstances. Campbell offered examples of empowerment from the Old Testament (i.e., Moses, Elijah, Elisha, prophets, and priests) and New Testament examples (i.e., Jesus, the disciples, and Paul) but offered little insight on how God empowers other than stating, "The Holy Spirit delegates His power to emerging leaders in the form of spiritual gifts" (p. 14).

Christian leaders have acknowledged there is a divine aspect to leadership empowerment and have attempted to address this mystery. Many writers have insisted that empowerment (or receiving power) comes from closeness to God (e.g., Dorman, 1985; Fee, 1994, 1996; Miller, 2008; Wilkes, 1998). Other writers have attributed empowerment to the work of the Holy Spirit (e.g., Dodd, 2003; Hammet, 2005), although they did not explain how this empowerment happens other than to use phrases such as connected to God; aligned with God; dependence on the Spirit's gifting and empowerment; being Spirit-led; and being renewed in the person, presence, and power of the Holy Spirit. Yet, other Christian writers have made general statements about being empowered by God such as "Jesus appeared to them with a word of empowerment and a directive of mission" (Stetzer & Rainer, 2010, p. 84). The point is not to argue with these valid statements but to show the lack of conceptualizing the divine aspect of empowerment.

Pentecostals and Charismatics almost universally attribute divine empowerment to the baptism in the Holy Spirit (e.g., Bottoms, 2011; Kärkkäinen, 2002a; Keener, 1996, 2001, 2007; Macchia, 2006, 2008; Miller, 2005; Stronstad, 1984) for the primary purpose of evangelization/mission/witness (e. g. Bottoms, 2011; Dorries, 2006; Fettke, 2011; Keener, 1996, 1997, 2001, 2007, 2009; Klaus & Triplett, 1991; Land, 2010; Macchia, 2006; Menzies, 2004; Miller, 2005; Pate, 1991; Yong, 2006). Other purposes for this Spirit empowerment are help in doing God's will (e.g., Miller, 2008); doing exploits, signs, and wonders (e.g., Keener, 1996, 1997); and living an obedient, holy, and pure life (e.g., Cerillo, 1991; Keener, 1997; Miller, 2009). Acts 1:8 is foundational for the Pentecostal/Charismatic notion of spirit empowerment. This verse explicitly promises power (*dunamis*) and connects that power with being witnesses (*martureo*) to the ends (*exousia*) of the earth (*gé*). In Acts 2.4f, the promise of power is clearly and unarguably fulfilled. This explicit promise and fulfillment of power in Acts 1-2 has resulted in minimizing the attention toward the empowering work of Christ.

Therefore, the problem is twofold. The first aspect of the problem is the lack of an integrated definition of empowerment that includes all aspects—social, structural, psychological, and especially the spiritual. Second, and most important, empowerment in a Christian or church context is generally seen as the work of the Holy Spirit, and the role of Christ in the empowering process has been ignored at worst and given a background role at best. Although ecclesial leaders and theologians speak of the finished work of Christ, the ascended Lord still plays an active role in leadership empowerment.

Section 1.03   Purpose of this Research

This study examines the Christological connection to leadership empowerment. Specifically, this study analyzes the relationship between the ascension/exaltation of Christ and leadership functions listed in Ephesians 4:11 (i.e., apostle, prophet, evangelist, pastor, and teacher) with special attention to the empowering aspect of the relationship. This relationship is examined in light of the current study of organizational empowerment and leadership theories. The findings of this study aid in the understanding of the spiritual (divine) aspect of leadership empowerment and assist in developing a comprehensive and integrated theory of leadership empowerment. This study addresses the critical need for leadership development and succession in the church today.

The New Testament does not give explicit instructions for the structure and the function of church leadership. It is not easy to classify the various ministers and officers mentioned in the New Testament (Duffield & Van Cleave, 1987). While there are no models of church leadership plainly given in scripture (Warrington, 2008), three Greek words found in Paul's writings give an indication of explicit leadership assigned to the church: elder (Titus 1:5, *presbuteros*), overseer (1 Tim 3:1, *episkopos*), and deacon (1 Tim 3:8, *diakonos*). Nevertheless, it is generally thought that elders and overseers (sometimes translated as bishops) are synonymous. Scriptural evidence that elder and overseer are one office is convincing. Paul commissioned Titus to appoint elders and then described them immediately as overseers (Titus 1:5-7); when Paul called the elders of the church of Ephesus to meet him at Miletus, he described their position as overseers (Acts 20:17, 18); when Paul listed qualifications for the overseer and deacons he did not mention elders (1 Tim 3:1-13); and in Philippians 1:1, Paul mentioned only overseers and deacons (Ryrie, 1999). *Elders* emphasizes maturity and dignity, usually denoting an older person, and *overseer* denotes the work of shepherding by the elder. Both terms are basically the same, but elder signifies the office, whereas overseer emphasizes function (Enns, 1989). Erickson (1998) suggested that the titles of overseer, elder, and pastor are different names for the same office but designate different functions or different aspects of the ministry. The third office or ministry, deacon, means servant or to serve.

Clarke (2008) argued against forming an ecclesiology based on these titles for six reasons: (a) it often fails to identify the presence, influence, or type of leader in the communities where Paul did not use these titles; (b) it gives undue significance to these titles to the neglect of other terms used elsewhere; (c) these titles give us little information about the actual function of these posts; (d) this approach is often used in conjunction with an interpretive model of straight-line institutionalizing development that has not sufficiently evaluated that these titles occur very rarely in Paul's corpus; (e) insufficient distinction is often made between the letters written to individuals whose concern is local church government and order and those letters that are written to larger communities, where there is less need to mention titled officers or discuss their qualifications; and (f) analysis of leadership structures is often pursued independently from critical reflection on the size, structure, and congregational context of the historical church communities. It is not clear the specific function or hierarchy of these ministry offices and functions, but it does indicate a new way for God's people to accomplish God's mission (*Missio Dei*), ultimately separating from the Jewish temple worship and traditions.

Historically, the church has organized around three types of government: episcopal where authority resides with the bishop to varying degrees, presbyterian where authority rests with a body of representatives, and congregational that makes the local congregation the seat of authority; a possible fourth type is combining elements of each (Erickson, 1998). It should be noted that power and authority are the distinguishing variables between these types of church government. Although the Bible does not teach one particular type of government, scriptural support can be found for each. Considering the lack of specifics for a biblical leadership model, leaders have looked for scriptures that address leadership issues. Paul listed five leadership ministries of the church: apostle, prophet, evangelist, pastor, and teacher (Ephes 4:11). Although the word leader or leadership is not used to describe these ministries, they are readily associated with leadership development in Christian literature (e.g., Elliston, 1992; Ford, 1991; Hemphill, 1992; Warrington, 2008). This pericope (Ephes 4:1-16) assumes an already established functional leadership group (Barentsen, 2011). While definitions and understanding of each of the five ministries can be deduced from scripture, the social relationships between each of these ministries and the offices of elder, overseer, and deacon is less obvious. Pentecost seemed to have brought about a decentralizing of authority and a democratizing of power, especially in the divine impartation of ministry gifts. No longer was God's people under a Levitical priesthood with centralized authority and structure, they now had the priesthood of every believer.

The exact form of church government and leadership in the New Testament remains obscure, yet we see the New Testament church as a powerful and organized body that was successful in planting churches and making converts throughout the Roman Empire. The key to the success of the church was the result of Pentecost. Pentecost initiated the equipping for ministry through gifts often referred to as spiritual gifts (Rom 12:6-8; 1 Cor 12:8-10, 28-30; Ephes 4:11). Every Christian is given at least one ministry gift (Hemphill, 1992; Ryrie, 1999; C. P. Wagner, 1979). The gifts or ministries listed in Ephesians 4:11 are often listed alongside the other lists of spiritual gifts (Duffield & Van Cleave, 1987; Enns, 1989; Thiessen, 1979). However, the gifts listed in Ephesians 4:11 are distinct from the other lists in two main ways. First, these are persons who are given to the church (Barentsen, 2011; Enns, 1989; Erickson, 1998; Holdcroft, 1999; Warrington, 2008); and these gifts of persons are given, distributed, or allotted by Jesus Christ (Buswell, 1962; Fee, 2007; Ryrie, 1999).

Paul stated that these ministries or functions (Bayes, 2010) were given by Christ who had ascended and is sitting at the right hand of God, thus indicating the direct relationship of Christ's ascension to the leadership gifts of apostle, prophet, evangelist, pastor, and teacher:

> But to each one of us grace was given according to the measure of Christ's gift. Therefore it says, "When He ascended on high, He led captive a host of captives and He gave gifts to men." (Now this *expression*, "He ascended," what does that mean except that He also had descended into the lower parts of the earth? He who descended is Himself also He who ascended far above all the heavens, that He might fill all things.) And He gave some *as* apostles, and some *as* prophets, and some *as* evangelists, and some *as* pastors and teachers, for the equipping of the saints for the work of service, to the building up of the body of Christ; until we all attain to the unity of the faith, and of the knowledge of the Son of God, to a mature man, to the measure of the stature which belongs to the fullness of Christ. (Ephes 4:7-12, New American Standard)

According to scripture, Christ ascended and is now seated at the right hand of God (Ephes 1:20; Hebrews 12:2). *Session*, from the Latin word *sessio*, refers to Christ *sitting* on the right hand of the Father (Guynes, 1986). "Session of Christ at the right hand of God means . . . the investment of power and authority, dominion, and rule" (Williams, 1996, Vol. 1, p. 403). Session is for the sake of exercising power and authority. The basic definition of empowerment is to give power and/or authority to another (Campbell, 2005); therefore, Christ's ascension (and ultimate session) is directly tied to the giving of power (empowerment) to the apostle, prophet, evangelist, pastor, and teacher in Ephesians 4:11.

The relationship of Christ's ascension and session to the ministry gifts are diagramed in Figure 1.

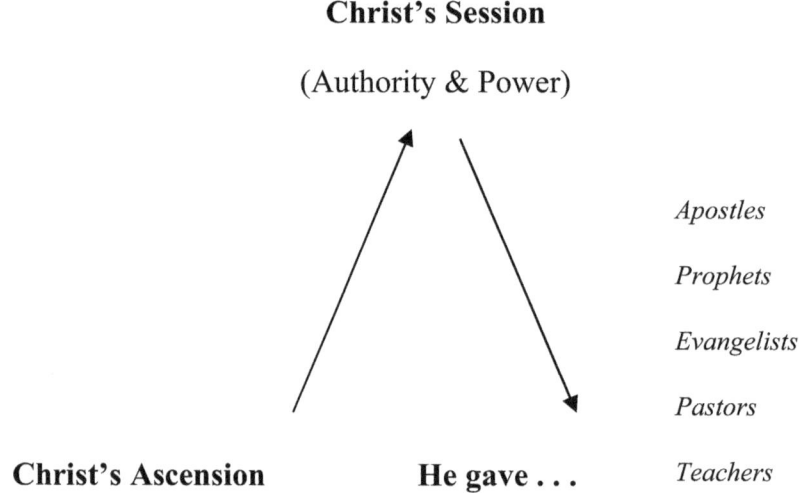

Figure 1: Ascension and empowerment—the relationship between the ascension of Christ and empowerment.

The ascension of Christ as a Christological topic has been neglected in the study of theology. Often it is relegated to an exclamation point at the end of the study of Christ or as an event that takes place before the Second Coming. In *The Gospel of the Ascension*, Guynes (1986) articulated the neglect of this very important doctrine:

> The ascension of Jesus Christ as compared to His birth, death, and resurrection has not been the topic of a great amount of preaching, teaching, or writing. It has been looked upon as post-climatic to the primary redemptive work of Christ, i.e., His death and resurrection. In most minds the ascension is His "going away," the losing of Jesus from the earthly scene. The mental concept was and is that Jesus, having completed His task, returned to heaven to await the final outcome. (p. 1)

Whereas the divine or spiritual aspect of empowerment has not been studied in organizational literature and the nature of divine empowerment in scripture has not adequately addressed the Christological link, the purpose of this study is to examine the empowering aspect of the Christological event of Jesus' ascent and exaltation to the leadership ministries in Ephesians 4:11. This relationship is examined in light of current empowerment and leadership theory.

Section 1.04   Research Question

A research question is asked to act as a guide and focuses the study (Creswell, 2009; Patton, 2002). The objective of this study is achieved by addressing one research question: What is the empowering relationship between the ascended Christ and the leadership ministries in Ephesians 4:1-16 (see Appendix A)? This question is addressed using Socio-rhetorical analysis of the chosen text. Specifically, inner texture, cultural and social textures, and sacred texture analysis are used to mine the text for information that answers the research question. Inner texture, cultural and social textures, and sacred texture analysis are subsets of Socio-rhetorical analysis (V. K. Robbins, 1996a, 1996b).

Section 1.05   Significance of This Study

This research addresses several areas of leadership study. First, this study addresses leader–follower empowerment as it is theorized and practiced in organizations. Additionally, this study addresses the biblical or divine aspect of leadership empowerment. This research is significant in that it addresses several areas of leadership that have not previously been studied. The result of this study furthers the understanding of leadership empowerment.

Several researchers have proposed integrated models of empowerment for organizational leadership (Cho, 2008; Laschinger, Gilbert, Smith, & Leslie, 2010; T. L. Robbins, Crino, & Fredendall, 2002) or a multilevel approach to empowerment (Seibert et al., 2004), but to date, there are no integrated models of empowerment that include a divine component of empowerment. This research is significant in that it contributes toward an integrated model of empowerment that includes the social, structural, psychological, and spiritual aspects. An integrated model of empowerment helps toward a more complete taxonomy of power and empowerment and adds to the nomological network for the construct validity of empowerment in future quantitative research.

Additionally, there exists a gap between the perception of empowerment between leaders and followers (Applebaum & Honeggar, 1998). That is, employees' perception of their empowerment does not always correlate to the perception the leader has of his or her own empowering efforts. Often, empowering actions of leaders can be misinterpreted as micromanagement or manipulation. A misunderstanding of these empowering efforts and motives can lead to leader–employee mistrust. A better understanding and an integrated model of empowerment will help close the gap between leader-empowering actions and followers' perception of their own empowerment.

Organizational leaders have used empowerment models as a pattern for empowering their followers; however, these models do not include a spiritual component. An integrative model that includes a spiritual aspect will be more likely used in Christian organizations and churches. An understanding of this divine or spiritual empowerment assists in taking the concept of empowerment from descriptive to prescriptive. This has great implications for leadership development in the Christian context.

Spiritual empowerment as currently conceptualized is often defined heuristically and tends to be ideological and subjective. This study is significant because it defines empowerment from a divine perspective. A better understanding of empowerment from a biblical perspective helps move the conceptualizing of divine or spiritual empowerment toward objectivity and, therefore, be of practical use to ecclesial leaders.

This study introduces a divine aspect to the current understanding of leader empowerment in leadership theories. Transformational leadership, spiritual leadership, servant leadership, and authentic leadership explicitly state that empowerment is a significant aspect of their theories. (Empowerment is implicit in other leadership theories such as Situational Leadership II, leader–member exchange theory, and Theory Y). Leadership theories with an explicit inclusion of empowerment are considered in light of theories of empowerment, including this proposed model of divine empowerment.

Finally, it has been shown that the cultural value of power distance moderates the effect of empowerment on job satisfaction (Eylon & Au, 1999; Hui et al., 2004). Given the cultural differences regarding power distance, there is a need for an integrated model of leadership empowerment. This model should include an understanding of the divine aspect of empowerment. Questions in a cross-cultural context—such as should employers empower employees, in what ways do our employees perceive empowerment, and how can we best empower our employees?—depend upon a clear understanding of empowerment.

Section 1.06   Scope and Limitations

This study adds to the knowledge regarding the concept of empowerment as an organizational construct. The particular addition is the divine component of empowerment, specifically the empowering aspect of Christ's act of ascension found in Ephesians 4:1-16 in relationship to the leadership ministries listed in verse 11. Therefore, the scope of this study is limited to the mentioned pericope.

Other scriptures allude to a connection between Christ's ascension ministry and the empowering or equipping of ministry leaders. One, for instance, is the Great Commission found in Matthew 28:18-20 (New International Version):

> Then Jesus came to them and said, "All authority in heaven and on earth has been given to me. Therefore go make disciples of all nations, baptizing them in the name of the Father and of the Son and of the Holy Spirit, and teaching them to obey everything I have commanded you. And surely I am with you always, to the very end of the age."

It is significant that Jesus spoke these words to his disciples after the resurrection and before he ascended. He was about to ascend to heaven, yet he promised the disciples that he would be with them for all time. This indicates an ongoing relationship between the disciples and the ascended and exalted Christ. Also, when Jesus gave his disciples authority and sent them out to minister (Matt 10; Luk 9) foreshadows the day when the disciples would be in the world ministering and Christ would be sitting at the Father's right hand in heaven. There is also a direct connection between the events of Pentecost and Christ's ascension ministry. Jesus told his disciples that it was best for them that he went away (John 16:7), because if he did not go, he could not send the Holy Spirit. Then Jesus promised that when he departed, he would send the Holy Spirit. Luke is more specific about Christ's promise to send the Holy Spirit in Acts 1:8 (preascension) and the fulfillment of this promise in Acts 2 (postascension). Therefore, any act of the Spirit empowerment is in a sense an empowering act of the ascended Christ. Though several texts offer insight into the relationship between Christ's ascension ministry and leadership empowerment, Ephesians 4:1-16 has the clearest connection and, therefore, is the focus of this study.

Exegesis is the historical investigation into the meaning of the biblical text. This study investigates a portion of scripture taken from Paul's epistle to the church in Ephesus. The epistles are, for the most part, comprised of paragraphs of argument or exhortation. The exegete must trace the flow of the writer's argument in order to understand any sentence or paragraph (Fee, 1983). To trace the flow of the argument, this research applies Socio-rhetorical analysis to the text of Ephesians 4:1-16. Because there are multiple textures in a given text (V. K. Robbins, 1996a), several textures are analyzed in this study. DeSilva (2004) pointed out that Bible interpreters will not always use all the resources of Socio-rhetorical interpretation and that some textures are more suited to one kind of text than to another. The scope of this study is purposely narrow, focusing on one portion of scripture and just applying several textures of Socio-rhetorical analysis, in order to add to the present knowledge of Christ's active participation in the empowering process of Christian leaders by examining Ephesians 4:1-16.

Section 1.07   *Definition of Terms*

Every research project and every researcher uses words in a particular fashion. Often, words can have several meanings or connotations. Such is the case with this study. This study defines the concept of empowerment from a spiritual or divine point of view. Therefore, this section highlights and defines terms that are important to this research.

(a) Power and Authority

The term *power* is an important concept when researching the construct of empowerment. Oftentimes, this term incorporates both the concepts of power and authority. This research uses each concept distinctively, and when both concepts are intended both are used (i.e., power and authority). As previously noted, power—taken from the Greek word *dunamis*—is having the ability and/or resources to accomplish desired outcomes and to control one's environment (Kanter, 1993; Salancik & Pfeffer, 2001; Weissberg, 1999); and possessing power means the ability to get others to do something or to change their behavior (Burns, 1978; Hersey et al., 2001; Ivancevich et al., 2008).

Authority (*exousia*) is a closely related concept to that of power (*dunamis*). Nevertheless, there are differences between the two concepts. Authority has several general meanings. The first, similar to *dunamis*, is the power to do something because nothing stands in the way. The distinguishing factor between the two is that power/*dunamis* is intrinsic ability, and authority *exousia* is power based on extrinsic considerations. The second meaning is that of authorization. This power has been conferred by a superior power, court, or norm. Bromiley (1979) suggested that the right expressed by *exousia* is not abstract but carries with it real power, even though this is extrinsically rather than intrinsically derived. The third meaning, similar to the first and also similar to *dunamis*, is authority that is innate such as the authority of a ruler or king. This kind of authority can be rendered power just as easily as authority. The final meaning of authority is the same as *office*. The main concept is that of wielding a conferred power. For this study, references to authority indicate an authorization or power conferred by an outside source—or legitimate power.

(b) Empowerment

Empowerment is the primary topic of this study. However, as seen in the literature review in Chapter 2, empowerment is defined from several theoretical points of view and is fully defined according to the theoretical basis as this study progresses. Unless otherwise defined, the basic meaning of empowerment is to give power and/or authority to another (Campbell, 2005).

(c) Spiritual/Divine Empowerment

Use of the word *spiritual* has become vogue in contemporary leadership writing (Fry, 2003, 2008; Fry & Cohen, 2009; Korac-Kakababse, Kouzmin, & Kakababse, 2002; McCormick, 1994; Poole, 2008). Spirituality used in organizational literature usually takes on a general meaning, such as the presence of a relationship with a higher power or being that affects the way in which one operates in the world and is defined broader than any single formal or organized religion with its prescribed tenants, dogma, and doctrines (Fry, 2003). However, for the purposes of this study, spiritual as a descriptor of empowerment means that it is attributed specifically to the Holy Spirit.

The use of the word *divine* has also been used to describe empowerment (Michel et al., 2012; Petrucci, 2011). Sometimes the words spiritual and divine are used interchangeably. For the purpose of this study, divine empowerment is designated for the work of the Trinity collectively or of Christ specifically in the empowerment process to distinguish it from spiritual empowerment as a direct work of the Holy Spirit.

(d) Theology

Enns (1989) pointed out that there are several ways *theology* is studied: Biblical theology takes its material in a historically oriented manner to arrive at theology, historical theology examines Christian theology throughout the centuries, and dogmatic theology reflects the interpretation of a particular ecclesial body. Nevertheless, references to theology usually refer to systematic theology where biblical material is collected, arranged, compared, exhibited, and defended according to theological topics. These topics include bibliology (study of the Bible), theology proper (study of God), Christology (study of Jesus Christ), pneumatology (study of the Holy Spirit), ecclesiology (study of the Church), and eschatology (study of last things). Theology comes from the Greek words *theos* meaning god and *logos* meaning word. Theology as a discipline has numerous definitions: the doctrine of God (Thiessen, 1979), the rational interpretation of the Christian faith (Ryrie, 1999), the study that deals directly with God and His relationship to the world and to man (Buswell, 1962), discourse about God (McGrath, 1994), and the ordered consideration or study of God (Garrett, 1990).

(e) Ascension Ministry of Christ

The term *ascension ministry of Christ* or *ascension ministry* is used in this study, especially in the context of the empowering work of Jesus. This term was coined by Delmar Guynes (1986) and combines the distinct works of Christ's ascension, exaltation, and session into a single concept that captures the continuing work of Christ. Guynes explained,

> The ascension truth is vital to all aspects of the redemptive work of Christ. In this sense the ascension and exaltation of Christ are the culmination of all redemptive work, linking all other redemptive events into one unbreakable chain and fashioning an inseparable tandem of inter-related redemptive truth. (p. 7)

This study refers to the ascension ministry when making reference to the postresurrection and current ministry of Christ; otherwise, the individual term (ascension, exaltation, or session) for the specific redemptive act is used when referring to the specific event.

Section 1.08   Organization of Study

All research is built upon previous research findings and theories. The literature review (Chapter 2) builds the foundation for which the findings of this study are laid. The primary area of interest is in the construct of empowerment, but there are three theoretical disciplines on which this research depends. The construct of empowerment is complex, and there has been much study in this area. Empowerment theories are dependent upon the conceptualizations of power. Therefore, the first area of literature reviewed is the topic of power. There has also been much written about power, but this study reviews the important works and research that have come about the past 50 years.

The second area of interest is in empowerment itself. Empowerment theories are considered: critical social empowerment, structural empowerment, and psychological empowerment. The purpose in reviewing literature regarding empowerment is twofold: discover the theoretical bases for empowerment (how it has been conceptualized and how empowerment theories have been used in research) and develop a taxonomy that includes all theoretical aspects of empowerment. The third area of interest for this study is theology as it relates to leadership. Theology has not been used to a large degree in leadership studies (Ayers, 2006), but there is some recent leadership research based in theology (Crowther, 2012). Conceptions of leadership should begin with the doctrine of the Trinity (Horsthuis, 2011), therefore theology as it relates to leadership is reviewed (i.e., theology proper, Christology, and pneumatology). A thorough review of literature on these topics is necessary to determine the empowering relationship between the leadership ministries in Ephesians 4:11 and the ascension ministry of Christ.

To extract data from Ephesians 4:1-16, this study utilizes Socio-rhetorical analysis developed by Vernon K. Robbins. Socio-rhetorical criticism is an approach to literature that focuses on values, convictions, and beliefs both in the texts we read and in the world in which we live (V. K. Robbins, 1996a). V. K. Robbins (1996a) stated that socio as a prefix refers to the rich resources of modern anthropology and sociology that Socio-rhetorical criticism brings to the interpretation of a text. The aim of good interpretation is to get at the plain meaning of the text (Fee & Stewart, 1982). Socio-rhetorical analysis helps the interpreter consider all aspects of the communication process, including the social aspect to arrive at the meaning of the text. Theologians do not agree upon the nature of the church (*ekklēsia*) or assembly (Giles, 1995). Whether scripture reveals the church as the assembly of God's people or merely an assembly of people or if the church is revealed as a formally organized structured society or an informal interpersonal community (Dulles, 2002), the social aspect of scripture cannot be denied. Therefore, we need to explore how a passage orients its audience to the world of everyday life and how it seeks to shape their relationships and interactions with one another (DeSilva, 2004).

The rhetorical aspect of Socio-rhetorical criticism refers to the way language in a text is a means of communication among people (V. K. Robbins, 1996a). Whether you believe that Paul's epistles were private letters, public epistles, or treatises (Osborne, 2006), they are without doubt a communication tool. People use language in many ways. They use it to establish relationships, to set some people off as enemies, to negotiate with kinsmen, to pursue interests, and so forth. Socio-rhetorical criticism integrates the ways people use language with the ways they live in the world (V. K. Robbins, 1996a). V. K. Robbins (1996b) used the metaphor of tapestry to describe how Socio-rhetorical criticism works. He identified five levels (i.e., textures) of social and rhetorical analysis: inner texture (getting inside the text), intertexture (entering the world of a text), social and cultural texture (living with a text in the world), ideological texture (sharing interests in texts), and sacred texture (seeing the divine in the text).

The method of research is a qualitative, hermeneutical approach toward mining the text for the understanding of leadership empowerment in this text as a part of the larger body of scripture. This method of qualitative research is especially useful toward the understanding of biblical texts (Patton, 2002). Specifically, this research examines the inner texture, the social and cultural textures, and sacred texture of Socio-rhetorical analysis as conceived by V. K. Robbins (1996a, 1996b). Some textures are more suited to one kind of text than others (DeSilva, 2004); this study applies only the subtextures that are relevant to the stated purpose of this study.

Section 1.09   Summary

Leadership is a social relationship with three key components: leaders, followers, and the context in which they interact. One cannot lead without power (Nye, 2010). Leadership essentially is about how and why people use their power. Issues of power may be the single most important leadership topic, yet the concept of power is an elusive concept to define and categorize.

Power is everywhere. We see power at work every day. We can hardly interact with a group without sensing power relationships. Kids in the playground, high school freshmen, new employees, and corporate executives are all cognizant of power. Power is a dynamic that is constantly at move. Some are using it, some are wanting it, and each of us are aware of it. There are many ideas of what make people powerful—how people get, use, and keep power. One example of the diverse views of leadership distinguishes between what is referred to as soft power and hard power. Soft power, attraction and persuasion, is the ability to shape the preferences of others to want what you want while hard power is coercive, rests on inducements and threats, and has the ability to hire and fire; and smart power is the ability to combine soft and hard power into an effective strategy (Nye, 2010; E. J. Wilson, 2008).

Power sharing is known as empowerment. Questions regarding the sharing of power abound: when do we empower, what kind of power should be shared, whom should we empower, how do we empower, do they want to be empowered, and will I lose control if I empower others? Some see power in a social context that categorizes groups of people with power and those without power. Empowerment in this context, critical social empowerment, states that groups and individuals seek control and mastery over the social, economic, and political aspects of their lives (Jennings et al., 2006). Others see true empowerment by equipping others with knowledge and resources and to be given sufficient knowledge, guidance, and support to be successful for the organization and as an individual (Kanter, 1979). This empowerment is referred to as structural empowerment. One of the most popularly conceived and often used theories of empowerment is psychological empowerment. This motivational aspect of empowerment encourages followers and helps build their self-efficacy and competence; thus, they have the feeling of power (Conger & Kanungo, 1988).

Empowerment is a common topic in Christian literature. Empowerment, in this context, is usually conceived in two ways. The first is an organizational type empowerment where the leader empowers followers structurally by giving the proper information, resources, and support to accomplish challenging organizational goals. The second concept of empowerment is spiritual or divine empowerment. This type of empowerment is not well defined but generally understood by the context. Yet, this allows for a subjective understanding of how God empowers followers. Many times, empowerment is seen strictly as a work of the Holy Spirit, and the work of Christ in the empowering process is largely missing. There are no comprehensive integrated models of empowerment that includes the divine aspect. This study examines the Christological aspect of empowerment in leadership ministries and suggests a model of divine empowerment and its inclusion into an integrated model of empowerment.

Chapter 2 – Literature Review

Literature reviews are used to frame the problem of the research study to the larger ongoing dialogue of the issues being considered (Creswell, 2009). The current review examines several topics that aid in the understanding of the ideas and theories concerned in this study before exploring their relationships. Whereas the current study examines the relationship of Christ's ascension and leadership empowerment in Ephesians 4:1-16, it begins with an examination of current literature concerning Ephesians 4:1-16. The primary focus of this research is leadership empowerment; therefore, this review of literature focuses upon power, empowerment, and theology as they lay the theoretical foundation for studying the empowerment of followers in contemporary leadership research. As with most theoretical constructs and concepts, there is little agreement and many divergent ideas regarding power and empowerment. Although power is an ancient concept (Dahl, 1957) and theoretical conceptualizing about power can be traced back to Plato (Baruch, 1998), this review presents only the thinking about power in modern times. The many definitions of power reveal differing approaches to the ontology, sources, substance, and uses of power.

Following the critical review of power, the conceptions of leadership empowerment are reviewed. It logically follows that if the conception of power is diverse, then the conceptualization of empowerment is also diverse. Literature regarding modern theories and use of empowerment as a leadership construct is examined. Finally, whereas the need and use of biblical theology in contemporary leadership research has increased (Ayers, 2006; Crowther, 2012) and given that this research examines the relationship of a theological topic (Christ's ascension and session) to leadership empowerment, theology as it relates to leadership research is reviewed.

Section 1.10   Ephesians 4:1-16

This section briefly reviews literature regarding the text of Ephesians 4:1-16. This review addresses some issues specific to this pericope but also addresses some general issues to the epistle of Ephesians that are germane to this study.

(a) General Issues

The six chapters of Ephesians are naturally divided into two divisions. Chapters 1-3 comprise the first division; Chapters 4-6 comprise the second division. The pericope under consideration in this study, Ephesians 4:1-16, is the opening section of the second division of Ephesians. The "Amen" at the end of Chapter 3 and the change to direct exhortation at the beginning of Chapter 4 are clear division markers (Lincoln, 1990). Scholars have noted that the first division is more theological or doctrinal, and the second division is ethical or practical (Ballenger, 1997; Foulkes, 1983; Lincoln, 1990; Patzia, 1990; Stern, 1992). Gundry (2010) wrote that Paul detailed the privileges of Christians (Ephes 1:3-3:21), then he detailed the responsibilities that come along with those privileges (Ephes 4:1-6:24). The first half of the letter is distinguished by its epistolary use of liturgical forms and elements of anamnesis—the memorial character of the Eucharist or the passion, resurrection, and ascension of Christ (Lincoln, 1990). The second half is given almost entirely to ethical appeal—"to walk in a manner worthy of the calling with which you have been called" (Ephes 4:1b).

This pericope is the introduction to the paraenetic nature of the second division of Ephesians. Paraenesis, a New Testament innovation to epistolary form, is a section of moral commands and normally comes after the doctrinal section of an epistle (Ryken, 1987). Paraenesis is used to describe a text containing a series of admonitions, usually ethical and eclectic in nature; it exhorts or gives advice (Huey & Corely, 1983; Schreiner, 1990). In Ephesians 4:1-16, the readers are exhorted to play their part in maintaining unity in the church, which is on its way to maturity through its ministers and the love of its members. Everything that follows this section describes how they should live this worthy calling. In 4:17-24, they are urged to live as those who have been taught the Christian tradition and are members of the community. The next two sections (4:25-5:14) indicate that their words and deeds should reflect a distinct difference between their old lives and new. They are exhorted to live wisely and to live in the power of the Spirit resulting in corporate edification and worship (5:15-20). Relationships should be modeled after the relationship of Christ and the church (5:21-6:9). The paraenesis culminates in 6:10-20 with a call to the readers to be strong and stand firm in the spiritual battle against the powers of evil that are arrayed against them and to engage in constant prayer (Lincoln, 1990).

Ephesians 4 begins "Therefore I, the prisoner of the Lord, implore you" (v. 1). This is a reference back to the beginning of the book (1:1) where Paul is named as the author of this work. Paul's autograph is repeated in 3:1. In spite of Paul's signature on this letter, Pauline authorship has been disputed. Ephesians was generally regarded as the work of Paul until the rise of rationalistic criticism at the turn of the 18th century when some theologians were not able to reconcile the contents of Ephesians to contents of the undisputed writings of Paul (Patzia, 1990; Wood, 1978). The theological differences between Ephesians and the undisputed writings are often the decisive proof that Paul did not write Ephesians (Witherington, 2007). Complaints of Pauline authorship include supposed conflicts regarding the teaching of law; Ephesians lack of "justification by faith" language; a more developed ecclesiology; an enhanced interpretation of marriage; Ephesians' cosmic posture of Christ; and possible eschatological emphasis, style, and language differences (Patzia, 1993; Witherington, 2007; Wood, 1978).

Lincoln (1990) submitted the probability that a later follower of Paul writing in Paul's name is responsible for the portrait of Paul that can be constructed from the letter by the reader and for its other features. Patzia (1993) posited the possibility of pseudonymity (writing in someone else's name) as a possibility in first century and lists Timothy, Luke, and Tychicus as potential deutero-Pauline writers. However, with only a few exceptions, evangelical scholars have believed that no one but Paul could have written this letter. If the epistle to the Ephesians was not written by Paul, but by one of his disciples in the apostle's name, then its author was the greatest Paulinist of all time—a disciple who assimilated Paul's thoughts more thoroughly than anyone else did. The man who could write Ephesians must have been the apostle's equal, if not his superior (Bruce, 2012). Witherington (2007) rhetorically asked: Who is this marvelous mysterious theologian who mirrors and even exceeds Paul, but has left no other known trace? If the Ephesian epistle were written by anyone but Paul, then the "I" in Ephesians 4:1 would have no authoritative standing.

In Ephesians 4:1, Paul entreated Christian brethren in Ephesus to walk in a manner worthy of the calling with which they had been called. The identity of the recipients of the letter has also been disputed but with more reason. Uncertainty as to the destination of this letter arises from a textual problem in the opening verse. "In Ephesus" is not found in some of the oldest and most reliable manuscripts, including the Chester Beatty papyrus—the earliest known manuscript of Paul's letters dating to A.D. 200 (Foulkes, 1983; Metzger, 1971; Wood, 1978). Westcott and Hort (1988) indicated that it is more likely "in Ephesus" was added to later manuscripts than purposely omitted from earlier ones. The most acceptable explanation for this discrepancy is that it was intended to be circulated to all the churches of the province of Asia—some known to Paul and others not (Bruce, 2012). This *circular letter* theory seems to be the most plausible explanation. This view states that the letter was intended to be read by Christians living in the Roman province of Asia of which Ephesus was the capital and from Ephesus it was circulated (Wood, 1978). This would help explain the general nature of the letter (Patzia, 1993). Ephesians does not deal with any particular problem of the church (Witherington, 2007). Ephesians 4:1-16 attests to the general nature of the letter. For example, Paul's appeal for unity in Ephesians 4 is a general appeal for unity throughout the church and not in response to the sectarianism we find in Paul's first letter to the Corinthian church.

Ephesians 4 has a clearly paraenetic nature, but Ephesians as a whole resists clear-cut classification in terms of ancient epistolary and rhetorical categories (Lincoln, 1990). Witherington (2007) referred to Ephesians as a circular homily rather than a circular Pauline letter. Evidence points away from Ephesians being an epistle in the traditional sense and toward being a sermon or homily. Ephesians does not include a typical Pauline opening and 1:1-2 is the bare minimum of typical epistolary opening. The lack of an opening personal prayer, rehearsal of relevant events or travelogue, and no mention of individuals (other than Tychicus) is unusual for Paul to omit in a personal letter to a church that he founded and spent a great amount of time at and at which no doubt had many friends. Nevertheless, elements of traditional rhetoric are evident in Ephesians. The first division of Ephesians is epideictic, and the second division is deliberative (Lincoln, 1990). Cooper (1960) pointed out that overlapping rhetorical style are common; Lincoln's Gettysburg address is primarily a speech of praise (epideictic) but ends in advice for the future (deliberative). The liturgical nature of Ephesians and that it reads more like a sermon than a letter has been noted by many writers (Foulkes, 1983; Lincoln, 1990; Patzia, 1993; Witherington, 2007). For Witherington, Ephesians is a circular homily probably written in Asiatic rhetorical style. Witherington noted that Ephesians has elements of Asiatic rhetoric and even suggested that Ephesians might be an exercise in an Asiatic style of rhetoric. There are two styles of Koine Greek. Atticizing style attempts to emulate Classical Greek and the Asiatic style that is "a highly artificial, self-conscious search for striking expression in diction, sentence structure and rhythm" (Witherington, 2007, p. 4) that is found in Ephesians. A homily or sermon is intended to inspire the audience. "Asiatic rhetoric in an epideictic mode appeals very strongly to the emotions to persuade the audience under the assumption that right belief and behavior will result if one wins the hearts and not just the minds" (Witherington, 2007, p. 217). Although Ephesians has elements of deliberative rhetoric and epistolary form, it is better characterized as epideictic rhetoric in sermonic form.

(b) Specific Issues

Two verses in Ephesians 4:1-16 present two of the most difficult interpretive problems in Ephesians. The first is Paul's use of Psalm 68:18 in verse 8, and the second is the meaning of "he also had descended into the lower parts of the earth" in verse 9. In the first interpretive problem, the writer of Ephesians quoted Psalm 68:18 in Ephesians 4:8 in order to give scriptural warrant for Christ giving gifts to the church. Textually, the citation of Psalm 68:18 does not correspond exactly to the Hebrew Masoretic text or to the Greek Septuagint (G. V. Smith, 1975). The major interpretive difficulty in this text is that while in Psalm 68:18 Yahweh *receives* gifts from men, in Ephesians 4:8 Christ *gives* gifts to the church—a change that almost reverses the meaning of the actual text (Gombis, 2005). Summarizing the possible explanations for the discrepancy between Psalm 68:18 and Ephesians 4:8, R.

A. Taylor (1991) listed (a) possible misquotation of the Psalm, (b) the possible use of a quotation of an earlier unidentified Christian hymn, (c) possible quotation from a collection of Old Testament texts (*testimonia*) strung together, (d) a correction of a Jewish interpretation, (e) a consistency of meaning but not of wording, (f) a *Midrach pesher*—a common early Jewish hermeneutic in which the exposition of the text determined the textual form of the quotation itself, or (g) the difference is explained by the existence of a variant text-form of the psalm. The last two seem to be the most plausible. Ellis (1989) favored the *Midrach pesher* view. The last view and closely related to the *Midrach pesher* view is the variant text option supported by R. A. Taylor:

> The use of the verb "gave" in Ephesians 4:8 for "received" in Psalm 68:18 may be explained by the existence of a variant text-form of the psalm passage. Being aware of a wording of Psalm 68:18 that had the verb "gave," the apostle realized that it was more appropriate to his Christological application of the psalm (i.e., Jesus *gave* gifts to the church; He did not *receive* gifts from the church), and Paul therefore employed this alternative text-form because of its suitability to his argument. (p. 329)

The Coptic translations, Targumic readings, and most Syriac Peshitta manuscripts of Psalm 68:18 have agreed with the wording of Ephesians 4:8 (R. A. Taylor, 1991), indicating that there is some support for variant text theory.

Though Psalm 68 has the most interpretational difficulties of all the psalms and is difficult to classify, the overarching message of this psalm is that God is to be praised as the one whose past acts of deliverance and provision for his people give confidence of his continuing care for his people. The message of verse 18 is that in the person of the victorious king, God ascended Zion in triumph over his enemies, receiving from submissive people congratulatory gifts of honor (R. A. Taylor, 1991). Gombis (2005) submitted that the change from receive in Psalm 68:18 to give in Ephesians 4:8 is not a reversal of meaning at all; rather, the writer is looking to the movement of the psalm as a whole depicting Christ as the triumphant Divine Warrior who, after he has ascended his throne, blesses his people with gifts. According to Gombis, Paul employed the ideology of divine warfare (widely used in ancient Near East and Old Testament writings) in order to state and defend the claim that Christ has been exalted over the powers and authorities ruling the present evil age. Ideology of divine warfare was used to assert the supremacy of a nation's deity and had a specific pattern: deities engage in conflict, an eventual victor is proclaimed supreme, the victor builds a house or temple, and then people gather to celebrate the deity's ascendency. Psalm 68 celebrates Yahweh as the conquering Divine Warrior and utilizes this pattern of divine warfare to portray him as such. In Gombis' view, Paul was not simply quoting Psalm 68:18 in abstraction from the rest of the psalm, but "rather appropriating the narrative movement of the entire psalm" (p. 375).

Given the difficulties interpreting Psalm 68, definitive pronouncements for or against certain theories are probably ill advised, but it seems best to think that Paul himself changed the Greek rendering of the text to suit his argument at this point in the letter (Thielman, 2007). Calvin and others have not tried to reconcile the textual difference but thought that Paul changed the words quoting the Psalm for its word that applies to the triumph and exaltation of Jesus and altering it to express the giving rather than the receiving of gifts in accordance with the truth expressed in such a passage as Acts 2:33 (Foulkes, 1983). Regardless of textual difficulties, Psalm 68 fits Paul's purpose exceptionally well. The psalm depicts God as mighty to empower and save his people in their struggle with their enemies. In the past, God demonstrated his power by defeating and scattering his enemies. This resulted in receiving gifts and booty from the captured foe. The psalmist prays that God will once again give his people the requisite gifts, power, and strength to overcome their enemies (Arnold, 2010).

The second interpretive difficulty in Ephesians 4:1-16 is the meaning of the text "he also had descended into the lower parts of the earth" in verse 9. Paul argued that Psalm 68:18's mention of an ascent implies a prior descent. He then said that the one who both descended and ascended must be Christ—the same person God exalted over all invisible and cosmic powers after his descent into the "lower regions of the earth" (Thielman, 2007, p. 824). There are three interpretive options: (a) the descent was the descent into hell (*Descensus ad Infernos*) during which Christ visited hell during the three days (*triduum*) he was dead, (b) the descent was the incarnation of Christ, (c) or the descent was the coming of the Holy Spirit at Pentecost to give spiritual gifts to believers (Hinson, 2007). The view that Christ descended into hell, written of in Ephesians 4:9, is almost unanimously the view of the church fathers. Proponents of the descent as a trip into hell maintain that this interpretation shows the true parallelism between the depths of the descent with the height of Christ's ascension "far above all the heavens" in Ephesians 4:10. Scriptures thought to support this view are Acts 2:27, Romans 10:6-7, 1 Peter 3:18-30, and 1 Peter 4:6—the most important being 1 Peter 3:18-20. A problem with this view is that the descent according to this view is from earth into Hades—not from heaven to earth. Also, this view presumes a three-story cosmology (heaven, earth, and underworld) where Ephesians seems to portray a heaven and earth only cosmology (Lincoln, 1990).

The second view claims that the descent is the incarnation of Christ. While this view was known to the church fathers, it was adopted by very few. This view gained support during the medieval period; but, in recent years, this view has become the majority view among scholars (Hinson, 2007). This view takes the reference of the descent to be a prior descent in the incarnation and has the advantage of following the order of the original meaning of Psalm 68 (Lincoln, 1990). Witherington (2007) gave three points in support of the view that the descent is of the preexistent Christ in the incarnation: (a) the focus of verses 8-9 is ongoing up and on the giving of gifts as a result of going up, (b) early manuscripts added the word "first" before "came down" in verse 9 indicating an attempt to make it clear that the descent preceded the ascent, and (c) the contrast is between descent to earth and ascent to the heavenlies by the same person.

The third view is that the descent of Christ refers to the descent of the exalted Christ in the Spirit to give gifts at Pentecost. Some have noted that in the Jewish liturgy Psalm 68 was used at Pentecost and have surmised that this prescribed reading was taken over into the Christian celebration of Pentecost.

The descent would then be Christ's coming in the Spirit when gifts were given to the church (Wood, 1978). This view takes the descent as subsequent to the ascent and thus as a descent in the Spirit. It is argued that the ascent and the giving of gifts can maintain their central function in the passage (Lincoln, 1990). This view has no supporters before the 19th century (Hinson, 2007). W. H. Harris (1994) supported this view. The event of the descent in Ephesians 4:9 may not be clear, but the ascent is clear and is the point Paul made and the reason for his use of Psalm 68:18. The issues in the quotation of Psalm 68 are complex and show the sort of creative use of the Old Testament scriptures that characterizes various early Jewish exegetes (Witherington, 2007).

Section 1.11 Power

The concept of power is related to leadership because it is part of the influence process (Northouse, 2007). Interest in power as a means of gaining and keeping control over others is centuries-old, but understanding power as an organizational construct is fairly recent. Dahl (1957) stated that the idea that some groups or individuals have more power than others is one of the most palpable facts of human existence, and Burns (1978) wrote that people are bewitched or titillated by power. According to Lord Acton, "Power tends to corrupt and absolute power corrupts absolutely" (Coll, 1986, p. 412). Kets de Vries (1991) posited that being in a position of power can be as intoxicating as any drug, and because of the possibility of the corruption of power, it was Plato's conviction that power would continue to corrupt unless philosophers become rulers and rulers become philosophers. In modern times, the understanding of power has become one of the most central concepts to the social sciences and is foundational to the understanding of society (Gjerstad, 2005; Willer, Lovaglia, & Markousky, 1997). However, the concept power has proven to be amongst the most slippery concepts in the whole of the social sciences (Crewe, 2010).

(a) Theoretical Roots of Power

Since the 16th century, there have been two avenues of thought regarding the concept of power. The first avenue sees power as decentralized, strategic, and available to anyone who seeks to gain power, particularly dynasties that have had power or seek to regain power (Sadan, 2004). This concept comes from the works of Niccolò Machiavelli (2012) who lived from 1469 to 1527. The unemployed Machiavelli wrote his treatise, *The Prince*, in dedication to the son of Piero de Medicci, Lorenzo the Great, for the probable purpose of gaining favor and being brought back into public service (Holler, 2007). In Chapter 1 of *The Prince*, Machiavelli wrote how principalities—ruling families—come to power. If they do not come to power by heredity, they come to power by arms, fortune, or ability. Later writings by Machiavelli, *Discourses on the First Decade of Titus Livey*, extolled government by the people (republics) and probably reflected his own philosophy and politics more accurately (Machiavelli, 2012). Yet, advocating total power at any cost and gaining power by justifying the means of getting that power (as Machiavelli wrote about in *The Prince*) has caused controversy and captured imaginations to the point that Machiavellianism has become a label for amoral power-hungry leaders.

In the similar vein as Machievelli's decentralized notion of power are the conceptualizations of the French philosopher, Michel Foucault (1925-1984), who has been recognized as one of the most influential theorists of power of the late 20th century (Gaventa, 2003). Foucault never clearly or concisely elaborated his conception of power (Kearins, 1996) and was often ambiguous (Newman, 2005) because his theory and methods tended to be implicit within his work on other subjects like discipline, sexuality, and madness. Also, where Foucault more explicitly explained his thoughts, he tended toward hyperbole and abstraction (Gaventa, 2003). Explaining his work, Foucault (1982) said that instead of addressing theory, his real objective was to relate a history of the different modes by which, in our culture, human beings are made subjects. Yet, Foucaultian thoughts about power have been summarized by writers: Foucault saw power as omnipresent because it originates from everywhere (Kuokkanen & Leino-Kilpi, 2000); power is exercised rather than possessed (Bradbury-Jones, Sambrook, & Irvine, 2008); power is pervasive and subtle, it is not something that is acquired, seized, or shared, but is exercised from innumerable points (Ailon, 2006); power is ubiquitous—it appears in every moment of social relations (Gaventa, 2003);

and power is not something that can be owned but rather something that acts and manifests itself in a certain way—it is more a strategy than a possession (Bălan, 2010). Synthesizing these ideas, Foucalt's view of power is a sytem or network of relations that encompasses all of society and not a mere relation between those with power and those with no power. Bălan (2010) added that people are not just the subjects of power but the locus where the power and resistance to it are exerted. The exercise of power, according to Foucault, is not just a relationship between individuals or groups but a way in which certain actions modify or change other actions. Power, for Foucault, exists only when it is put into action and not the renunciation of freedom, a transference of rights, or power delegated to a few. The value of Foucault's conception of power for leadership studies is that it causes the researcher to look for the cause and effect of the power relationship and not focus upon power as a commodity.

In contrast to the view of power inspired by Machiavelli and advanced by philosophers such as Foucault, the second avenue of thought conceptualizes power as centralized and located in a sovereign entity. This thought traces back to Thomas Hobbes (Sadan, 2004). For Hobbes (1651), there exists a total political community, the embodiment of which is the state, commonwealth, or society. Hobbes referred to this political community that holds power as the leviathan, a commonwealth, state, artificial man, or sovereign. Hobbes tended to use these terms interchangeably. Hobbes explained how this political community (commonwealth) gains power:

> A Common-wealth is said to be Instituted, when a Multitude of men do Agree, and Covenant, Every One With Every One, that to whatsoever Man, or Assembly of Men, shall be given by the major part, the Right to Present the Person of them all, (that is to say, to be their Representative;) everyone, as well he that Voted For It, as he that Voted Against It, shall Authorise [sic] all the Actions and Judgments, of that Man, or Assembly of men, in the same manner, as if they were his own, to the end, to live peaceably amongst themselves, and be protected against other men. (p. 82)

This sovereign power, commonwealth, or artificial man attains power by natural force (coercion or might) or when men voluntarily agree to submit to this man or assembly of men for their protection and well-being. Whereas neither Machiavelli nor Foucault offered a definition of power, Hobbes, arguing for a social contract and rule by an absolute sovereign, wrote that "the power of a man, (to take it Universally,) is his present means [ability], to obtain some future apparent Good" (p. 36). Hobbes further divided power into natural power and instrumental power. Natural power is strength, form, prudence, arts, eloquence, liberality, and nobility that come from the facilities of the body and mind. Instrumental powers are riches, friends, reputations, and the working of God (men call good luck) that are acquired by natural power or fortune and are the means for obtaining more power.

That Hobbes (1651) did not write for a critical audience is evidenced by his inconsistencies regarding his conceptualization of power. For example, it is widely accepted that Hobbes has a zero sum understanding of power; that is as one individual gains power another's power necessarily decreases (Read, 1991). Nevertheless, Read (1991) stated that Hobbes' definition of power— the means to obtain some future apparent good—does not logically require that gaining power comes at the expense of another. (This foreshadows a discussion about power to and power over, which is presented later.) Because contemporary research has sought precision and logic and asked how we can observe, measure, and quantify power, Hobbes' language and images are more suited for the modern scientific approach than Machiavelli's images or Foucault's poststructuralist conceptualization of power. Therefore, it seems that Hobbes thought won out over Machievelli's (Sadan, 2004).

(b) Modern Conceptualization of Power

German sociologist, philosopher, and political economist Max Weber (1864-1920) serves as a point of departure for thought about power because he continued the rational Hobbesian line and developed organizational thinking that links power with concepts of authority and rule (Sadan, 2004). Power is the main element in Weber's model of social stratification (Pyakuryal, 2001). Weber viewed society as stratified or divided in three dimensions: (a) economic class represented by income and resources the individual possesses, (b) social status with the prestige and honor enjoyed, and (c) political power represented by the power exercised by the individual. Weber's concept and definition of power has often been used by organizational writers: Power is the probability that an actor within a social relationship would be in a position to carry out his will despite resistance to it (Barbalet, 1985; Barnett & Duval, 2005; Pyakuryal, 2001; Ryan, 2006; V. Smith & Smith, 2003).

Robert Dahl (1957), clearly influenced by Weber, wrote about the difficulty of defining power:

> To define power could push us into some messy epistemological problems that do not seem to have any generally accepted solutions at the moment. I shall therefore quite deliberately steer clear of the possible identity of "power" with "cause," and the host of problems this identity might give rise to. (p. 203)

Noting the difficulties of defining power, Dahl desired to define the intuitive nature of power that all human-kind experiences. Therefore, he offered a definition as a starting point. Dahl's intuitive notion of power is that A has power over B to the extent that he can get B to do something that B would not otherwise do. Hardy and Clegg (1999) wrote that this seemingly simple definition that presents the negative rather than the positive aspects of power has been challenged, amended, critiqued, extended, and rebuffed over the years but remains the starting point for a remarkably diverse body of literature.

Barnett and Duval (2005) said that in terms of sheer influence, arguably no definition surpasses that of Dahl's (1957). Barnett and Duval noted that Dahl's concept has three defining features: (a) there is intentionality on the part of A, (b) there is conflict of desires to the point that B feels compelled to alter his behavior, and (c) the ability of A implies that A has the resources that leads B to alter his or her actions. Crewe (2010) stated that one limitation of Dahl's definition is that it does not allow for latent power. Crewe explained that when the police officer is not arresting someone, he or she is not bringing about the consequence. According to Dahl's definition, when the police officer is not actually arresting someone, he or she would not have power to do so. To be technically accurate, power must exist latently within A.

Additionally, Ailon (2010) asserted that Dahl's (1957) conception of power must include two things for power to be present. The first is that a change in the behavior of B is necessary; second, the thing that B would otherwise do must be known by A before he or she attempts to influence B's behavior. If B was going to do what A desired in the first place, then power has not been exercised. Therefore, according to Ailon, A must know what B would otherwise do. Dahl, anticipating the shortcomings of his definition, listed other variables that impact a power relation. He stated that the bases of power are innumerable and consist of all of the resources, opportunities, acts, and objects that one can exploit in order to effect the behavior of another. Also, the means of power (instruments used to exercise power), the scope of power (possible responses to power by B), and the amount of power (the probability of successfully changing the behavior of B) are all variables in a power relation, and each of them are numerous; therefore, a more exact definition of power is difficult.

Bachrach and Baratz (1962) labeled theorists, such as Weber and Dahl, who believe that power is centralized as elitist. Whereas, pluralists are those who believe that power is widely diffused. Bachrach and Baratz, distinguishing between the two, explained that pluralists are interested in only the effects of power—not the individuals who hold power. This distinction has caused researchers to examine the elitist perspective (centralized power) more closely. Power, as defined by Weber and Dahl, is exercised when A participates in the making of decisions that affect B, but Bachrach and Baratz explained that power is also exercised when A devotes his or her energies to creating or reinforcing social and political values and institutional practices that limit the scope of the political process to public consideration of only those issues that are comparatively innocuous to A. This use of power controls the agenda for the decision-making process, thus A indirectly has power over the actions and outcomes of B. Weber and Dahl's view of power has been called the first dimension of power. The view of power explained by Bachrach and Baratz is referred to as the second dimension of power (Fairhead & Griffin, 2000; Hardy & Clegg, 1999; Hardy & Leiba-O'Sullivan, 1998; Kearins, 1996). The first dimension of power is described as the most overt and visible kind of power. According to Kearins (1996), first-dimensional power is characterized by its emphasis on concrete, observable behavior. Bachrach and Baratz's concept of second-dimensional power is power used to exclude certain issues and individuals from the decision-making process (Fairhead & Griffin, 2000; Hardy & Clegg, 1999; Hardy & Leiba-O'Sullivan, 1998; Kearins, 1996).

Because second-dimensional power uses power to control the decision-making process and to deliberately head off conflict (Fairhead & Griffin, 2000), the questions of why grievances do not exist, why demands are not made, and why conflict does not arise should be examined (Hardy & Clegg, 1999). Steven Lukes (1975) looked into the societal and class functions that perpetuate this status quo. Lukes, noting that the system is sustained by socially structured and culturally patterned behavior of institutions, pointed to power as a means of shaping the perceptions and cognitions of others, so that what they (those in power) consider to be in their best interest is changed (Kearins, 1996). Organizations and power brokers use third-dimensional power to establish values and norms to the point where followers do not question the organization or those in power. This is the most insidious (stealthy or deceptive) and important form of power (Dowding, 2006). Lukes wrote,

> Is it not the supreme and most insidious exercise of power to prevent people, to whatever degree, from having grievances, shaping their perceptions, cognitions, and preferences in such a way that they accept their role in the existing order of things. (p. 24)

In this way, power operates even when there are no instances of A acting to exercise control over B (Barnett & Duval, 2005). Whereas first-dimension power is visible and seen in the actions of the leader, and second-dimension power is hidden because those in power control the agenda for decision making, third-dimension power is invisible because this unseen power shapes the psychological and ideological boundaries by influencing how individuals think about their place in the world to the point they do not question their current status and position (Gaventa, 2006).

Organizational interest in power once stopped with the structuralist ideas of theorists like Dahl and Lukes, but the past 30 years have seen interest in Foucaultian expressions of power or a fourth dimension of power (Hardy & Leiba-O'Sullivan, 1998). Hardy and Lieba-O'Sullivan (1998) listed the important points that are addressed in their four-dimensional model of power: (a) Foucault's work contests the concept of sovereign power found in the first three dimensions of power; (b) Foucault draws attention to how the subject is socially produced by the system of power that surrounds it; (c) as the status of the subject is challenged, so too, is that of the researcher; and (d) Foucault's work illuminates the limitations of resistance. Their model suggests that power can work at a number of levels. On the surface (first dimension), power is exercised through manipulating resources and managing decisions; at a deeper level (third dimension), power is exercised by managing the meanings that shape others experiences; still deeper (fourth dimension), power is embedded in the fabric of the system (organization) and directs what and how we see and how we think—that in turn limits the capacity for resistance. This fourth dimension suggests that followers cannot control or escape the power relations that are embedded in the system. In this model, also called system power, power is not consciously manipulated by actors but is embodied in impersonal and invisible forces that produce advantages and disadvantages for organizational members—leaders and followers; this power is not susceptible to deliberate manipulation by any one actor, but is impersonally embedded within larger systems (Fairhead & Griffin, 2000). Table 1 shows the four dimensions of power for comparison. This table shows how the four dimensions of power are conceptualized—how the dimensions are seen, how power is achieved, and who controls power.

Table 1: Details of Power Dimensions

First dimension	Second dimension	Third dimension	Fourth dimension
Dahl	Bachrach & Baratz	Lukes	Foucault
Visible power	Hidden power	Invisible power	Invisible power
Power by controlling resources and decisions	Power by controlling decision making agendas	Power by establishing meaning and values	Power is not controlled
A directly controls B	A subtlety controls B	A subtlety controls B	A does not control B

This discussion shows the complexity of conceptualizing and defining power that captures every nuance and application of power. Modern structuralists who have researched power in organizational contexts have been particularly interested in the effects of power and the locus of power (Gjerstad, 2005). Addressing these questions, Gjerstad (2005) noted that, in addition to the four power dimensions, power can be defined by senses: power over, power to, and power with. Each sense elucidates an aspect of the power relationships—that is the direction and use of power between those with power and those without power. Power over refers to the ability of the powerful to affect the actions and thoughts of the powerless (Gaventa, 2006) and is reflected in the definitions of power given by Weber and Dahl. This distributive power is about who has power over whom and what (Domhoff, 2005). According to Gjerstad, this is the most common conception of power and is often seen as a relationship of dominion, conflict, violence, evilness, selfishness, hierarchy, and victimization. Power to is the capacity to act (Gaventa, 2006). On an organizational level, this power is collective power; concerns the capacity of a group to realize its common goals; and is the combination of organization, morale, and technology that allows one group or nation to grow and prosper (Domhoff, 2005). On an individual level, power to is the ability of an individual actor to attain an end or series of ends (Allen, 1998; Gjerstad, 2005).

The third sense of power, power with, is the synergy that can emerge through partnerships and collaboration with others or through processes of collective action and alliance building (Gaventa, 2006). Allen (1998) summed up the complexity of the relationship between each of these senses: These three senses of power are not necessarily opposed to each other; having power-over presupposes having power-to and having power-with presupposes having power-to. Thus power-over, power-to, and power-with are not distinct types or forms of power; they represent analytically the distinguishable features of a situation. These views alone are one-sided and incapable to handle complex, multifarious power relations. The picture is more complex in reality; the subjects of power can for example be both dominated and empowered.

The likelihood of developing a single concept or definition of power is small considering its complexity. While some may hold that there may exist a single concept that captures the essence of power, Haugaard (2010) proposed that power consists of a cluster of concepts, each of which qualifies as power and where the different perspectives are not necessarily in mutually exclusive competition. Using Ludwig Wittgenstein's concepts of meaning and family resemblance, Haugaard resisted the quest for a single meaning of power and offered a plural view of power. Haugaard wrote that Wittgenstein developed the concept of family resemblance concepts to "denote concepts that overlap in usage while there is no single essence that unites all these usages" (p. 424). He suggested three "family members" of power: episodic power, dispositional power, and systemic power. Episodic power refers to the exercise of power that is linked to agency, dispositional power is the inherent capacity of an agent irrespective of whether or not he or she exercises that capacity, and systemic power refers to the ways in which social systems confer differentials of dispositional power to agents. In light of this family resemblance concept, Dahl's (1957) concept of power is the exercise of A's power over B that is episodic power and allowing A to exercise this power is a dispositional aspect of power that reflect a larger system of power. Haugaard stated that the better definition is the one that accomplishes the task the theorists set for themselves. Therefore, for Haugaard, these related or family conceptualizations are tools to be utilized by the researcher or theorist:

> The assertion that the episodic view of power fits poorly with Luke's characterization of the third dimension of power is one which tells us

that this particular conceptual tool was inadequate to its task. It was inadequate because it was inappropriate to the phenomenon analyzed, thus not the right tool for the objective at hand, which was the theorizing the three dimensions of power. (p. 426)

Haugaard indicated that the importance of family resemblance classifications and other language games is because—particularly in the study of power—various disciplines speak their own languages. The political scientist and the social psychologist work with differing defintions, paradigms, and purposes. Therefore, a cluster of concepts allow for researchers or writers to better explain their work.

(c) Bases of Power

Adding to the taxonomy of power for organizational behavioralists is the seminal article by French and Raven (2001)—*The Bases of Social Power*. It has been one of the most influential works in the area of power as it relates to organizational behavior (Northouse, 2007). Inquiry into the effects of power in the studies of social influence led French and Raven to examine the different types of power. The result of their work was identifying the major types of power and defining them systematically. Their theory of power bases considers power as influence and influence as psychological change; therefore, the theory is about the influence O (a social agent) has upon P (the person). The social agent can be a person, group, role, or norm. The basis of power is the relationship between O and P, which is the source of that power. The five power bases they identified are (a) reward power, (b) coercive power, (c) legitimate power, (d) referent power, and (e) expert power. French and Raven defined reward power as power whose basis is the ability to reward. Reward power rests upon the ability that P perceives that O can mediate rewards to him or her and the ability of O to administer positive valences and remove or decrease valences. There is also a latent aspect to reward power, that is the promise of rewards have power to influence P's behavior. Coercive power is similar to reward power in that it also depends upon O's ability to manipulate valences. Coercive power stems from the expectation of P that he or she will be punished by O if he or she fails to conform to the influencing action. French and Raven noted that there can be some difficulty distinguishing reward from coercive power. Is the withholding of a reward a punishment, and is withholding a punishment a reward?

Legitimate power, the most complex power base, is defined by French and Raven (2001) as "that power which stems from internalized values in P which dictate that O has a legitimate right to influence P and that P has an obligation to accept this influence" (p. 260). Valences, in the case of legitimate power, are induced by some internalized norm or value. They noted that legitimate power is similar to the notion of legitimate authority, but legitimate power is not always associated with an official position. The power that comes from close identification with someone is called referent power. Referent power is when P sees qualities in O that he or she identifies with and wants to establish a relationship on that basis even if O is not aware of the influence he or she has upon P. Expert power is the influence O has over P where P evaluates O's expertness in relationship to his or her own as well as an absolute standard. The strength of expert power varies with the extent of the knowledge or perception that P attributes to O in a given area.

Lusch and Brown (1982) categorized these power sources into economic and noneconomic sources. Reward and coercive sources correlate to economic incentives and disincentives, while referent, expert, and legitimate power are noneconomic sources. Northouse (2007) divided these powers into position power and personal power. Position power is the power a person derives from a particular office and rank in a formal organizational system, and personal power is the capacity a leader derives from being seen by followers as likable, knowledgeable, and acts in ways that are important to followers. Northouse listed legitimate, reward, and coercive power under positional power and referent and expert power under personal power.

After the publication of *Bases of Social Power*, French and Raven (2001) added informational power, which was originally included as an influence within expert power (French, 1956; Raven, 1999). Informational power is the intrinsic persuasiveness of the influencing message (Litman-Adizes, Raven, & Fontaine, 1978). This power is based on the potential use of informational resources and can influence through means such as rational argument, persuasion, and factual data. Other potential sources of power such as charisma, credibility, and rational persuasion have also been suggested (Christman, 2007) and Hersey et al. (2001) added connection power as a base of power. Connection power is based on the leader's connections with influential or important persons inside or outside the organization. They suggested that a leader with high connection power can induce compliance from others because they aim at gaining the favor or avoiding disfavor of the powerful connection.

Henry Mintzberg (2005) also addressed the subject of power bases. Mintzberg stated that the power of an individual, in an organizational context, reflects some dependency or gap in an individual's power as a system. He stated that a resource, a technical skill, or a body of knowledge are three prime bases of power. For a resource, technical skill, or body of knowledge to be a power base, they must be essential to the functioning of the organization, they must be concentrated (i.e., be in short supply or in the hands of one or just a few individuals), and they must be nonsubstitutional and cannot be replaced by other resources, skills, or knowledge. In addition to these three prime bases, Mintzberg wrote that a fourth general basis of power stems from legal prerogatives, which are the exclusive rights or privileges to impose choices. This correlates to French and Raven's legitimate power and is sometimes referred to as formal power or positional power. Mintzberg added a fifth general basis of power that is derived from access to those who can rely on the other four bases of power. This power correlates with connection power where the power is extrinsic and exists only in the close ties to the individual or individuals with power. In spite of the additional conceptualizations of power bases, the original five by French and Raven (2001) remain the most widely used in studying organizational behavior.

(d) Power in Organizational Leadership

Two of the most influential works on leadership power have been produced by Rosabeth Moss Kanter (1993) and James MacGregor Burns (1978). Kanter's *Men and Women of the Corporation* is not just a book about leadership but a theoretical account of how consciousness and behavior are formed by positions in organizations. The contribution Kanter made to the study of organizational behavior, leadership in general, and the concept of empowerment specifically is her structural concept of power. Kanter wrote that power is a virtual requisite for the effective performance in jobs with accountability for others, especially if power is defined as efficacy rather than domination. These assumptions led Kanter to define power as the ability to get things done, to mobilize resources, and to get and use whatever it is that a person needs for the goals he or she is attempting to meet. Power in organizations is analogous to physical power; it is the ability to mobilize human and material resources to get things done. Kanter (1979) posited that accomplishment is the true sign of power. Two capacities bring effectiveness to power: first is access to the resources, information, and support necessary to carry out a task, and second is the ability to get cooperation in doing what is necessary. Kanter wrote that the sources of these capacities come from three lines: lines of supply, lines of information, and lines of support. Possessing lines of supply means that those in power have the capacity to bring the materials, money, rewards, prestige, and other resources needed into the organization. Lines of information are important, Kanter asserted, because those in power need to be "in the know." Lines of formal and informal support are also important sources of power. Formal support is essential so that the manager can make innovative and risk-taking decisions without going through the "stifling and multi-layered approval process" (Kanter, 1979, p. 2), and informal support of more powerful influencers becomes another resource. Kanter's theory of power moves beyond social influence made popular by French, Raven, and others and focuses upon the literal or structural aspects of power. This theory gives rise to the structural theory of empowerment.

Burns (1978), in his seminal work on leadership, wrote that to understand the nature of leadership requires understanding of the essence of power. Burns is one of the most influential writers on leadership and his concepts of transactional and transformational leadership have been the basis and inspiration for a multitude of leadership studies. Burns brought the concept of power into practical application in leadership studies. Diverging from

Kanter's structural view of power, Burns stated that we must see power and leadership not as things but as relationships. For Burns, the two essentials of power are motive and resource. Both are interrelated, and both must be present or power collapses. If the motive is missing, resources diminish; lacking resources, motives are idle. Burns explained that many individuals have the power to act but lack the motive, while others have the motive but lack the resources. Many have the resources to get a gun and slaughter people (according to Burns' example), but the motive to do so is not there. Many may have the motive to be president or own a yacht but have no resources to make it a reality. Using Weber's definition of power (the probability an actor within a social relationship will be in a position to carry out his or her own will despite resistance) as a starting point, he stated that power and leadership become part of a system of social causation. The relationship between P (power holder) and R (power recipient) is not certain but is a degree of probability. Burns defined the power process as

> one in which power holders (P), possessing certain motives and goals, have the capacity to secure changes in the behavior of a respondent (R), human or animal, and in the environment, by utilizing resources in their power base, including factors of skill, relative to the targets of their power-wielding and necessary to secure such changes. (p. 13)

This concept deals with three elements necessary to the process: (a) the motives and the resources of power holders, (b) the motives and resources of power recipients, and (c) the relationship between these. Burns replaced the traditional picture of a single-minded power yielder that is bent on usurping his power over others with a picture of power as a "relationship in which two or more persons tap motivational bases in one another and bring varying resources to bare in the process" (p. 15).

Burns (1978) posited that all leaders are actual or potential power holders, but not all power holders are leaders. He wrote that leadership over human beings is exercised when persons with certain motives and purposes mobilize—in competition or conflict with others—institutional, political, psychological, and other resources so as to arouse, engage, and satisfy the motives of followers. Burns added that like power, leadership is relational, collective, and purposeful. For Burns, leadership is primarily about the use of power as reflected in his concepts of transactional and transformational leadership. Kanter and Burns have dramatically differing views of power, where power originates from, and how power is used, but the works of both writers have left a lasting contribution to the study of power and leadership.

(e) Concepts Related to Power

The concept of authority is closely related to the concept of power. For some, organizational power is defined as the authority to use or withhold resources such as people, time, skills, tools, materials, energy, information, and money (Babson, 1995). Others explicitly have stated that authority and power are not the same (Bass, 2008). For Weber, authority is a potential determinate of power (Keltner, Gruenfeld, & Anderson, 2003). Bass (2008) wrote that authority is power legitimized by tradition, law, agreements, religion, and the rights of succession and is derived from the implicit or explicit contracts concerning the individual's position or knowledge. Authority involves the rights, prerogatives, obligations, and duties associated with particular positions in an organization or social system (Yukl, 2010). Leaders have authority only to the extent that their followers are willing to accept the authority. Bass used the illustration of having the authority to rid an area of bears, but having the power to do so is quite a different thing. According to Bass, in traditional societies, authority is the legitimate support for the father, the priest, and the noble and comes from a higher power—God, heaven, or nature. By contrast, in modern societies, formal authority derives from man-made constitutions, charters, legislation, judges' rulings, and due process. In any social context, there are beliefs and practices that become accepted in that particular setting. The acceptance of these beliefs and practices binds the individuals belonging in that setting. The distribution of power within a social setting can become legitimate over time. When power is legitimized this way, it is denoted as authority (Pfeffer, 2005). Pfeffer stated that the transformation of power into authority can be seen most clearly in the relationship between supervisors and subordinates in work organizations. Bromiley (1979) distinguished between power and authority in the New

Testament. Two words reveal the meanings: power/dunamis and authority/exousia. Power, in this sense, is having the ability and/or the resources to accomplish desired outcomes, and authority primarily has the meaning of authorization. What distinguishes these two is the source. Power is based on intrinsic ability, while authority is based on extrinsic considerations (Bromiley, 1979).

Influence is another concept highly related to power. Bass (2008) and Crewe (2010) asserted that power is not synonymous with influence, but that influence is a function of power. Power, for Bass, is the potential for influence; power is quantified by the amount and type of influence. C. Anderson, Spataro, and Flynn (2008) argued that power comes from access to and control over important resources such as information, equipment, decision premises, monetary rewards, and alliances with prominent colleagues or the possession of personal characteristics that others admire and respect. They asserted that influence stems from power and influence tactics such as ingratiation, use of reason and logic, and coalition building. Willer et al. (1997) believed that a narrow definition of power and influence separating the two concepts may have important advantages for social analysis. They defined power as the structurally determined potential for obtaining favored payoffs in relations where interests are opposed. Influence is defined as the socially induced modification of a belief, attitude, or expectation effected without recourse to sanctions. Power occurs in relations where the interests of the actors are opposed but complementary, and influence occurs when actors change their behaviors because they expect that change to benefit them or the group to which they belong. Although separate concepts, they are linked. Willer et al. saw a symbiotic relationship where power may produce influence, and influence may produce power.

Section 1.12   Empowerment in Leadership

More than 70% of organizations surveyed have adopted some sort of empowerment initiative for some portion of their workforce (Casey et al., 2010). Concepts having similar meanings as empowerment occur in literature. They include delegation of authority, motivation, self-efficacy, job enrichment, employee ownership, autonomy, self-determination, self-management, self-control, self-influence, high-involvement, and participative (M. Lee & Koh, 2001). Yet, there is much discussion and debate about empowerment in spite of the ambiguity of empowerment as a concept (D. Collins, 1999). Serious study into empowerment began in the late 1980s and continues today. Empowerment as an organizational concept has had some difficulty gaining support. Argyris (1998) wrote that despite all the talk and the change programs, empowerment is still mostly an illusion. He insisted that managers like empowerment in theory but have less trust than the command-and-control model, and employees are often ambivalent about empowerment. Landes (1994) is more critical toward empowerment, stating that employee empowerment is a misguided notion that is mostly a myth in many organizations. He explained by saying that, ultimately, management must take responsibility for maintaining control in the organization and executing the master plan. Landes said that employees need to be equipped—not empowered. D. Collins (1999) wrote that management literature on empowerment is notable for its avoidance of conceptual reflection and methodological investigation resulting in the processes and problems of empowerment being all but ignored by management authors. Ciulla (2004) warned about bogus empowerment—that is when employees are told that they are being empowered, but they know that they are not.

In spite of the criticisms (or maybe because of them), organizational writers and researchers have put forth several empowerment theories and models. There is now a body of research that lends legitimacy to their theories. There are three primary avenues of conceptualizing empowerment: the critical social, the structural, and the psychological. This section reviews the important works that have contributed to the understanding of leadership empowered from these perspectives.

(a) Critical Social Empowerment

A popular conceptualization applies critical social theory to empowerment (Bay, 2007; Bradbury-Jones et al., 2008; Casey et al., 2010; Fulton, 1997; Jennings et al., 2006; Koukkanen & Leino-Kilpi, 2000). Critical social theory can be traced back to the Frankfurt School in Germany and was inspired by the critical Marxist philosophy. Critical social theory assumes that certain groups are in a subordinate position (Bradbury-Jones et al., 2008), that institutions are often the bastions of unequal distribution of power and privilege (Casey et al., 2010), and that empowerment is equal to liberation (Fulton, 1997). Koukkanen and Leino-Kilpi wrote (2000) that the use of critical social theory for research is based on the assumption that people are capable of self-reflection and that all people have a basic need to act independently. Social critical empowerment is aimed specifically at the third dimension of power where unseen institutional power shapes the ideas and values of the individual and the organization. Social activists and proponents of critical social theory such as Paulo Freire have believed that social conditions distort the individual's self-perception and that insights from critical social theory will enable people to see their conditions for what they are and find ways of ousting them to become free (Fulton, 1997). For Freire, education is the key to empowerment (Weissberg, 1999). The premise of his work is that liberating and empowering education is a process that involves listening, dialogue, critical reflection, and reflective action (Jennings et al., 2006). Engagement between teacher and pupil reveals powerless situations; together, a social action agenda can be formulated. Thus, the fresh situational awareness inspires the beliefs of capacity to change. Because the state of the oppressed or unempowered varies, the nature of empowerment is different depending upon the condition and situation of the subordinate individual or group.

Although research is limited, it has shown the validity of critical social empowerment in organizations. In a qualitative study, Fulton (1997) found that teaching critical social theory was an important empowerment paradigm relevant in nursing education today. Nursing in the United Kingdom has been found to be an oppressed group because of gender, occupational bias, and class inequality. In two focus groups, Fulton found that the nurses did not feel empowered and had a lack of confidence and low self-esteem. Fulton found the focus groups conceptualized empowerment in terms of freedom—freedom to make decisions with authority and to have choices. In another study, Casey et al., (2010) found that critical social empowerment shows that to reach their potential organizational contribution, nurses should be empowered, having an equal voice in decision making with doctors and managers.

Critical social empowerment is still in the early stages of development (Casey et al., 2010), and a comprehensive model has not been developed. However, Jennings et al. (2006) suggested a critical social empowerment model among youth having six dimensions: (a) safe, supportive environment; (b) meaningful participation; (c) shared power; (d) individual and community level orientation; (e) sociopolitical change goals; and (f) critical reflection. Social awareness is the starting point in social critical empowerment in extant literature. Additional models will be developed as critical social empowerment research continues.

(b) Structural Empowerment

A second important concept of empowerment in organizational literature is structural empowerment (Faulkner & Laschinger, 2008; Laschinger, Finegan, et al., 2004; Laschinger, Gilbert, et al., 2010; Laschinger, Leiter, et al., 2009; S. S. Lee, 2008; Ning et al., 2009; O'Brien, 2011; Sun, Zhang, Qi, & Chen, 2010; J. I. J. Wagner et al., 2010). This model of job-related empowerment comes from Rosabeth Moss Kanter's conception of power (Casey et al., 2010) and has been theoretically defined as access to organizational structures in the work environment through lines of communication, support, information, and resources, which offer workers opportunities to share in decision-making processes, assist in control of resources, and grow in their jobs (O'Brien, 2011). For Kanter (1979), empowerment evolves from two kind of capacities: (a) access to the resources, information, and support necessary to carry out a task and (b) ability to get cooperation in doing what is necessary. These capacities are provided by informal and formal power in the workplace. The basic idea of Kanter's model lies in the power and the opportunity structures created by the organization, not in an individual's qualities and reflection within the environment (Kuokkanen & Leino-Kilpi, 2000).

Structural empowerment consists of four components (Ning et al., 2009): information, support, resources, and opportunities. Kanter's empowerment structures in the workplace are outlined in Table 2 below. The structural component of information means having the knowledge of organizational decisions, policies, goals as well as the data, technical knowledge, and expertise required to be effective. Having information gives a sense of purpose and meaning for employees and enhances their ability to make judgments and influence organizational decisions. The structural component of support includes feedback and guidance received from superiors, peers, and subordinates and may also consist of emotional support, helpful advice, and assistance. The structural component of resources refers to the capacity of the individual to access the materials, money, supplies, time, and equipment required to accomplish organizational goals. Opportunities, as a structural component, are opportunities for mobility and growth that entail having access to challenges, rewards, and professional development experiences to increase knowledge and skills. Opportunities may be provided through participation on committees, task forces, and interdepartmental work groups that give opportunities to work with individuals in other areas of the organization.

Table 2: Components of Structural Empowerment

Component	Description
Opportunity	A sense of challenge and chance to grow and develop
Information	Data, knowledge and expertise, and awareness of organizational goals
Support	Problem-solving advice and feedback and guidance received from senior managers, peers, and direct reports
Resources	Time, supplies, and equipment to accomplish organizational goals
Formal power	Jobs that afford flexibility and visibility and that are relevant to key organizational processes
Informal power	Network of alliances with sponsors, senior managers, peers, and direct reports within and outside the organization

Note. Reprinted from "Impact of Critical Social Empowerment on Psychological Empowerment and Job Satisfaction in Nursing and Midwifery

Settings," by M. Casey, J. Saunders, and T. O'Hara, 2010, *Journal of Nursing Management, 18*, p. 24. Copyright 2010 by M. Casey, J. Saunders, and T. O'Hara.

Structural empowerment is a relational construct that describes the perceived power or control that a leader has over others (Conger & Kanungo, 1988). The sources of power over others are said to be the office or structural position, the personal characteristics of the person (French & Raven, 2001), the expertise of the person, and/or the opportunity for the person to access specialized knowledge or information (Bacharach & Lawler, 1980). Conger and Kanungo (1988) stated that this theory of empowerment has led to the focus on the sources of power, to the conditions that promote these conditions, and ultimately to development of strategies and tactics of resource allocation for increasing the power for subordinates. Spreitzer (2008) referred to this empowerment theory derived from Kanter's notion of power as social–structural empowerment. Spreitzer wrote that Kanter's research showed how women lacked certain "power tools," that is opportunity, information, support, and resources. Employees at low levels of hierarchy can be empowered if they have access to these "power tools." The essence of the social–structural perspective on empowerment is the idea of sharing power between superiors and subordinates with the goal of cascading relevant decision-making power to lower levels of the organizational hierarchy. According to Spreitzer, many—in spite of having these empowerment tools—still feel unempowered, while others lacking these tools can feel and act in empowered ways. Psoinos and Smithson (2002) wrote that management rhetoric may be so effective that employees perceive themselves to be empowered but they may not match empowerment criteria. This limitation helped spur the emergence of the psychological perspective on empowerment.

(c) Psychological Empowerment

The primary conceptualizing of psychological empowerment comes from the works of Conger and Kanungo (1988), Thomas and Velthouse (1990), and Sprietzer (1995). Conger and Kanungo argued that delegating or resource sharing (structural empowerment) is only one set of conditions that may—but not necessarily—enable or empower subordinates. Therefore, they offered an alternate definition of empowerment:

> Empowerment is defined here as a process of enhancing feelings of self-efficacy among organizational members through the identification of conditions that foster powerlessness and through their removal by both formal organizational practices and informal techniques of providing efficacy information. (p. 474)

This concept of empowerment is a motivational construct based on two types of expectancy: that their effort will result in a desired level of performance and that their performance will produce desired outcomes. Bandura (1977) referred to the first as self-efficacy and to the second as the outcome expectation. According to Conger and Kanungo, when individuals are empowered, their personal efficacy expectations are strengthened. Thus, empowerment refers to a process whereby an individual's belief in one's self-efficacy is enhanced and to empower means either to strengthen this belief or to weaken one's belief in personal powerlessness.

Thomas and Velthouse (1990) further developed Conger and Kanungo's (1988) theory and conceptualized empowerment in terms of cognitive variables or task assessments that determine motivation. They argued that empowerment is a multifaceted construct and that its essence cannot be captured by a single concept. They defined empowerment as increased intrinsic task motivation manifested in a set of four cognitions reflecting an individual's orientation to his or her work role: (a) impact, (b) competence, (c) meaningfulness or meaning, and (d) choice or self-determination. Meaning is the value of a work goal or purpose; competence (self-efficacy) is an individual's belief in his or her capability to perform activities with skill; self-determination is an individual's sense of having choice in initiating and regulating actions; and impact is the degree to which an individual can influence strategic, administrative, or operating outcomes at work. Components of psychological empowerment are outlined in Table 3.

Table 3: Components of Psychological Empowerment (Spreitzer, 1995)

Component	Description
Meaning	Congruence between job requirements and a person's beliefs
Competence	Person's beliefs in capability to accomplish work to be done
Self-determination	Autonomy in work behaviors and processes
Impact	Sense of being able to influence organizational activities and outcomes

Note. Reprinted from "Impact of Critical Social Empowerment on Psychological Empowerment and Job Satisfaction in Nursing and Midwifery Settings," by M. Casey, J. Saunders, and T. O'Hara, 2010, *Journal of Nursing Management, 18*, p. 24. Copyright 2010 by M. Casey, J. Saunders, and T. O'Hara.

Sprietzer (1995) constructed and validated a measure of psychological empowerment for the workplace context that builds upon Thomas and Velthouse's work that defines psychological empowerment as a motivational construct manifested in these four cognitions. This measure has become widely used in organizations to determine employees' perception of empowerment in the workplace environment. Organizational researchers have seen the validity in both structural empowerment and psychological empowerment and the need to examine the relationship between the two concepts and to integrate both concepts into their research (Bradbury-Jones et al., 2008; Casey et al., 2010; Chang & Liu, 2008; Cho, 2008; Dewettinck & Van Ameijde, 2011; Faulkner & Laschinger, 2008; Khan, Saboor, Khan, & Ali, 2011; Laschinger, Gilbert, et al., 2010; Menon, 2001; O'Brien, 2010; T. L. Robbins et al., 2002; Seibert et al., 2004; J. I. J. Wagner et al., 2010).

To distinguish between structural empowerment and psychological empowerment, it has been said that structural empowerment is the perception of the presence or absence of empowering conditions in the workplace and that psychological empowerment is the employee's psychological interpretation or relation to these conditions (Laschinger, Finegan, et al., 2004). Psychological empowerment represents a reaction of followers to structural empowerment. Most authors have viewed empowerment as change in an employee's intrinsic motivation resulting from changes in organizational structures, policies, or practices (Seibert et al., 2004) implying the presence of both structural and psychological empowerment. There has been a consensus that structural empowerment is a management technique used to increase organizational outcomes and builds on the notion that superiors distribute power, responsibility, and information to subordinates (Cho, 2008). Structural empowerment is the application of management practices, and psychological empowerment is how these applications are understood (Çavuş & Demir, 2010). Research has shown that structural empowerment and psychological empowerment are two distinct constructs, but it is also acknowledged that the best method of empowerment is integrating the two constructs (Çavuş & Demir, 2010; Cho, 2008; Menon, 2001).

Few researchers have conceptualized an integrated model of empowerment. However, Seibert et al. (2004) developed a multilevel model of empowerment that integrates these empowerment constructs (see Figure 2). Their model of empowerment addresses both the group or team level and the individual level. The empowerment model conceived by Seibert et al. was developed with macro- and microperspectives. The macroperspective focuses upon organizational structures and policies. The macroperspective is conceived as a climate construct and is labeled *empowering climate*. This construct influences the work group or team as a whole. The microperspective focuses upon empowerment as an intrinsic motivation construct. This aspect allows leaders or managers to directly influence or motivate their subordinates. Their research found positive relationships between empowerment constructs and work performance and job satisfaction. They also found that psychological empowerment fully mediated the effect of empowering climate on job satisfaction. Because empowering climate is significantly related to psychological empowerment and psychological empowerment is significantly related to individual job performance, their results demonstrated an indirect relationship between empowerment climate and job performance. Research has suggested that implementing both structural and psychological empowerment has positive organizational impact. Therefore, more research and development of integrated empowerment models are needed.

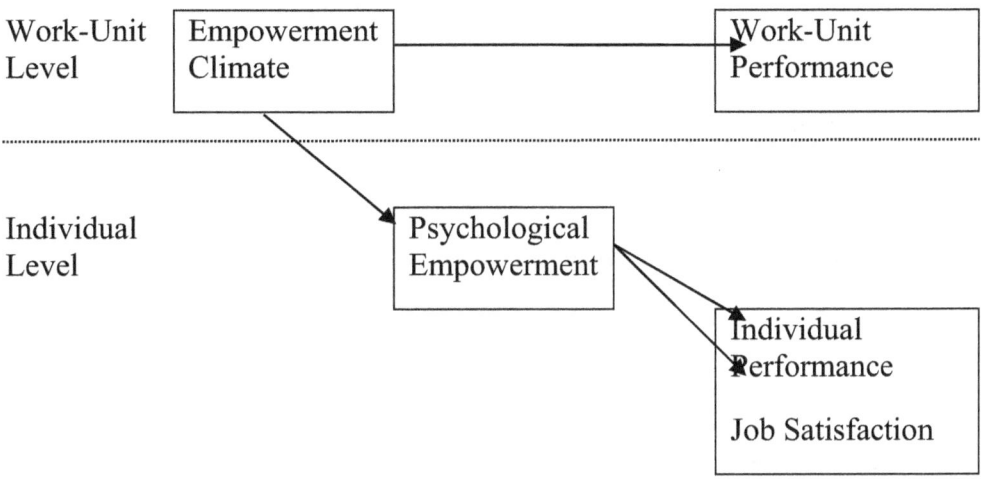

Figure 2: Multilevel (integrated) empowerment model. Reprinted from "Taking Empowerment to the Next Level: A Multiple-Level Model of Empowerment, Performance, and Satisfaction," by S. E. Seibert, S. R. Silver, and W. A. Randolph, 2004, *Academy of Management Journal, 47*(3), p. 333. Copyright by S. Seibert, S. Silver, and W. A. Randolph.

(d) Concepts Related to Empowerment

Organizational writers have often equated numerous concepts with the empowerment of employees. For example, releasing self-motivation of employees, delegation of authority, delegation of decisions, participative leadership, access to organizational structures, levels of employee input, power sharing, employee involvement, and equipping are often used as synonymous to or in place of empowerment (Aamodt, 2010; Bass, 2008; Coleman, 1996; Edwards & Collinson, 2002; Yukl, 2010). Some see effective empowerment inclusively, which includes providing inspirational goals, resources and information, removing organizational constraints, encouraging participation in decision making, and rewarding staff initiative and development (Offerman, 2010). Most of these concepts fall under the category of social, structural, or psychological empowerment. For example, equipping as an empowering behavior is structural empowerment because the leader makes available information and resources to accomplish tasks.

Some writers have equated delegation with empowerment. Delegation is a distinct type of power-sharing process that occurs when subordinates are given responsibility and authority for making some types of decisions formerly made by the manager (Yukl, 2010). Bass (2008) said that delegation is similar to but not the same as empowerment. The delegation of decision-making authority falls on a continuum that begins with autocratic decisions where the top leaders make all of the decisions that affect the organization. The second level of decision making is consultative where leaders gather information from subordinates but make all of the final decisions. The next level of decision making is joint decisions. Joint decisions are made in a group environment with many inputs, and the final decision is made collectively. The final level of decision making is delegation. Delegation gives the authority and responsibility for making a decision usually over the subordinate's direct work. These decisions are usually within established limits and approved boundaries. Bass pointed out that responsibility and authority should always accompany delegation. Delegation is never absolute; the manager always bears the final responsibility. Delegation is only empowering when the responsibility is given within the ability and knowledge of the employee and can have an unempowering effect if the employee fails or makes a series of bad decisions.

(e) Spiritual Empowerment

Feature articles from *Newsweek, Time, Fortune,* and *Business Week* have chronicled the growing presence of spirituality in corporate America (Fry, 2008). Issues regarding workplace spirituality (Giacalone & Jurkiewicz, 2010) have been receiving increased attention in the organizational sciences (Fry, 2005), and there has been a move toward spirituality in leadership studies (Crowther, 2012). Influenced by the interest in spirituality in the workplace, Fry (2003) developed a theory of spiritual leadership for organizations. Fry (2006) defined spiritual leadership as the values, attitudes, and behaviors that are necessary to intrinsically motivate one's self and others so they have a sense of spiritual survival (well-being) through calling and membership. Operationally, spiritual leadership is conceived as a causal theory within an intrinsic motivational model that incorporates vision, hope/faith, altruistic love, and theories of workplace spirituality and spiritual survival. The ultimate purpose of spiritual leadership is to create vision and values congruence across all organizational levels and to foster higher levels of organizational commitment and productivity. Spiritual leadership is accomplished by creating a vision wherein leaders and followers experience a sense of calling where life has meaning and makes a difference and by establishing a social or organizational culture based on the values of altruistic love where leaders and followers have a sense of membership, feel understood and appreciated, and have genuine care, concern, and appreciation for self and others.

A special issue of *The Leadership Quarterly* on the subject of workplace spirituality and spiritual leadership revealed three themes required for workplace spirituality: (a) an inner life that nourishes and is nourished by (b) calling or transcendence of self within the context of (c) community based on the values of altruistic love (Fry, 2006). Fry's (2008) definition of spirituality is nonreligious, and he admitted that "religious ideology has been virtually disregarded" (p. 89) in the study of workplace spirituality. He cited the possibility of division, religious exclusivity, arrogance, zealotry, offense, and the potential for a decrease in morale, employee well-being, and organizational goals for this nonreligious conceptualization of spirituality. Instead of a deity, Fry stated that spirituality reflects the presence of a higher power (that may or may not be centered in a particular god) that affects how individuals operate in the world, and spirituality is broader than any organized religion with tenets, doctrines, and dogma. This nonreligious spirituality has at least four characteristics: (a) a belief in a higher power or higher meaning, (b) conscious attempts to understand and connect with a higher power or meaning, (c) transcendence of self, and (d) connectedness to others (Koch, 1998). Ultimately, for these organizational writers, spirituality is necessary for religion but religion is not necessary for spirituality. Fry (2003, 2006, 2008) made several references to empower or empowered. It may be assumed employees feel empowered if spiritual leadership successfully motivates employees, but the empowering aspect of spiritual leadership has not been adequately explored.

Few articles consider spiritual empowerment in an organizational context. A search for academic articles on spiritual empowerment from Academic OneFile, EBSCO, and JSTOR revealed only three articles: one in a clinical/counseling context (Koch, 1998), one in a Christian/biblical context (Makau-Olwendo, 2009), and one in an Islamic context (Buturovic, 1996)—but none in an organizational or leadership context. One study attempted to combine current organizational empowerment with a biblical or spiritual type of empowerment (Campbell, 2005). Campbell's (2005) expressed purpose for his study was to introduce a model of leadership development for churches based on a theological and organizational understanding of the processes of empowerment. Campbell's model of leadership development emphasizing the empowering aspect includes sharing information, creating autonomy, and replacing hierarchical leadership with teams. This model also includes mentoring models, coaching, and redefining failure. Campbell defined empowerment: to empower someone is to give that person the authority, ability, or strength to control or influence surrounding circumstances. The spiritual nature of empowerment comes from the example of the Christian Bible. In the Old Testament, man (represented by Adam) was given authority over creation and was made regent over God's creation (Gen 1:26). In the New Testament, the Holy Spirit becomes the agent by which God equips and empowers men and women to function as God's representatives in the world. According to Campbell, the spiritual aspect of empowerment comes when the Holy Spirit delegates his power to emerging leaders in the form of spiritual gifts and existing leadership gives space and opportunity to allow this to happen. This model can be summarized by saying that leaders who have been authorized by God and having been given gifts by the Holy Spirit empower others by sharing knowledge, creating autonomy, establishing teams, modeling leadership, coaching, and redefining failure. This first attempt at integrating aspects of organizational empowerment and spiritual empowerment failed to consider other aspects of critical social, structural, and psychological empowerment.

The need remains for an integrated model of empowerment that considers all aspects of empowerment.

Section 1.13   *Theology and Leadership*

Whereas empowerment is the distribution of resources, authority, power and building self-efficacy in others, and that Christian scripture says that God is the source of everything, this section reviews the topic of theology as it relates to empowerment. Ayers (2006) asserted that leadership literature and research does not generally embrace theology. In spite of the recent interest of spiritual matters in leadership, the relationship between theology and organizational leadership in scholarly writing and research is tenuous. There has always been a strained relationship between the philosophy of the day and theology as reflected in Tertullian's famous line: What is there in common between Athens and Jerusalem (Erickson, 1998)? While there has not been a convergence of theology and leadership in organizational literature and research, Christian leadership literature regularly has used theology to inform leadership thought and practice (e.g., Bekker, 2006; Clarke, 2008; Howell, 2003; Niewold, 2006).

Horsthuis (2011) suggested that conceptions of leadership should begin with the doctrine of the Trinity. The ancient concept of *perichoresis* (can be equated to the Greek "dance around") refers to the mutual interaction of the threefold nature of God and offers a participative understanding of leadership. *Perichoresis* is not actually derived from the root of the verb "to dance around," *perichoreuo* (related to *choreia* from which the English "choreography" is derived), but the play on words illustrates the dynamic sense of *perichoresis* (Fiddes, 2000). *Perichoresis* was first used in patristic times to explain how the two natures of Christ—human and divine—function together in unity. The term was later applied to the Trinity to temper the suggestion of tri-theism. Horsthuis defined *perichoresis* as the mutual indwelling, without confusion, of the three persons of the one God. Horsthuis pointed out that the use of *perichoresis* is not limited to early Christian usage but that Karl Barth, among many theologians, made use of the term, suggesting that the divine modes of existence condition and permeate one another mutually with such perfection and that one is as invariably in the other two as the other two are in the one. The patristic and the modern use of *perichoresis* contain two features: (a) the three persons of the Trinity mutually dwell in one another, and (b) there is no confusion of the persons of the Godhead in the mutual indwelling of divine persons. Thus, despite this mutual indwelling, the Son is never the Father, the Spirit is never the Son, and so forth.

Horsthuis (2011) wrote that the use of the well-established doctrine of *perichoresis* welcomes Christ's disciples as participants in the mutuality of Father, Son, and Spirit (as suggest by Jesus' high priestly prayer in John 17). For Horsthuis, a theology of leadership including the notion of being drawn into participation with God has profound implications.

> A cluster of scholars share a favorite image of the perichoretic union of the Father, the Son, and the Holy Spirit. This image aids us in understanding how disciples might be included in such a profound relational space. This favorite image of a dance is compelling because it incorporates both movement and participation as it provides a measure of definition to dynamics of the Triune God. (p. 93)

Perichoresis traditionally expresses participation in the triune life and participation has been suggested to be a Trinitarian virtue (Pembroke, 2006). The image of a dance is used to illustrate the *perichoretic* unity of the Godhead and how individuals might participate in that unity. "It roots all leading not in the leader's capabilities or techniques, but in a movement of grace that begins with and in the Triune God" (Horsthuis, 2011, p. 94). As a result, leaders will view their ministry as a means of participation in the mutual ministry of the Trinity.

The dynamic of different entities working in harmony can also be expressed in the term *polyphony*. Polyphony is a musical term that denotes the simultaneous singing or playing of two or more melodic lines that fit together as equally important parts in the overall structure of a piece. In relation to the Triune God, polyphony refers to the way in which simultaneous difference exists as a homogeneous unity (Pembroke, 2006). The standard definition of participation is "to take part in" and usually refers to an activity in which we are joined by others but becomes a significant Trinitarian concept as we begin to think about what it might mean to dwell in and be indwelt by the lives of others (Cunningham, 1998). The Trinitarian virtue of participation can come to mark our own lives as we contemplate participating with God in pastoral ministry (Fiddes, 2000; Penbroke, 2006) and Christian leadership (Horsthuis, 2011). *Perichoresis* and polyphony offer a limited but significant understanding of human participation in divine activity (Cunningham, 1998). This section reviews the pertinent literature on each of the *perichoretic* partners: the Father (theology proper), the son (Christology), and the Holy Spirit (pneumatology).

(a) Theology Proper

Study of theology in the narrow sense of the term is largely the study of the triune nature and attributes of God. The Trinity is the central mystery of the Christian faith (Williams, 1996). Grudem (1994) defined the Trinity as "God eternally exists as three persons, Father, Son, and Holy Spirit, and each person is fully God, and there is one God" (p. 226). A proper definition of the Trinity must include the distinctness and equality of the three persons within the Trinity as well as the unity within the Trinity (Enns, 1989). Some theologians have used the term *Triunity* (or Tri-unity; Duffield & Van Cleave, 1987; Ryrie, 1999) to emphasize the dual distinctive of perfect unity among the Godhead yet the individual distinction of the three persons of the Godhead (Father, Son, and Spirit).

God has revealed himself to man and man can know him by his attributes (Thiessen, 1979). Attributes of God are those qualities of God that constitute what he is, the very characteristics of his nature (Erickson, 1998). For Enns (1989), the attributes of God may be defined as those distinguishing characteristics of the divine nature that are inseparable from the idea of God and that constitute the basis and ground for his various manifestations to his creatures. There is a great diversity of methods of classifying the attributes of God. Table 4 shows the diverse ways theologians have grouped God's attributes.

Table 4: Categories of Attributes of God

Author	Attribute	Characteristics
Bancroft (1946)	Absolute attributes	Life Personality Self-existence Immutability Unity Truth Love Holiness
	Transitive attributes	Eternity Immensity Omnipresence Omniscience Omnipotence Veracity and faithfulness (transitive truth) Mercy and goodness (transitive love) Justice and righteousness (transitive holiness)
Berkhof (1938)	Incommunicable attributes	Self-existence Immutability Infinity Unity

	Communicable attributes	Spirituality of God
		Intellectual attributes
		    Knowledge
		    Wisdom
		    Veracity
		Moral attributes
		    Goodness
		    Holiness
		    Righteousness
		Attributes of sovereignty
		    Will of God
		    Power of God

Buswell (1962) Hodge (1940)	From the *Westminster Catechism*	God is spirit, infinite, eternal, and unchangeable in his being, wisdom, power, holiness, justice, goodness, and truth.
Enns (1989)	Absolute attributes	Spirituality Self-existence Immutability Unity

Author	Attribute	Characteristics
	Relative attributes	Truth
		Love
		Holiness
		Eternity
		Immensity
		Omnipresence
		Omniscience
		Truth
		Mercy
		Grace
		Justice
Erikson (1998)	Attributes of greatness	Spirituality
		Personality
		Life
		Infinity
		Constancy
	Moral qualities	Moral purity
		Holiness
		Righteousness
		Justice
		Integrity
		Genuineness
		Veracity
		Faithfulness
		Love
		Benevolence
		Grace
		Mercy
		Persistence
Garrett (1990)	Natural attributes	Self-existence
		Immutability
		Omnipresence
		Omniscience
		Omnipotence
		Eternity
		Immensity
	Moral attributes	Holiness
		Love
		Righteousness
		Truth
Grudem (1994)	Incommunicable attributes	Independence
		Unchangeableness
		Eternity
		Omnipresence

Author	Attribute	Characteristics
	Communicable attributes	God's being Spirituality Invisibility Mental attributes Omniscience (knowledge) Wisdom Truthfulness Moral attributes Goodness Love Mercy (grace) Holiness Peace (order) Righteousness (justice) Jealousy Wrath
	Purpose attributes	Will Freedom
	Summary attributes	Omnipotence (power and sovereignty) Perfection Blessedness Beauty Glory
Ryrie (1999)	Perfections of God	Eternity Freedom Holiness Immutability Infinity Live Omnipotence Omnipresence Omniscience Righteousness Simplicity Sovereignty Truth Unity
Shedd (1888)	Passive attributes	Self-existence Simple Eternal Immense Omnipresence Immutability

Author	Attribute	Characteristics
	Active attributes	Unity Omnipotence Omniscience Wisdom Goodness

Strong (1889)	Absolute attributes	Spirituality
		  Life
		  Personality
		Infinity
		  Self-existence
		  Immutability
		  Unity
		Perfection
		  Truth
		  Love
		  Holiness

	Relative attributes	To time and space
		  Eternity
		  Immensity
		To creation
		  Omnipresence
		  Omniscience
		  Omnipotent
		To moral beings
		  Veracity and faithfulness (truth)
		  Mercy and goodness (love)
		  Justice and righteousness (holiness)

Thiessen (1979)	Essence of God	Spirituality
		  Incorporeal
		  Invisible
		  Alive
		Self-existence
		Immensity
		Eternity

	Attributes of God	Nonmoral
		  Omnipresence
		  Omniscience
		  Omnipotent
		  Immutability
		Moral
		  Holiness
		  Righteousness and justice
		  Goodness (love/benevolence/mercy/grace)

Author	Attribute	Characteristics
	Nature of God	Truth
		Unity
		Trinity
Williams (1996)	Identity of God	God is living
		God is personal
		God is spirit
	Transcendence of God	God is infinite
		God is eternal
		God is unchanging
	Character of God	God is holy
		God is love
		A God of truth
	Perfections of God	God is omnipresent
		God is omniscient
		God is omnipotent
	Nature of God	One God/three persons

Ryrie (1999) and Williams (1996) used the term *perfections* of God because, as Ryrie stated, "all of the qualities or attributes of God are perfect" (p. 39). God also reveals himself through the titles and names by which he is called. The names of God are descriptions of his character (Grudem, 1994). Names are the self-revelation to the creation from the Creator. A name was regarded as an expression of the nature of the thing designated (Berkhof, 1938). God's power and authority are the attributes that relate most directly to leadership. The Hebrew names for God *Adonai, Yahweh,* and *El Shaddai* sum up God's power and authority (with direct implications for spiritual empowerment).

Adonai means lord, master, owner, or ruler. This term can be used to describe the relationship among men—master/slave (e.g., Exo 21:1-6). Ryrie (1999) wrote that when *Adonai* is used of God's relationship to men, it conveys absolute authority (e.g., Josh 5:14; Isa 6:8-11). The Greek *kurios* is the equivalent word for Lord or master in the New Testament (Duffield & Van Cleave, 1987). It was often used to address Jesus. It emphasizes authority and supremacy; when used of God, it expresses his creatorship, power revealed in history, and just dominion over the universe (Ryrie, 1999). *Kurios* can also refer to an authority relationship among men or between God and man.

El Shaddai is a compound word from *El* meaning God (a very ancient name for God) and *shaddai*. The derivation of shaddai is unknown, but it could have derived from *shad* meaning "breast" (Duffield & Van Cleave, 1987) or from *shadad* meaning "to be powerful" (Berkhof, 1938). Together, this divine name means "the Satisfier," "All Sufficient One," "Almighty," or "Almighty God." This name points to God as possessing all power in heaven and on earth. This name was the name by which God appeared to the patriarchs to give comfort and confirmation of the covenant with Abraham (Ryrie, 1999). Duffield and Van Cleave wrote that the emphasis derived from this name is God's omnipotence.

The most revealing name for God is *Yahweh*. This personal name for God is also the most sacred name for God. Because of the sacred nature of this name, the real derivation, the original pronunciation, and its meaning are more or less lost in obscurity (Berkhof, 1938). Nevertheless, Berkhof (1938) wrote that the Pentateuch connects *Yahweh* (YHWH) with the Hebrew verb meaning "to be" (Exo 3:13-14). On the strength of this passage, we may assume that the name is probably derived from an archaic form of the verb. The meaning, explained in verse 4, is "I am that I am," or "I shall be what I shall be." Thus, the name indicates the immutability or unchanging nature of God. More than that, Berkhof noted, it points to the unchangeableness of his relation to his people.

Father is a common title for God in the Bible, especially in the New Testament (Erickson, 1998), and is the label that distinguishes the first *perichoretic* partner. The use of the divine title of Father occurs 245 times in the New Testament, and it also occurs some 15 times in the Old Testament (Ryrie, 1999). The use of father and son describes the relationship of the two persons of the Trinity in the context of redemption and does not mean that the Father once existed alone and begot a son at some point in time (Duffield & Van Cleave, 1987). God the Father and God the Son (as well as God the Holy Spirit) are coequal and coeternal. Garrett (1990) pointed out that God's fatherly relation to the Israelites was expressed in Egypt and in the wilderness (Exo 4:22-23; Deut 1:31, 8:5, 14:1), and in the Psalms divine fatherhood is an analogy describing the relationship between God and his people rather than a title (Pslm 68:5; 103:13). Jesus' favorite designation for God was Father, and Jesus made fatherhood the controlling idea in God's relation to man (Garrett, 1990). Therefore, father not only describes the relation between the first two members of the Godhead, but it also describes the relation between God and man. The names and titles of God reveal that the Godhead possesses all authority and power. Each divine *perichoretic* partner equally possesses these attributes.

(b) Christology

Christology is the study of the person or nature and works of Jesus Christ. Early Christianity was filled with controversy surrounding the ontology of the second member of the Trinity. Orthodox Christianity has affirmed that Christ in his incarnation was at once fully God and fully human, or as Fee (2006) wrote, "The common faith of the one historic church is that, in the Jewish Messiah Jesus, God was living out a genuinely human life on planet earth" (p. 25). Jesus, the God–man (Gruden, 1994; Ryrie, 1999; Shedd, 1888) and third person of the divine Godhead, shares equally all of the attributes of God.

After the nature and attributes of Christ, Christology focuses upon the acts of Christ. Most conservative theologians have agreed on the basic acts or events of Christology: preexistence, virgin birth, sinless life and ministry on earth, atoning death and burial, resurrection from death, postresurrection ministry on earth, ascension, and session. Figure 3 below diagrams the basic events of Christology.

A Model of Divine Empowerment 71

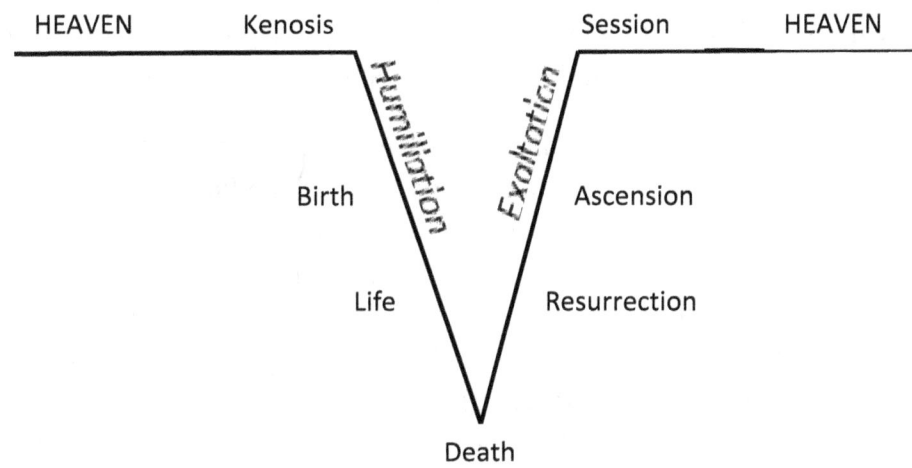

Figure 3: Christological events. Reprinted from *Renewal Theology: Systematic Theology From a Charismatic Perspective* (p. 381), by J. R. Williams, 1996, Grand Rapids, MI: Zondervan. Copyright 1996 by Zondervan.

The incarnation is the doctrine that maintains that the eternal, preexistent Son of God became human in the person of Jesus (Reymond, 1991). Incarnation has given Kenotic theory a special place in the field of systematic theology (Martin, 1997). The word *kenosis* is taken from the Greek verb *kenóō*, which generally means "to empty" and is translated "emptied himself" in Philippians 2:7 (Evans, 2006). Kenosis or the humiliation of Jesus includes his birth through his death, whereas the exaltation of Jesus includes his resurrection, ascension, and session in heaven (Williams, 1996). Theologically, kenosis and session are bookends to the earthly ministry of Christ. Kenosis or the kenotic theory has been associated with the ontological controversy regarding the nature of Christ (Erikson, 1998; Grudem, 1994). According to Grudem (1994), the kenosis theory derived from Philippians 2:5-11 holds that Christ gave up some of his divine attributes while on earth as man. Erikson wrote that this theory sees Jesus not as God and man simultaneously, but successively. Grudem contends that the real meaning of kenosis is revealed in the context of the verse: "being found in human form he humbled himself and became obedient unto death" (Phil 2:8). This emptying is equivalent to humbling himself and taking on a lowly status and position—kenosis equals humility, not relinquishing divine attributes.

Bekker (2006) eruditely explained that recent studies have attempted to escape the controversy around Philippians 2:5-11 (The Philippian Hymn) and explore the hymn as "an alternative and exemplary model . . . of ethical leadership rooted in a first-century, mimetic Christological spirituality" (p. 2). Bekker (2009), therefore, submitted a model of mimetic Christological leadership that is marked by (a) Christological mimesis, (b) kenosis (self-emptying), (c) servant posturing, (d) humane in its orientation, (e) active humility, and (f) missional obedience. Mimesis and kenosis (humility) are two issues addressed by this model. Mimesis is the ability to imitate someone or something in action, speech, and behavior, while the cognitive function of mimesis allows one to recognize the reality of that which is being mimicked (Crowther, 2012). The Philippians Hymn is a call to imitate Jesus, who is shown as divine (Phil 2:6), and is thus a call in a sense to "imitate God" (Bekker, 2006). Mimesis is human participation in the *perichoretic* union—not deification as some in eastern theology uses the word *perichoresis* (Kärkkäinen, 2002b).

While the humiliation of Jesus is finding its place in leadership research and literature, the exaltation aspect of Christology has been largely neglected. The exaltation of Christ includes the resurrection, ascension, and session. Christ's death, burial, resurrection, ascension, and session are each integral to the gospel, but the ascension has not aroused as much reflection and devotion as the other aspects of Christ's mission (Haroutunian, 1956). The ascension of Christ is the event by which Jesus decisively ended his time on earth in terms of his physical presence on earth by ascending—by going up to the place from where he had come (A. Wilson, 2007). Ascent is the reversal of descent (Farrow, 2011). The actual event of the ascension is recorded in Luke 24:50-53, Acts 1:9-11, and Mark 16:19-20 (although the Mark passage is generally thought to be a later addition to the text). Toon (1984) listed six results of Jesus' ascension: (a) the ascension follows and completes the resurrection; (b) Jesus becomes the first fruits of his people that guaranteed the final redemption and sanctification of those in union with him; (c) the ascension implies exaltation; (d) Jesus ascended to begin his heavenly ministry as high priest, making intercession for his people; (e) Jesus ascended to bestow the gift of the Holy Spirit; and (f) the ascension inaugurates a new era. The ascension of Christ is important to Christian leadership studies because Paul tied the leadership gifts of apostle, prophet, evangelist, pastor, and teacher directly to the ascension of Christ in Ephesians 4:1-16.

Session is the climactic stage in the exaltation of Christ and concerns the present locus and sphere of the exalted Lord (Williams, 1996). Daniel foresaw the disrupting and transforming power of the ascended Jesus and what Paul encountered on the road to Damascus (Farrow, 1999):

> In my vision at night I looked, and there before me was one like a son of man, coming with the clouds of heaven. He approached the Ancient of Days and was led into his presence. He was given authority, glory and sovereign power; all peoples, nations, and men of every language worshipped him. His dominion is an everlasting dominion that will not pass away, and his kingdom is one that will never be destroyed. (Dan 7:13-14)

The earliest New Testament reference to the phase of Christ's existence following his burial cast it in terms of exaltation (Fritzmyer, 1984):

> Therefore God exalted him to the highest place and gave him the name that is above every name, that at the name of Jesus every knee should bow, in heaven and on earth and under earth, and every tongue confess that Jesus Christ is Lord, to the glory of God the Father. (Phil 2:9-11)

The present locus of Christ's being is enthroned in heaven (Haroutunian, 1956) at the right hand of the father. The present position of Christ at the right hand of the Father is mentioned in many scriptures (Ps 110:1; Matt 22:44; Mrk 12:36, 16:19; Luk 20:42-43, 22:69; Rom 8:34; Ephes 1:20; Col 3:1; Hebrews 1:3-13, 8:1, 10:12, 12:2; 1 Pet 3:22). The implication is that all glory, authority, and power are shared by the Father with the Son (Walvoord, 1964). Jesus returned to his rightful place beside the Father in a place of authority and rulership so that he could send the Holy Spirit on the day of Pentecost. Christ's exalted presence and ascension ministry is of great significance to church leadership (Guynes, 1986).

(c) Pneumatology

Pneumatology is the study of the Holy Spirit. The Holy Spirit is the third person of the Godhead, equal to the Father and the Son in every way, and the third parichoretic partner. While most Christians have little difficulty relating to God the Father and the Son because of personal images, the Christian understanding of the Holy Spirit often comes considerably short of personhood (Fee, 1996). We tend to think of the Spirit in nonpersonal terms because of the nonpersonal titles and symbols used for the Holy Spirit: Holy Spirit, Spirit of God, Spirit of Christ, Spirit of Grace, Spirit of glory, Spirit of truth, Spirit of life, Spirit of adoption/sonship, Spirit of promise, Spirit of Wisdom, Spirit of understanding, Spirit of power, Spirit of knowledge, eternal Spirit, comforter (helper, counselor, guide), power of the Most High, and breath of the Almighty (Holdcroft, 1999; McRoberts, 1994). Symbols for the Holy Spirit include dove, wind, breath, fire, water, seal, deposit, clothing, finger of God, and oil (Holdcroft, 1999; Kärkkäinen, 2002a; McRoberts, 1994).

Christ's ascension and Pentecost are inseparable (Brunback, 1955). It was in connection with the sending of the Holy Spirit that Christ stressed the necessity of his going away from the disciples, "But I tell you the truth: It is for your good that I am going away. Unless I go away, the Counselor will not come to you; but if I go, I will send him to you" (John 16:7). "This indicates that Pentecost is a primary, and not a secondary, benefit of the departure of the Lord" (Brumback, 1955, p. 97). Peter's sermon on the day of Pentecost affirms that it was the ascended Jesus who was given the promise of the Spirit and sent him on the day of Pentecost (Witherington, 1998): "God has raised this Jesus to life, and we are all witnesses of the fact. Exalted to the right hand of God, he has received from the Father the promised Holy Spirit and has poured out what you now see and hear" (Acts 2:32-33).

The Holy Spirit's role as comforter reveals much of the work he was sent to do. This Greek word can also be translated as helper, counselor, intercessor, advocate, or guide. In light of Jesus' promise to send another comforter in John 14-16, Toon (1984) made seven statements concerning the prophetic ministry of Jesus and the coming of the Holy Spirit: (a) the coming of the Holy Spirit is dependent upon the going away of Jesus; (b) the Holy Spirit comes in the name of the Son to abide with the disciples forever; (c) the Holy Spirit comes to the disciples to testify of the exalted Christ; (d) the Holy Spirit comes as the Spirit of truth to guide the disciples into all truth; (e) the Holy Spirit discloses to the disciples what Christ has received of the Father and thus what Christ offers to them now as Savior and mediator; and (f) the Holy Spirit, whom the world cannot naturally receive, nevertheless comes to the world to convince people of their need of Christ.

The importance of the Holy Spirit's role as counselor to leadership should not be underestimated; however, the Holy Spirit as giver of gifts and power more directly relates to leadership and leadership empowerment. Spiritual gifts can be defined as any ability that is empowered by the Holy Spirit and used in any ministry of the church (Grudem, 1994) or a divine endowment of a special ability for service upon a member of the body of Christ (Enns, 1989). Table 5 shows the lists of gifts in the New Testament.

Table 5: Lists of Spiritual Gifts

1 Cor 12:1-11	1 Cor 12:27-31	Rom 12:6-8	Ephes 4:11
Wisdom	Apostles	Prophesy	Apostle
Knowledge	Prophets	Serving	Prophet
Faith	Teachers	Teaching	Evangelist
Healing	Miracles	Encouraging	Shepherd
Miracles	Healing	Giving	Teacher
Prophecy	Helps	Leading	
Discernment	Administration	Mercy	
Tongues	Tongues		
Interpretation	Interpretation		

These lists should not be viewed as comprehensive or exhaustive but as representative (Grudem, 1994; Warrington, 2008). Other gifts are mentioned in scripture; for example, 1 Peter 4:10-11 lists speaking and service as gifts (Erickson, 1998), and 1 Corinthians 7:7 lists marriage and celibacy as gifts (Grudem, 1994). Attempts to categorize these gifts are tentative at best (Fee, 1996). One reason is that a variety of terminology is used to describe these gifts. Three primary words are used to explain the giving of spiritual gifts: first is pneumatikos and means spirituals or spiritual things and is often translated "spiritual gifts," second is charisma that means grace gift, and third is the general word for give is didomi. Each list shown in Table 5 uses different words to describe the gifts. For example, the spiritual things (pneumatikon) being given (didotai) in 1 Corinthians 12:1-11 are called grace gifts (charismaton), services (diakonion), or operations (energematon). The word for spiritual things, pneumatikon, is used only in 1 Corinthians 12. Neither pneumatikon nor charisma is used to describe the ministries Christ gave (edoken) in Ephesians 4:11 (Holdcroft, 1999).

Another distinction between the three main gift lists is that each list has a different primary divine agent. In Romans 12:3b, Paul stated that "God has given" each of these gifts to the members of the body of Christ, these gifts could be properly called the gifts of the Father (Miller, 2008). Ephesians 4:7 states that these gifts are given "as Christ apportioned" and are sometimes referred to as the ministry gifts of Christ. Paul referred to the manifestation of the Spirit and used the phrase "by the Spirit" throughout the list in 1 Corinthians 12—they alone can accurately be called "gifts of the Spirit" (Miller, 2008). Each person of the Trinity plays a vital part in the manifestation of gifts. The persons of the Godhead have different roles, yet vitally work together, blending into a perfect unity of expression (Lin, 1994). This is an example of the divine *perichoretic* partnership at work.

There has been a great controversy regarding the baptism of the Holy Spirit (often *of*, *with*, or *in* the Holy Spirit are used interchangeably). Most Pentecostals and charismatics have believed that the baptism in the Holy Spirit is an experience subsequent to salvation, whereby the third person of the Godhead comes upon the believer to anoint and empower him for special service (Duffield & Van Cleave, 1987; Keener, 2001; Miller, 2005). Others have believed that the baptism with the Holy Spirit happens upon conversion and is a baptism into the body of Christ (Grudem, 1994; Thiessen, 1979). A difficulty in finding consensus of meaning is the diverse language used to explain the relationship of the Holy Spirit to man. For example, the Holy Spirit has been said to be "poured out" (Isa 44:2-3; Ezek 39:29; Joel 2:16-18; Acts 2:33, 10:45), "fallen on" (Acts 10:44, 11:15), "coming upon" (Acts 1:8, 19:6), "baptizing with" (Acts 1:5, 11:16; 1 Cor 12:13), and believers are "filled with" or "full of" the Holy Spirit (Acts 2:4, 6:5, 7:55; Ephes 5:18). Grudem wrote that the phrase "baptism in the Holy Spirit" is divisive and suggests that Pentecostals and Charismatics use terms such as "fullness of the Holy Spirit" or "new empowering for ministry." Different phraseology will not settle the "subsequence" issue or having two categories of Christians—"Spirit-filled Christian" and "ordinary Christian." There is, however, a commonly held belief among evangelicals of subsequent and additional "fillings" of the spirit separate from what they view as baptism by the Holy Spirit into the body of Christ (Enns, 1989; Ryrie, 1999; Thiessen, 1979). This may provide some common ground.

G. L. Anderson (2005), in a major Pentecostal journal, stated that believers who have not experienced the baptism in the Holy Spirit (according to the Pentecostal formula) can still minister with supernatural signs following. Yet, G. L. Anderson stated that the Spirit-baptized believer will have more power for ministry. A more thorough examination of the controversy over the baptism of the Holy Spirit is beyond the scope of this paper. Nevertheless, even with disagreements regarding an experience with the Holy Spirit subsequent to salvation and an enduement of additional power, there are several areas regarding the Holy Spirit where evangelical Christians and Pentecostals can agree: (a) the Holy Spirit indwells all Christians; (b) the Holy Spirit is the paraclete that comes alongside the Christian to counsel, help, teach, and guide; (c) the Holy Spirit gives gifts to Christians; and (d) the Holy Spirit empowers Christians by his presence and empowering gifts.

Section 1.14   *Summary*

The use of power and power distribution has become a major topic of organizational writing because power is part of the influence process (Northouse, 2007). Empowerment as an organizational strategy and leadership method has captured the attention of many writers and researchers. This interest has spurred much research and theorizing. Power in literature has found four conceptualizations or dimensions. The first dimension of power is overt and direct. This power influences the actions of others, usually by coercion and/or controlling resources and decision making. The second dimension of power is more subtle. It generally controls the agenda and the decision-making process, eliminating subordinate participation in the process. The third dimension of power is even more subtle than the second dimensional power. This dimension establishes the values and meaning of the organization. The fourth dimension of power is embedded in the system. It directs how and what we see and think. This power is controlled by the invisible forces operating in the organization and is beyond the manipulation of leader or follower.

An examination of how organizations view and use empowerment reveals three basic conceptualizations of empowerment. First is the critical social view of empowerment and makes aware social injustice and inequity. Critical social empowerment makes subordinates aware of their circumstances and works toward a social action agenda to better their situation. The second conceptualization is structural empowerment and gives access to organizational structures (information, support, resources, and opportunities). Third is psychological empowerment—the process of enhancing feelings of self-efficacy among members by removing conditions that foster feelings of powerlessness. It should be noted that in spite of a growing interest in spirituality in the workplace, there has been a failure to significantly investigate spiritual empowerment.

There is a lack of theological consideration in organizational leadership. Horsthuis (2011) suggested that conceptions of leadership should begin with the doctrine of the Trinity and that the ancient concept of *perichoresis* offers a participative understanding of leadership. *Perichoresis* allows that man might participate with God by rooting leadership in movement of grace that begins with and in the Triune God and not in the leader's capabilities or techniques (Horsthuis, 2011). Thus, leadership in general and leadership empowerment specifically should incorporate the attributes of the Father, the humility and exaltation of the Son, and the empowering practices of the Holy Spirit.

Chapter 3 – Method

This study examines the relationship between the ascension of Christ and leadership empowerment in Ephesians 4:1-16. Christianity is a historical religion with events and teachings that took place in time and space and ultimately recorded in writing. Therefore, the research method for this study is a qualitative hermeneutical method, drawing insight from several sources. The biblical text of Ephesians is the primary source for this study, but qualitative data consist of quotations, observations, and excerpts from other written documents (Patton, 2002).

The meaning of a text does not reside alone in the creative genius of its author; there is a complex correlation between a text and the contexts in which a text has been read and reread, including various dynamic interrelations between creator and contemplators, past and present (Gowler, 2010). Traditional exegesis tends to focus on the lexical meaning of words and their use in scripture without understanding how the culture and social framework of the original author affects the meaning of words (Buchanan, 2009). What a text means depends upon the cultural context in which it was originally created as well as the cultural context within which it is subsequently interpreted. Hermeneutics provides a theoretical framework for interpretive understanding, or meaning, with special attention to context and original purpose (Patton, 2002). Hermeneutics is derived from the Greek word meaning *to interpret* (Osborne, 2006). In modern usage, hermeneutics offers a perspective for interpreting legends, stories, and other texts, especially biblical and legal texts (Patton, 2002). The *hermeneutical circle* is an analytic process aimed at enhancing the understanding that relates parts to whole and the whole to parts. Constructing the meaning of the whole means making sense of the parts, and grasping the meaning of the parts depends on some sense of the whole. Knowing the meaning of lines of poetry requires an understanding of the poem, and knowing the meaning of the poem requires understanding the lines. Understanding the meaning of a text comes in layers. Each layer gives meaning or understanding to the other layers. Liberal interpreters of the Bible have used the term hermeneutical circle leading to where the text is interpreting us; therefore, *hermeneutical spiral* is a better metaphor because it is not a closed but rather an open-ended movement from the horizon of the text to the horizon of the reader (Osborne, 2006).

For Osborne (2006), the hermeneutical spiral is biblical interpretation that entails a spiral from text to context, from the original meaning to its contextualization or significance spiraling toward the true meaning. The interpreter can eventually step outside of the hermeneutical circle or spiral to grasp the meaning of a text in which the whole, its parts, and layers are in agreement. The meaning of a text is negotiated among a community of interpreters, and to the extent that some agreement is reached about meaning at a particular time and place, that meaning can only be based on consensual community validation (Patton, 2002). Interpreters, using acceptable methods of hermeneutics, should come to similar or complementary conclusions.

This research utilizes a hermeneutical method known as Socio-rhetorical interpretation or analysis. Emerging in the 1970s, Socio-rhetorical interpretation received its name in study of the Gospel of Mark that integrated rhetorical, anthropological, and social–psychological insight (V. K. Robbins, 2004). V. K. Robbins first introduced the term *Socio-rhetorical* into New Testament studies in 1984 (Gowler, 2010). Socio-rhetorical analysis is not just another method for interpreting texts, it is an interpretive analytic or an approach that evaluates and reorients its strategies as it engages in multifaceted dialogue with the texts and other phenomena that come within its purview (V. K. Robbins, 1999). Socio-rhetorical analysis begins with detailed attention to the text itself, then moves into the world of the people who wrote the texts, and then into our own world.

Socio-rhetorical comes from the combination of two words—socio and rhetorical. The hyphenated prefix, *socio,* refers to the rich resources of modern anthropology and sociology, while the term *rhetorical* refers to the way language in a text is a means of communication among people (V. K. Robbins, 1996a). Socio-rhetorical analysis integrates the ways people use language with the ways they live in the world. Socio-rhetorical analysis fosters a dialogic relationship with scholars of various approaches and disciplines, and its connection with reception history in particular is multifaceted, beginning with its foundational assumptions about the nature of texts and discourse (Gowler, 2010). Socio-rhetorical analysis is not just interested in the meaning of the text but also in how the text lived and breathed in its original context (V. K. Robbins, 2004). At the most basic level, the textures of Socio-rhetorical analysis can serve as a taxonomy of the various approaches an interpreter should utilize to create a more comprehensive interpretation of a text and its reception (Gowler, 2010).

Section 1.15   Research Design

Ephesians 4:1-16 is examined using Socio-rhetorical analysis to gain insight into the relationship between the historical event of Jesus' ascension and the leadership ministries of apostle, prophet, evangelist, pastor, and teacher. The research question that guides this study follows: What is the relationship between the ascension of Christ and leadership empowerment in Ephesians 4:1-16? The purpose of this study is to conduct a multifaceted hermeneutical analysis of a portion of Paul's epistle to the Ephesian church to discover the relationship and affects that Christ's ascension had upon leadership. This study explains the intent of Paul, the author, in connecting the ascension event to giving the leadership gifts of apostle, prophet, evangelist, pastor, and teacher. This study intends to be introductory into the examination of divine empowerment for leaders.

The method of research is a qualitative hermeneutical approach toward mining the text for the understanding of leadership empowerment in this text as a part of the larger body of scripture. This method of qualitative research is especially useful toward the understanding of biblical texts (Patton, 2002). Specifically, this research examines the inner texture, the social and cultural texture, and the sacred texture of Socio-rhetorical analysis as conceived by V. K. Robbins (1996a).

Section 1.16   Socio-rhetorical Analysis

Socio-rhetorical analysis draws a number of temporary boundaries around a text for the purpose of close examination from one point in time (V. K.

Robbins, 1996b). This approach presupposes that what is discovered within one bounded area will be put in dialogue with discoveries in other bounded areas (Snodderly, 2008). It can be compared to piecing together patterned squares that have been sewn separately; only when the squares are placed in right relation to each other does the overall design emerge. V. K. Robbins (1996a, 1996b) referred to these bounded areas as textures. By changing the interpreter's angle a number of times, the interpreter is able to bring multiple textures of the text into view. Socio-rhetorical analysis, as developed by V. K. Robbins (1996a), exhibits five different angles to explore multiple textures within texts: (a) inner texture, (b) intertexture, (c) social and cultural texture, (d) ideological texture, and (e) sacred texture. V. K. Robbins' (1996b) systematic approach asks the interpreter to develop a conscious strategy of reading and rereading a text from different angles. This study analyzes the inner texture, the social and cultural texture, and the sacred texture of Ephesians 4:1-16.

(a) Inner Texture

Inner texture concerns relationships among word–phrase and narrational patterns that produce argumentative and aesthetic patterns in texts (V. K. Robbins, 1996b). Historically, this texture has been called exegesis and could include textual criticism, literary analysis, rhetorical analysis, narrative analysis, linguistic and discourse analysis, and genre analysis, but V. K. Robbins (1996b) promoted his own set of six ways to explore the inner texture of a text: (a) repetitive, (b) progressive, (c) narrational, (d) opening-middle-closing, (e) argumentative, and (f) sensory-aesthetic (Snodderly, 2008). See Table 6 for descriptions of each.

Table 6: Six Kinds of Inner Texture (V. K. Robbins, 1996a)

Inner texture	Description
Repetitive	Resides in the recurrence of works and phrases more than once in a portion of text.
Progressive	Resides in the progressions of words and phrases throughout the text and is a logical progression (step-by-step advancement) or qualitative

Inner texture	Description
	progression (one quality introduces or prepares another quality).
Narrational	Resides in voices through which the words of the text speak; the narrator introduces characters, actions, other narrators, or other texts.
Opening–middle–closing	Resides in the nature of beginning, body, and conclusion of a section of discourse.
Argumentative	Found in the inner reasoning of the discourse with logical assertions, supporting clarifications, or qualitative images for persuasion.
Sensory–aesthetic	Resides in the range of senses the text evokes or embodies and the manner in which the text evokes or embodies them.

(b) Social and Cultural Texture

While inner texture and intertexture are concerned with the rhetorical aspect of interpreting texts, social and cultural texture and ideological texture are concerned with the social and cultural aspect of textual analysis. V. K. Robbins (1996b) defined culture as a system of patterned values, meanings, and beliefs that give cognitive structure to the world and provide a basis for coordinating and controlling human interactions to constitute a link as the system is transmitted from one generation to the next. Social and cultural texture is where a text interacts with society and culture by sharing in the general social and cultural attitudes, norms, and modes of interaction that are known by everyone in a society and by establishing itself in relationship with the dominant cultural system as sharing, rejecting, or transforming those attitudes, values, and dispositions. Analysis of the social and cultural texture takes the interpreter into social and anthropological theory that addresses the issue of the social and cultural nature of the text that searches out the kind of person who lives in the world of a particular text (V. K. Robbins, 1996a). The investigation of the social and cultural texture of a text includes exploring the type of social and cultural world the language evokes or creates. The language of a text reveals the social and cultural world in which the text is a part. This texture of texts emerges from specific social topics, common social and cultural topics, and final categories (V. K. Robbins, 1996a). Table 7 lists the seven types of specific social and cultural topics (social responses).

Table 7: Social Responses (Specific Social Topics; V. K. Robbins, 1996a)

Social response	Description
Conversionist	Considers the outside world to be corrupted and salvation is available only through a profound and supernatural transformation of the person.
Revolutionist	Declares that only the destruction of this world will be sufficient to save people.
Introversionist	Sees the world as irredeemably evil and encourages retreat from the world and to enjoy the security granted by personal holiness.
Gnostic–manipulation	Does not reject the world and its goals, but says that salvation is possible in the world and that evil can be overcome if people learn the right means to deal with their problems.
Thaumaturigical	Seeks immediate relief from their present circumstances through an act of divine intervention and seeks compensation for personal losses rather than the specific quest for cultural goals.
Reformist	Believes that the world is corrupt because its social structures are corrupt, but if the structures can be changed then salvation will be present in the world.
Utopian	Asserts that people should establish a new social system free from evil and the corruption to run the world.

Social and cultural texture of a text concerns the social and cultural systems and institutions that it both presupposes and evokes (V. K. Robbins, 1996b). Common topics of social and cultural texture reveal the overall environment of the text. Knowing the common social and cultural topics in a text can help the interpreter avoid ethnocentric (based one one's own culture, values, and experience) and anachronistic (chronological inconsistencies or mistakes) interpretation (V. K. Robbins, 1996a). V. K. Robbins (1996a) listed examples of common social and cultural common topics: (a) culture of honor, guilt, and rights; (b) dyadic or individualistic personalities; (c) dyadic and legal contracts and agreements; (d) challenge–response; (e) agriculture, industrial, or technological based economic exchange systems; (f) peasant, laborer, craftsmen, or entrepreneurs; (g) limited, insufficient, or overabundant goods; and (h) purity codes. Analysis of common cultural and social topics can thicken the analysis and interpretation of the text.

The cultural location of a reader, writer, or the text is categorized in final cultural categories of social and cultural textures (V. K. Robbins, n.d.). They are concerned with the manner in which people present their propositions, reasons, and arguments both to themselves and to other people. Determining the cultural location (in contrast to the social location) of a text reveals its writers' and readers' dispositions, presuppositions, and values, which influence the writing and reading of a text. Table 8 lists the final categories of social and cultural texture.

Table 8: Final Cultural Categories (V. K. Robbins, n.d.)

Final category	Description
Dominant culture	Presents a system of attitudes, values, dispositions, and norms that the speaker presupposes or asserts that are supported by social structures vested with power to impose its goal in a significantly broad region.
Subculture	Imitates the dominate culture and claims to enact them better than the members of dominant status.
Counterculture	Rejects the explicit and mutable characteristics of the dominant or subculture rhetoric to which it responds and evokes the creation of a "better society" by offering alternatives that the society will "see the light."
Contraculture	A short-lived, countercultural deviance; primarily a reaction-formation response to a dominant culture, subculture, or counterculture.
Liminal culture	Lasts only momentarily; they appear and disappear as people move from one cultural identity to another or consists of people who have never been able to establish a clear social and cultural identity in their setting.

(c) Sacred Texture

Sacred texture was added later by V. K. Robbins (1996a) and is considered by some to be a subset of ideological texture (Gowler, 2010). Sacred texture or theological texture (Snodderly, 2008) refers to the manner in which a text communicates insights into the relationship between the human and the divine. Sacred texture reveals insight into the nature of the relation between human life and the divine. It locates the ways the text speaks about God or about the realms of religious life. Table 9 shows the subtextures of sacred texture.

Table 9: Sacred Texture Subtextures (V. K. Robbins, 1996a)

Deity	Texts that decribe the nature of God
Holy person	Texts that reveal people who have a special relation to God or to divine powers.
Spirit being	Texts that reveal divine or evil beings who have the nature of a spirit rather than a fully human spirit.
Divine history	Texts that presuppose that divine powers direct historical processes and events toward certain results (eschatological, apocalyptic, or salvation history).
Human redemption	Texts that reveal the transmission of benefit from the divine to humans as a result of events, rituals, or practices.
Human commitment	Texts that portray humans who are faithful followers and supporters of people who play a special role in revealing the ways of God to humans (the other side of what God does for man).
Religious community	Texts that reveal the formation and nurturing of religious community; ecclesiology is concerned with the nature of community into which people are called by God.
Ethics	Texts that reveal the responsibility of humans to think and act in special ways in both ordinary and extraordinary circumstances.

Section 1.17   *Data Analysis*

Spiritual empowerment as a concept or construct implies the interaction of the divine with human. Within the Judeo–Christian tradition, the Bible is the ultimate record and authority for divine/human interaction. Self (2009) argued the validity of using sacred scriptures to investigate the construct of love by looking into the context of a New Testament text through lenses of social–rhetorical analysis. She posited that the Bible is a source from which the dominant philosophies of love stem. The same argument applies to empowerment and scripture. Although researchers have been slow to significantly use the Bible as a source for leadership research, some leadership writers have acknowledged that the Bible can inform leadership thought (Blanchard & Hodges, 2005; Kouzes & Posner, 2004). Yet some have still been puzzled that hermeneutical methods such as Socio-rhetorical analysis have not been more widely used to gain biblical insight into leadership thought (Self, 2009).

Socio-rhetorical analysis is particularly suited for examining relationships found in various cultural and social settings. This method allows the interpreter to examine how the meaning of the text is communicated, how the text lives in society, and how the text interacts with the divine. With each texture, the current study narrows the field of exploration to those aspects of texture (and subtexture) that are relevant to the research question.

Section 1.18   *Limitations of Study*

There are three potential limitations to this study. First, there are many biblical texts that address the issue of empowerment and many examples of leadership empowerment in the Bible. However, this study only considers one empowering relationship—the relationship of one event (the ascension of Christ) to leadership capacities (apostle, prophet, evangelist, pastor, and teacher) found in only a few verses in Ephesians. While the narrow focus on a few verses allows fuller interpretation, it also ignores other empowering relationships in scripture. Second, this study adds the divine aspect to leadership empowerment. Christian scripture is used as the primary source to inform our conceptualization of divine empowerment. No doubt, this will be rejected by many who wish to separate religion from spirituality. Third, this study does not look to other writings from other spiritual traditions.

Section 1.19   Summary

This study utilizes a hermeneutical method to inquire into the relationship of Christ's ascension to leadership empowerment in Ephesians 4:1-16 in light of contemporary theories of empowerment and organizational leadership. This research method uses qualitative analysis as suggested by Patton (2002) to gather information used to formulate a theory of divine empowerment. The multidimensional hermeneutic of Socio-rhetorical analysis as developed by V. K. Robbins (1996a, 1996b) is used to examine a portion of Paul's writing addressed to the Ephesians

Chapter 4 - Results

Constructing the meaning of the whole means making sense of the parts, and grasping the meaning of the parts depends upon some sense of the whole (Patton, 2002). To understand a text within a body of work, there must be a grasp of the overall meaning of the work. Authorship, date, and setting are important in understanding the social and cultural setting of the text. The presumed author of Ephesians is St. Paul. As mentioned in the literature review, many scholars have questioned the Pauline authorship of Ephesians. Several authors for Ephesians instead of Paul have been suggested, but no viable alternative has been accepted. Witherington (2007) astutely wrote that when a theory causes more problems than it solves, it should be abandoned. Such is the theory of Ephesians being written by an imitator of Paul. Whether written by an amanuensis, an associate, or by his own hand, Ephesians is decidedly Pauline.

Witherington (2007) suggested that Ephesians is not an epistle intended solely for the church in Ephesus; rather, it was intended to be a document circulated to the churches of Asia Minor where Ephesus served as its capital. Ephesus is located on long-established major roads leading eastward into the heart of Asia and Syria and adjacent to the Mediterranean Sea having a number of harbors was well situated to be the leading commercial center of Asia Minor (DeSilva, 2004). It would be accurate to characterize Ephesus as the leading city of the richest region of the Roman Empire. At this time, only Rome and Alexandria were larger (Arnold, 2010). Not only was Ephesus the greatest trading city of the province of Asia, it derived a certain religious authority in the whole province from the worship of Artemis (Ramsay, 1904) and was home of the great temple to her honor—one of the seven wonders of the ancient world. Ephesus was a city of wealth and of destination and the obvious choice for the provincial capital of Roman Asia Minor. Ephesus occupied an important place to the people of Asia as well as the ministry of Paul and the early church. Given the importance of this ancient city, it is logical that this circular document bears the name of the capital city.

Paul's reference to himself as a prisoner (Ephes 3:1& 4:1) and as an "ambassador in chains" (6:20) is good evidence that the date of the writing of this document came during a time of imprisonment. Several locations for Paul's imprisonment have been suggested, including Rome, Ephesus, Caesarea, and Philippi. The book of Acts records several occasions where Paul was incarcerated. Paul's brief confinement in Philippi (Acts 16:23f) for only one night can be eliminated from viable consideration. While tradition says that Paul was held captive for an extended period in Ephesus, there is no biblical evidence to support that claim (Ramsay, 1904). We have a subscript to Ephesians in several manuscripts (including codex Vaticanus) that says it was authored in Rome (Witherington, 2007), and this was the traditional view for 18 centuries (Wood, 1978). There is no compelling reason to reject Rome as the place of authorship. If written from Caesarea, the date of Ephesians falls between A.D. 59 and A.D. 61; if written from Rome, the date of Ephesians falls between the dates of A.D. 60 to A.D. 64 at the latest. In any event, we have a window of approximately 5-6 years for the date of authorship.

Exegetes generally interpret scripture according to the genre of the writing. Biblical scholarship has generally taken letter writing in the ancient Greco–Roman world as a model by which to describe the New Testament epistles (Ryken, 1987). It has been noted, however, that New Testament epistles differ from ancient letters. Epistles were artistically written for a wider public and intended for posterity, while letters were dashed off to address specific situations and problems and were never intended to be literary compositions (Schreiner, 1990). This has left some writers, in the case of Ephesians, to acknowledge the sermon-like qualities, but insist Ephesians is a letter (Arnold, 2010), and others acknowledging the qualities of a letter, but categorizing the document as a sermon or homily (Witherington, 2007). Acknowledging these two aspects, Lincoln (1990) described Ephesians as having the form of a letter meant to be read out loud, and the bulk of it is equivalent to a sermon. Witherington (2009) posited that understanding the oral culture of the Greco–Roman world in the time of Paul brings a greater understanding to the nature of sacred rhetoric. As far as can be determined, no documents in antiquity were intended for silent reading, and only a few were intended for private individuals to read. They always were meant to be read out loud, usually to a group of people (Witherington, 2009). The oral nature of literature is of necessity due to the estimated 80%-90% illiteracy rate and the great expense of written texts of the era. The New Testament epistles are generally longer than secular letters of the same period; although they sometimes have epistolary openings and closings, they are discourses, homilies, and rhetorical speeches that the authors could not deliver personally to the intended audience. Instead, they sent a surrogate to proclaim or deliver them, and the words themselves—especially religious words—were thought to have power and effect on people if they were properly communicated and pronounced (Witherington, 2009).

Paul wrote this letter to a large network of local churches in Ephesus and the surrounding cities to affirm them in their new identity in Christ as a means of strengthening them in their ongoing struggle with the powers of darkness, to promote a greater unity between Jew and Gentile within and among the churches of the area, and to stimulate an ever-increasing transformation of their lifestyles in a greater conformity to the purity and holiness to which God had called them (Arnold, 2010). The general purpose of Ephesians is to remind the Christian church of some central and distinctive features of their identity and to keep encouraging them to pursue the distinct values and behaviors that characterize them (DeSilva, 2004).

For Arnold (2010), four themes emerge in Ephesians. The first theme centers on the power of God over all other principalities, powers, and authorities. The threat of the spiritual powers should be seen in the light of the superior power of God and the power imparted by God to his people. The second theme is the unity of Jew and Gentile into one body in Christ. The cultural pressure of animosity toward Jews can and must be overcome in the church on the basis of Jesus' work of uniting Jew and Gentile into one community. The third theme is the appeal for maturity and holy living. All new Gentile believers need encouragement in continuing the process of ceasing their immoral practices and developing a lifestyle consistent with the holiness of God. The fourth theme is Paul's use of "in Christ" to characterize the new identity of these believers. Believers need to be well-established in an understanding of their new identity in Christ, understanding the implications for their spiritual struggle, their relationship to fellow believers, and their ability to live the virtue and moral imperatives of the Christian life.

Section 1.20   Socio-rhetorical Analysis of Ephesians 4:1-16

The goal of Socio-rhetorical analysis is to bring skills we use on a daily basis into an environment of interpretation that is both intricately sensitive to details and perceptively attentive to large fields of meanings in the world in which we live (V. K. Robbins, 1996a). It describes a set of integrated strategies that moves coherently through inner literary and rhetorical features of a text into a social and cultural interpretation of its discourse in the context of the Mediterranean world (V. K. Robbins, 1996b). Socio-rhetorical analysis is first concerned with rhetoric. Rhetoric is the faculty (power) of discovering, in the particular case, the available means of persuasion (Aristotle, 1960); in Paul's day, it is referred to as the art of persuasion (Buchanan, 2009). Rhetorical analysis concerns the interrelationship between language and human actions and how language attempts to create effects on an audience (Gowler, 2010). All language is a social possession that is an instrument of communication and influence. Therefore, rhetorical discourse is always situational, is generated to change reality, and is functionally a socially motivated mode of action (Wachob, 1993). Thus, Socio-rhetorical analysis is interested in how language is used to communicate within the social and cultural context of the text. Many methods can be utilized for Socio-rhetorical analysis. However, this study uses the method of Socio-rhetorical analysis developed by V. K. Robbins (1996a, 1996b). V. K. Robbins' (1996a, 1996b) method of Socio-rhetorical analysis is highly structured, dividing the analysis into divisions and subdivisions (he called textures). V. K. Robbins examined the rhetorical style by dividing the textual analysis into inner texture and intertexture and examines the social–cultural aspect of the text by dividing the textual analysis into cultural/social texture, ideological texture, and sacred texture. This study analyzes the inner, cultural/social, and sacred textures of Ephesians 4:1-16.

Section 1.21   Inner Texture Analysis

Inner texture focuses on words as tools for communication (V. K. Robbins,

1996a) and concerns relationships among word–phrase and narrational patterns that produce argumentative and aesthetic patterns in texts. At this stage, the interpreter assigns only basic lexical meanings to the words in the text and withholds fuller meanings to allow sign and sound patterns to emerge. The emphasis is on the relations of the signs and sounds rather than the content and meanings (V. K. Robbins, 1996b). According to V. K. Robbins (1996a, 1996b), Socio-rhetorical inner texture includes (a) repetitive–progressive, (b) opening–middle–closing, and (c) argumentative textures.

(a) Repetitive–Progressive

Repetitive texture resides in the occurrence of words, phrases, or concepts occurring more than once in a unit. Progressive texture resides in sequences or progressions of words, phrases, or concepts throughout the unit (V. K. Robbins, 1996a). Our pericope, Ephesians 4:1-16, contains 10 repetitive words, phrases, or concepts as shown in Table 10. A cursory look at the table reveals themes developing in the elementary structure of the text through the repetitive words, phrases, and concepts the author use to communicate his message.

Table 10: Repetitive Words, Phrases, and Concepts

Word	Verse	Concept
Calling	1	calling you have been called
	4	hope of your calling
Love	2	forbearance to one another in love
	15	speaking truth in love
	16	building up of [the body] in love
Unity	3	unity of spirit
	13	unity of the faith
	16	fitted and held together
Body	4	one body
	12	body of Christ
	16	whole body/causes the growth of the body
One	4	one body, one Spirit, one hope
	5	one Lord, one faith, one baptism
	6	one God
Authority (Power)	6	who is over all and through all and in all
	10	ascended far above all heavens
	15	him, who is the head
Gifts	7	grace was given according to the measure of Christ's gift
	8	he gave gifts to men
	11	and he gave
Maturity	12	building up
	13	mature man
	15	grow up in all aspects
	16	growth of the body / building up
Ascend	8	he ascended
	9	he ascended
	10	he who ascended
Descend	9	he who also descended
	10	he who descended

The most obvious use of repetitive texture is the repeated use of "one" in verses 4-6. The word translated as one comes from the Greek word *hen*; is the neuter primary numeral one; and precedes the words body, Spirit, hope,

Lord, faith, baptism, and God, which asserts God's oneness and unity with the body. This crescendo of nouns is used to preserve the unity of those belonging to Christ and unity in God (Wood, 1978). Some have seen a logical sequence to this series of seven acclamations of oneness (Lloyd-Jones, 1980). However, Lincoln (1990) wrote that the precise sequence is dictated more by compositional and rhetorical factors than by any deliberate preference for experiential rather than logical order in creedal formation. The repetitive words, however, are grouped around the three members of the Trinity: verse 4—one body, one Spirit, one hope; verse 5—one Lord, one faith, one baptism; and verse 6—one God and Father of all who is over all and through all and in all, which indicates not only the unity of the Godhead but also the unity with God and the body. This string of nouns, unconnected by conjunctions, has rhetorical force, adding to the weight of the exhortation to unity, which is a theme throughout the pericope (Witherington, 2007). The effect of the repeated use of one is to drive home the central theme of unity (Arnold, 2010). Significantly, the creedal tone of verses 4-6 establishes Trinitarian structure for a monotheistic Jewish audience living in a polytheistic Roman world. For Diaspora Jews accustomed to reading and hearing the Septuagint, the confession of "one Lord" would echo their daily confession of the Shema (Deut 6:4-9) where Yahweh is worshipped as the one Lord in the very same language (Arnold, 2010).

A second theme emerging from this textual analysis is calling. The references to calling are echoes from the introductory prayer in Ephesians 1:18 ("I pray that the eyes of your heart may be enlightened, so that you may know what is the hope of His calling") and helps connect the first division (theological) to the second paraenetic (exhortative) division of Ephesians. The redundancy in Ephesians 4:1 ("I . . . implore you to walk in a manner worthy of the calling with which you have been called") emphasizes the importance of this call (Arnold, 2010). The concept of calling is important in biblical thought (Patzia, 1990). Writers have identified three biblical calls. The first is the universal call for an individual to come into relationship with God. The second is a general call to Christian service. The third is to a specific call to a ministry or vocation (Iorg, 2008; Prime & Begg, 2004). This calling is primarily the first calling—the universal call to relationship with God—but may also include the others. The author addressed those who "were dead in [their] trespasses and sin in which [they] formerly walked according to this world" (Ephes 2:1) but now are a part of the community of God. This exhortation is directed toward all "the saints" in Asia, especially the converted Gentiles. The Jewish believer would be accustomed to the concept of "called" and "chosen," but this concept would be of great significance for the Gentile believers who are being told that they have full access to God and the Christian community. The expression "hope of your calling" (1:18 & 4:4) does not just refer to a future life; it is a reference to the present life of the believer that foreshadows a future life.

As with calling, a macroview of Ephesians reveals that power and authority are themes for the entire book as well. Ultimate power and authority are implicit in the phrases "who is over all and through all and in all" (Ephes 4:6) and "ascended far above all heavens" (v. 10). The headship (lordship) of Christ over the church is specified in Ephesians 4:15: "we are to grow up in all aspects into him who is the head, even Christ." Each of these phrases harken back to the prayer Paul offered in Ephesians 1 where the authority and headship of Christ is firmly established:

> I pray that the eyes of your heart may be enlightened, so that you will know what is the hope of His calling, what are the riches of the glory of His inheritance in the saints, and what is the surpassing greatness of His power toward us who believe. These are in accordance with the working of His might which He brought about in Christ, when He raised Him from the dead and seated Him at His right hand in heavenly places, far above all rule and authority and power and dominion, and every name that is named, not only in this age but also in the age to come. And He put all things in subjection under His feet, and gave Him as head over all things to the church, which is His body, the fullness of Him who fills all in all. (Ephes 1:18-23)

Ultimate authority and power is also implied in the repetition (and progression) of "descended" and "ascended" in verses 9-10; especially verse 10: "He who descended is Himself also He who ascended far above all the heavens, so that He might fill all things." Ascension also hearkens back to the prayer in Ephesians 1. The repetition of these phrases points directly to the authority and power of the ascended Christ that Paul had previously explicated.

(b) Opening–Middle–Closing

Opening–middle–closing texture resides in the nature of the beginning, the body, and the conclusion of a section of discourse (V. K. Robbins, 1996a). Other textures regularly work together to create the opening, middle, and closing of a unit of text. The opening, middle, and closing of our pericope becomes evident by examining the repetitive and progressive words in the text shown in Table 16 (p. 191), which reveals a distinct beginning, middle, and closing for this pericope and begins to reveal the theme for the paraenetic portion of Ephesians and reinforces the theme of the entire book of Ephesians.

The repetition of the phrases or words *calling*, *love*, *unity*, and *body* and the seven-fold use of *one* combine to reveal the beginning of this text is the author's call or appeal for unity within the body of Christ (Ephes 4:1-6). *Unity*, *love*, and *body* are found in the opening and closing. The middle portion of the text is clear through the repetition of *give* and *gift* (vv. 7-11). These gifts are directly linked to the exaltation of Christ through the repetition and progression of the *descent* and *ascent* of Christ (vv. 12-16). This equipping and appeal for unity culminates with an indication that unity and maturity in the body of Christ is the natural byproduct of empowered Christian living or service. The repetition of *love* in the beginning verses and the closing verses indicates that love is an important ingredient for accomplishing the unity desired. It is also noteworthy that the concept of authority appears in the opening, the middle, and the closing section signified by the use of the phrases *who is over all*, *above all heavens*, and *him who is the head*. The author's inclusion of phrases that indicate divine power and authority throughout this portion of text is most likely a sign that authority and power is foundational and integral to the additional points the author made.

Repetitive–progressive and beginning–middle–closing inner textural analysis is preliminary to our overall Socio-rhetorical analysis; however, a major theme is emerging: Believers are called to grow in maturity and maintain unity in the body of believers as the ascended Christ with all power and authority empowers them.

(c) Argumentative

Argumentative texture is interested in the rhetorical style as much as the words themselves. Study of argumentative texture investigates various kinds of inner reasoning in a discourse (V. K. Robbins, 1996a). Argumentative texture analysis attempts to integrate the tools of both ancient and modern rhetorical criticism into Socio-rhetorical analysis of the text (V. K. Robbins, n.d.). Argumentative texture looks for the logical reasoning in the text. Ephesians is a mixture of exhortation and argumentation. Ephesians 4:1-16 begins the section that is largely argumentation.

Rhetoric played a powerful role in the everyday life in the Roman Empire from the official courts to the marketplace (Buchanan, 2009). Traditional rhetoric is generally divided into three kinds or branches: (a) forensic, (b) deliberative, and (c) epideictic (Cooper, 1960). Forensic and deliberative rhetoric looks for judgments or verdicts, forensic rhetoric looks for judgments on past happenings as in judicial courts, and deliberative rhetoric looks for judgments in the future such as the legislature making laws. Epideictic rhetoric is ceremonial speech of praise (or blame) and does not look for a judgment. Its purpose is to inspire and motivate. Every Greco–Roman speech falls into one of these three branches, and identifying the branch of rhetoric scriptural text falls under gives the interpreter an important clue to understanding the intent of the author (Buchanan, 2009).

A biblical interpreter should be careful not to force rhetorical conventions upon a text that the author did not intend. However, whereas the art of rhetoric was well known in Paul's day, it is no surprise that typical rhetorical devices can be identified in New Testament writings. Ephesians 4:1-16 can be easily divided into three sections: (a) introduction and presentation of his argument (vv. 1-6), (b) the main part of the argument or body (vv. 7-13), and

(c) the conclusion of his argument (vv. 14-16). Ephesians 4:1-3 includes a brief *exordium* or introduction (I, the prisoner of the Lord), Paul then moved directly into his argument, "Therefore, I . . . implore you to walk worthy of the calling with which you have been called." The directive could end there, but in Pauline fashion, he offered an extended description of how to walk out this calling—with humility, gentleness, patience, tolerance in love, and unity. Verses 4-6 (an almost parenthetical description of unity) lists seven proofs for unity—one body, one Spirit, one hope of calling, one Lord, one faith, one baptism, and one God—supporting his admonition to strive for Christian unity.

Verses 7-13 include the main part of his argument—the *confirmatio* or the logical argument. The basic argument is that Christ gave the gifts of apostle, prophet, evangelist, pastor, and teacher to help in the walk that believers are called to and become mature as believers. These gifts are people with special abilities: leading, prophesying, proclaiming the good news, shepherding, and teaching. The author tied the giving of these gifted individuals directly to the ascension (and by implication to the session) of Christ. Again, this harkens back to Ephesians 1 where Christ is revealed as being resurrected and ascended to heavenly places: "[God] raised [Christ] from the dead and seated Him at His right hand in heavenly places" (Ephes 1:20b). These gifts of gifted individual are given for the specific purpose for maturing and unifying the body (vv. 12-13). To strengthen his argument, the author used the intertexture recitation of Psalm 68:18. This verse is quoted (if taken from Coptic translations, Targumic readings, or most Syriac Peshitta texts) or used in a similar context (if taken from the Masoretic text or the Greek Septuagint) to support the notion of Christ giving gifts. Psalm 68 is notoriously hard to interpret, but the key to understanding this verse is to recognize its original use as a liturgical text accompanying a ritual (Broyles, 1999). This psalm, governed primarily by ritual factors and not simply by literary and thematic considerations, is basically a psalm of military triumph (Boice, 1996). Boice (1996) explained Paul's logic in reciting Psalm 68:18:

> It is not so strange that Paul would take a verse that in the Old Testament refers to the arrival of the Ark of the Covenant at Mount

> Zion and refer it to Jesus who, in a similar way, ascended to the heavenly tabernacle after his resurrection to reign over the church. (p. 558)

The use of Psalm 68:18 to strengthen the concept of God giving gifts and also for the potential of every Christian to receive a gift from God would have been significant to the Jewish and Gentile believer alike.

Verses 14-16 are the *peroratio* or the conclusion. This conclusion is identified by the words "as a result." This indicates that the previous argument, when fulfilled, will accomplish or result in a desired state. This state includes maturity (no longer being children), confidence in the faith (not being carried about by every wind of doctrine, trickery of men, or deceitful scheming), and unity in the body of Christ (caused growth of the body for the building up of itself in love).

(d) Summary of Inner Texture Analysis

However preliminary in our investigation, themes can be seen developing that aid our understanding of the relationship between Christ's ascension to leadership empowerment. The first theme, calling, is evident in the repetitive texture in the opening portion of our pericope. Calling is also seen in the opening of the theological portion of Ephesians (i.e., Ephes 1-3) as well as in the opening of the exhortative section of Ephesians (i.e., Ephes 4-6). The second theme beginning to emerge is equipping through the gifts given by the authority and power of the ascended and seated Christ. The mediatorial role of the gifts of apostle, prophet, evangelist, pastor, and teacher are also beginning to form.

Section 1.22   *Cultural and Social Textural Analysis*

After rhetorical and textual considerations, the social and cultural aspects of the text are analyzed. What is significant here is the social and cultural nature or location of the text. The use of anthropological and social theory helps the interpreter understand the social and cultural voices in the text. V. K. Robbins' (1996a, 1996b) taxonomy of social and cultural texture considered specific topics, common topics, and final topics.

(a) Specific Categories

Specific social topics in the text reveal the religious responses to the world in its discourse. How the writer and audience of the text react to the world is of primary interest in specific topics. V. K. Robbins (1996b) wrote that people set themselves apart from others in the world. There are different ways in which people set themselves apart from others, and sociologists and anthropologists have given us language to describe different ways in which people do this. V. K. Robbins (1996a, 1996b) referred to the typology of sects developed by Bryan Wilson who conceptualized seven types of religious responses to the world: (a) conversionist, (b) revolutionist, (c) introversionist, (d) gnostic–manipulation, (e) thaumaturgical, (f) reformist, and (g) utopian. Each describes a possible reaction or response to the world from changing society by changing individuals to total destruction and reconstruction of society (see Table 7 page 85). Social and religious differences in the text are examined and then applied to social identity theory.

Ephesians 4:1-16 is the opening of the paraenetic portion of the book. Paul is exhorting the saints of Asia to live their lives worthy of their calling. The next verses read:

> So this I say, and affirm together with the Lord, that you walk no longer just as the Gentiles also walk, in the futility of their mind being darkened in their understanding, excluded from the life of God because of the ignorance that is in them, because of the hardness of their heart; and they, having become callous, have given themselves over to sensuality for the practice of every kind of impurity with greediness. (Ephes 4:17-19)

This suggests a conversionist reaction to the world. The conversionist response to society is characterized by a view that the world is corrupt because the people are corrupt; and if the people can be changed, the world will be changed (V. K. Robbins, 1996a). Paul's main concern is for individual change whether or not society changes. The Greek word for Gentile is *ethnā* from which we get the English word ethnic. In scripture, it can also be translated as nations, non-Jew, pagan, heathen, or unbeliever.

Paul addressed this discourse to "the Saints [*hagios*] who are at Ephesus." The reference to saints did not distinguish between ethnic identities but is an address to any believer in Christ regardless of his or her political or racial identity. The use of *hagios* and *ethnā* suggest a division between believer and nonbeliever, not a social distinction. The indication is that a Gentile believer is no longer part of the *ethnā* but is now a *hagios*.

Ephesians, as with all of Paul's writings, represents the intersection of three worldviews: Roman, Jewish, and the emerging Christian worldview. Roman society in the first century was very structured with distinct class stratification (Durant, 1971). At the very top of the society were the emperors. Becoming an emperor was by heredity. Emperors were not selected based on ability or honesty but because they were born in the right family—a divine right to rule. The Patricians comprised the privileged class with most of the wealth and power. Most Patricians came from families of wealth and land, but this class was open to a few who had been promoted by the emperor. Below them was the Equestrian class. They were the business class. Wealth could be achieved in this class as well. This class was made up of tax collectors, bankers, miners, traders, and so forth. Below the business class were the Plebeians. The Plebeians were the working class with jobs such as farming, baking, construction, or craftsmanship. Some Plebeians could eventually work themselves into the Equestrian class, but most lived the difficult life supporting their families and paying their taxes. At the bottom of the social structure were the slaves and freedmen. Slavery was common in the ancient world, and the Roman world was no exception. All slaves and their families were considered the property of their owners. Roman society practiced manumission or the practice of allowing slaves to be freed. Many freedmen became plebeians and worked the same job for their owners. Freedmen, although free, did not enjoy rights that other citizens enjoyed. For example, they were not considered citizens, could not own land, and any possessions went to their previous owner when they died.

Religion in the Roman Empire in the first century was polytheistic and very syncretistic (Durant, 1971). A typical household would have private gods like Janus and the goddess Vesta that watched out for their home and fields.

Romans also had national gods like Zeus and Jupiter (Diana or Artemis was the dominant god in the region of Ephesus). Durant (1971) wrote that some of the divinities (*di novensiles*) were not conquered but conquering; they seeped into Roman worship through commercial, military, and cultural contracts with Greek civilization. Thus, Roman gods became associated with Greek gods—Cronus with Saturn, Poseidon with Neptune, Artemis with Diana, Hades with Pluto, and so on. Religion permeated life in the Roman Empire. The innumerable deities and rites of polytheism were closely interwoven with every circumstance of business or pleasure, of public life or of private life; and it seemed impossible to escape the observance of them without renouncing the commerce of mankind and all the offices and amusements of society (Gibbon, 1845). Roman gods rewarded ritual and formulas, not goodness. Roman religion (heathenism) is a deification of the rational and irrational creative and a corresponding corruption of the moral sense, giving the sanction of religion to natural and unnatural vices—heathenism was a religion groping after the unknown god (Schaff, 1996).

Jewish life in the time of Paul was similar to that of the surrounding culture. They were involved in local commerce as shepherds, fishermen, carpenters, and so on. Yet, the theocentric nature of the Jews made them particularly stand out from society. Wherever a Roman or a Greek might travel, he could take his gods with him or find rites kindred to his own. It was far otherwise with the Jew. He had only one temple and only one God (Edersheim, 1890). The Assyrian and Babalonian captivities once caused the Jews to live away from their capital and temple, but by Paul's day, living away from Jerusalem and the temple was entirely voluntary. Edersheim (1890) described the Jew as being dispersed over the whole inhabited earth and become a world–nation, yet its heart still beat in Jerusalem. Gibbon (1845) described the diaspora Jews as being multiplied to a surprising degree in the East, and afterwards in the West, and soon exciting the curiosity and wonder of other nations and explained Jewish disposition toward Gentile cultures:

> The sullen obstinacy with which they maintained their peculiar rites and unsocial manners, seemed to mark them out as a distinct species of men, who boldly professed, or who faintly disguised, their

> implacable habits to the rest of human kind. Neither the violence of Antiochus, nor the arts of Herod, nor the example of the circumjacent nations, could ever persuade the Jews to associate the institutions of Moses [with] the elegant mythology of the Greeks. (p. 318)

Gibbon described the attitude of diaspora Jews as a narrow and unsocial spirit, which instead of inviting had deterred the Gentiles from embracing the Law of Moses. Jews, even in their disadvantaged state, still asserted their lofty and exclusive privileges, shunned, instead of courting the Gentiles. They still insisted with inflexible vigor to practice the parts of the law still in their power to practice with their distinction of days, of meats, and observances that probably seemed trivial and burdensome to Gentile neighbors. Gibbon suggested that even the rite of circumcision was alone capable of repelling a willing proselyte from the door of the synagogue. Schaff (1996) wrote that the Jews adhered most tenaciously to the letter of the law and to their traditions and ceremonies, cherished a bigoted horror of the heathen, and were therefore despised and hated by them as misanthropic. Thus, a strong line of demarcation between the Jews and Gentiles ran through the whole of the Roman Empire. The "middle wall" of partition was built up by diligent hands on both sides (Conybeare & Howson, 1980).

Under these circumstances, Christianity spread through Asia. At the time of Paul, the Christian worldview was emerging but was seen as a branch of Judaism. Soon Christians grew in number. Gibbon (1845) wrote that Christians had a similar inflexible and intolerant zeal as the Jew, but their zeal was "purified from the narrow and unsocial spirit" (p. 318) of Jewish zeal. It was this purified zeal, however, that helped Christianity to become influential. Doctrine of a future life, miraculous powers, Christian morality, and the unity and discipline of the Christian community were also influential, according to Gibbon. The enfranchisement of the Christian church from the synagogue was a work of some time and difficulty. Jewish believers tended to adhere to the customs of the law they were accustomed to and even desired to impose them upon Gentile converts. It was into this setting that Paul wrote his epistles, including Ephesians.

Application of social identity theory aids in the understanding of the conversionist disposition of our text. According to social identity theory, people tend to classify themselves and others into various social categories such as organizational membership, religious affiliation, gender, and age cohort (Ashforth & Mael, 1989). Group or group affiliation gives a sense of identity and belonging to the social world. People can belong to several groups depending on various factors such as ethnicity, location, belief, age, and gender. People have a tendency to divide themselves into us and them groups (labeled in-groups and out-groups). Tajfel and Turner (1985) identified three processes in distinguishing in-groups and out-groups. The first, social categorization is the simple process of deciding which group you and others belong to based on a variety of distinguishing factors. The second is social identification whereby individuals adopt the identity of the group they have categorized themselves with. The third process is social comparison. After identifying with a particular group (in-group), we have a tendency to compare our group with other groups (out-groups). Social comparison between groups is a decisive element in the process by which social categorization can turn into the creation of positive in-group distinctiveness. Social classification serves two functions: (a) it cognitively segments and orders the social environment, providing a systematic means of defining others, and (b) social classification enables the individual to locate or define himself or herself in the social environment (Ashforth & Mael, 1989).

Social identity is the perception of oneness with or belonging to some human aggregate (Ashforth & Mael, 1989). Ashforth and Mael (1989) identified three factors besides the typical factors for group formation (similarity, proximity, shared goals, etc.) that are most likely to increase the tendency to identify with a group: (a) group distinctiveness—values and practices in relation to the values and practices of other groups, (b) group prestige—individuals often cognitively identify themselves with winners, and (c) group salience (standing out relative to neighboring groups)—awareness of other groups tend to increase group homogeneity, reinforce boundaries, and underscore values. Ashforth and Mael also stated that group cohesion, cooperation, altruism, and positive evaluation of the group are results of an individual identifying with a group. Another result of group identification is that individuals tend to choose activities congruent with the salient aspects of the group identity, and they support the institutions embodying those identities.

Although there are three distinct worldviews, Paul drew the boundaries between two groups, the hagios and the ethna—the saints (believers) and Gentiles (unbelievers). The implication is that Jew and Gentile believers should identify with the Christian community. The first three chapters of Ephesians draw the boundaries for the Christian in-group and also help define the distinctiveness, prestige, and the salience of this in-group. The results of social identity as a saint will be group cohesion (unity), altruism (love), cooperation, and other activities congruent with the Christian identity—all of which are the ultimate goals of Paul's exhortation in Ephesians 4:1-16. So that Paul's message is clear, he listed behaviors or attitudes of their past that they should no longer associate with such as falsehood, anger, wrath, stealing, unwholesome speech, bitterness, clamor, slander, malice, immorality, greed, filthiness, silly talk, course jesting, and immorality. On the other hand, Paul listed in-group attitudes and behavior such as speaking words of edification, kindness, tender-heartedness, forgiveness, thankfulness, and being imitators of God. These behaviors clearly differentiate the groups. Drawing a comparison between the in-group hagios and the out-group ethna, as Paul did in Ephesians, helps increase their unity and strengthen their Christian values and behavior.

(b) Common Categories

Culture is a common or shared system of patterned values, meanings, and beliefs that give cognitive structure to the world, provide a basis for coordinating and controlling human interactions, and constitute a link as the system is transmitted from one generation to the next (V. K. Robbins, 1996b). Common social and cultural topics are instinctively learned. They are the overall environment for the specific social topics in a text. Knowing the common social and cultural topics in a text can help an interpreter to avoid ethnocentric and anachronistic interpretation (V. K. Robbins, 1996a). The emerging theme of Ephesians 4:1-16 is that Paul is exhorting Christians to walk worthy of their calling in maturity with altruistic behavior pursuing unity with other Christians. After this exhortation, Paul described the results as maturity and unity in the body of Christ. In verses 11-13, Paul introduced five gifts (or individuals with ministry gifts) that mediate the process of maturity and unity. These gifted individuals (apostle, prophet, evangelist, pastor, and teacher) are given by the ascended Christ specifically to help in the walk of maturity and unity. These gifts are culturally significant to the text.

For understanding the significance of giving in the first century, an examination of giving and the exchange of goods is examined. According to DeSilva (2000), the world of the authors and the readers of the New Testament was one in which personal patronage was an essential means of acquiring access to goods, protection, or opportunities for employment and advancement. Patronage is the giving and receiving of favors to relations and friends. In modern culture, patronage is seen as unfair advantage and despairingly called nepotism, but in the first century it was essential, expected, and even advertised. One particular kind of patronage was called benefaction. This relationship is where the wealthy person is the benefactor and there was a clearly articulated code that guided the noble exchange of graces (DeSilva, 2000). God is presented in the New Testament as the source of many gifts. God's patronage of the church is evidenced in the growth and building up of the churches and members. DeSilva (2000) asserted that benefaction within the church is a specific gift of God (Rom 12:6-8; Ephes 4:7, 11-12). It is a manifestation of God's patronage of the community, mediated through its members. DeSilva wrote,

> Alongside and among spiritual endowments and edifying services like prophesying, tongues, teaching and words of knowledge, God also bestows the gift of giving to achieve God's purposes in the family of God. God supplies all things, so that Christians are called to share on the basis of their kinship responsibly toward one another in the church rather than use gifts of money and hospitality to build up their client base (the source of local prestige and power). (p. 153)

Thus, God's purpose in patronage (giving graces) is to mature and build the body of Christ through the mediation of gifts given to individual members. These gifts for the building up of the body would include the apostle, prophet, evangelist, pastor, and teacher.

The disparity between the texts of Ephesians 4:8 and Paul's use of Psalm 68:18 to enforce the notion of the ascended Christ giving gifts may be understood in the context of patronage. Psalm 68:18 reads, "You have ascended on high, you have led captive your captives; you have received gifts among men," while Ephesians 4:8 reads, "When he ascended on high, he led captive a host of captives, and he gave gifts to men." This use of the Old Testament text seems to change or reverse the meaning of the text. However, patronage is seen as a reciprocal relationship where the more wealthy or powerful person or entity bestows gifts in return for services or even worship. At a time when patronage is the cultural norm, it would likely be understood that a conquering king would receive gifts from and also give gifts to their loyal subjects. One implies the other in Paul's world where patronage is the custom.

The gifts of apostle, prophet, evangelist, pastor, and teacher are common cultural topics. They each would have had a role in the life of a believer and a particular reason for Paul to list them as being important to the maturity of the church and establishing unity in the body of Christ. There has been, however, some disagreement whether Paul intended to list pastor and teacher as two separate gifts or as the combined gift of pastor/teacher. This disagreement comes from the anarthrous listing of teacher. Each of the gifts in the list is preceded by a definite article except for teacher, leading some to believe that Paul intended that pastor and teacher fulfill one role—that of a pastor/teacher. Ephesians 4:11 in the Greek reads και αυτος εδωκεν τους μεν αποστολους τους δε προφητας τους δε ευαγγελιστας τους δε ποιμενας και διδασκαλου. Note the use of a particle (μεν) and the use of two different conjunctions (δε and και). The author used δε before apostle, prophet, evangelist, and pastor, but he used και before teacher. The use of two different conjunctions could be a mere stylistic choice but may be an indication that the two functions of pastor and teacher were intended to be combined. The particle (μεν) is hard to translate and many English versions leave the particle untranslated. The UBS Greek New Testament (4th revised edition) indicates that when μεν and δε are used together, it is an indication of contrast or emphasis. With these factors in mind, Ephesians 4:11 could be translated "and he gave on the one hand apostles, and on the other hand prophets, and on the other hand evangelists, and on the other hand pastors and teachers." This has caused many (perhaps most) commentators to combine pastor and teacher into one role. However, it should be noted that the gifts listed in our text are individuals who operate in a particular function or functions (Bayes, 2010), and most of the other gifts that are listed (see Table 5 page 75) are functions (teaching, prophesy, serving, miracles, discernment, etc.), not people or offices. The list in 1 Corinthians 12:27 includes teacher separately with no mention of pastor, indicating that pastor and teacher are two distinct gifts. Regardless of whether Paul intended for teacher and pastor to be two gifts or one, they are two distinct functions—teaching and shepherding.

The ministry functions in Ephesians 4:11 provide a mediatorial role. God's expressed state for believers and his church is unity and maturity, according to his messenger Paul. The past state of his audience is implied in Ephesians 4 but made explicit in Ephesian 2:1, "And you were dead in your trespasses and sins." Ephesians 4:1-16 conveys that the past state of believers and the desired state of the church is mediated by the gifts (functions or ministries) of apostle, prophet, evangelist, pastor, and teacher (see Figure 4).

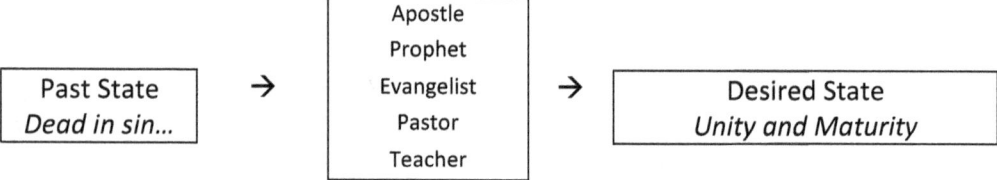

Figure 4: Mediatorial roles (leadership).

These mediatorial roles are indications of leadership. Each gift of apostle, prophet, evangelist, pastor, and teacher fulfills a leadership role in the church.

Northouse (2007) defined leadership as a process whereby an individual influences a group of individuals to achieve a common goal. The apostle, prophet, evangelist, pastor, and teacher each assert different influences upon saints and unbelievers to achieve a common goal. Each gift functions differently, but they have the shared goal of unity and maturity in the body of believers.

The first cultural item and leadership gift listed in Ephesians 4:11 is the apostle. Many scholars and commentary writers have believed that the office of the apostle has ended with the death of the last apostle. Numerous authors have followed the lead of Calvin (1548) who wrote in his commentaries of 1 Corinthians and Ephesians that only the "offices" of pastor and teacher were still functioning in the church in his day. Yet, Harnack (1904), pointing out that the term *apostle* is confined to the 12 only twice in Paul (1 Cor 9:5 and Gal 1:7), wrote,

> The term [apostle] cannot be sharply restricted at all; for God appoints prophets and teachers in the church, so also does he appoint apostles to be the front rank therein, and since such charismatic callings depend upon the church's needs, which are known to God alone, their numbers are not fixed. (p. 281)

Apostle is the transliteration of the Greek word *apostolos*, meaning "a messenger" or "one sent on a mission." Apostles were literally commissioned messengers fulfilling their sender's mission and were backed by the sender's authority to the extent that they accurately represented that commission (Keener, 1993). "Being sent" was known to the Jewish and ancient world (Bayes, 2010), but Paul's use of *apostolos* had a distinct meaning for the first-century believer. The New Testament used *apostolos* in the general sense as an apostle or sent one (Rom 16:7; 1 Thess 2:6), but in the majority of the approximately 80 times the word *apostolos* is used, it is in reference to the original 12 apostles (Bayes, 2010). However, Paul used this term to describe himself and his calling and used *apostolos* to describe a gifting for ministry (1 Cor 12:27; Ephes 4:11).

Much has been written about the criteria and function of apostleship. The concrete duties of an apostle are not clear, though they surely follow the example of the 12 and Paul. Although the apostolic functions are unclear, apostles have commonly been associated with authority to some extent. For centuries, apostleship has been held in high esteem and ascribed only to the original 12, Paul, and Matthias. J. B. Lightfoot and other scholars have concluded that direct commissioning from Jesus did not apply to Paul and Matthias; this raised theological problems about the significance of the derivation of apostle from the Jewish practice of legal representation (Schütz, 2007) and also about the authority of apostles in general. If those in the New Testament called apostles (namely Paul and Matthias) were not directly commissioned by Jesus, then where does their authority lie, and can others be named apostle as well? This raises questions about the continuation of the ministry or gift of apostle that Paul listed in Ephesians 4 and 1 Corinthians 12.

It is difficult to know what apostolic authority is and how it functioned in the New Testament (Schütz, 2007). The modern perception of authority, as with patronage, is not the perception of authority in the first-century Roman Empire. According to Schütz (2007), modern writing on authority is placed upon an implicit source alone; modern authority rests within the social organization and is constantly being underwritten by those who command and those who obey, presumably because the goals of the social organization benefit, and are shared by both. Authority in ancient times was more explicit. Authority should derive from an *auctor*. Schütz cited B. de Jouvenel:

> The *auctor* is, in ordinary speech, creator of a work, father or ancestor, founder of a family or a city, the Creator of the universe. This is the crudest meaning; more subtle meanings have become incorporated with it. The *auctor* is the man whose advice is followed, he instigates, he promotes. He inspires others with...his own purpose, which now becomes that of those others as well—the very principle of the actions which they freely do. In this way the notion of father and creator is illuminated and amplified: he is the father of actions and creator is illuminated and amplified: he is the father of actions freely undertaken whose source is in him through their seat in others. (p. 12)

For Schütz (2007), the *auctor* of apostolic authority is the power of the gospel (i.e., the news of the person and work of Jesus Christ). Nothing is more closely associated with the apostle Paul than the gospel ("Paul, a bond-servant of Christ Jesus, called as an apostle, set apart for the gospel of God" [Rom 1:1]). The one who knows himself to be sent, knows himself to be sent for the purpose of the gospel. (The distinction between the gift of apostle and Paul's own apostleship is not one that he made.) For the Jew, the ultimate source of authority is God through the law (i.e., Torah); for the first-century Roman, the ultimate source of authority is the Roman emperor through Roman law; for the Christian, the ultimate source of authority is God through the work of Christ. In the language of Schütz, the *auctor* or source of apostolic authority is the ascended and exalted Christ.

Whereas the specific role and function of an apostle is difficult to determine, the mediatorial leadership function of prophet, evangelist, pastor, and teacher are easier to recognize. The reason these roles are easier to determine is that they are known in the cultural and social context of the first century. It should be understood, first, that because each of the other ministry gifts share the mediatorial function with the apostle, they logically share in the authority given to them by the ascended Christ.

The English word prophet comes from the Greek *prophetes*, which signifies, in classical Greek, one who speaks for another, especially one who speaks for a god, and so interprets his will to man (W. Smith, n.d.). Prophesy and soothsaying were known in antiquity throughout the ancient Near East (Freeman, 1968). During the intertestamental times, the Jews recognized that prophecy had ceased, but they looked forward to a revival of prophecy during the messianic age (G. V. Smith, 1986). Certainly, prophets were known in Jesus' time: John the Baptist (Matt 11:9-14; Mrk 11:32), Jesus (Matt 21:11; John 4:19), Anna (Luk 2:36); Josephus reported that the first-century Essenes possessed the gift of prophesy, and the warning against false prophets presupposes the existence of authentic prophets (Matt 7:15; Acts 13:7; 2 Pet 2:1; 1 John 4:1). Whereas apostles, evangelists (those who deliver good news), shepherds, and teachers had a secular equivalent, prophets were distinctly religious whether Jewish, Christian, or heathen such as the well-known Oracle of Delphi said to be inspired by Apollo. Prophets were divinely inspired to communicate God's will to the people and to disclose the future to them (Unger, 1998). The mediatorial role for the prophet is to communicate God's message to his people.

Paul listed evangelists as the third mediatorial leader. In the literal sense, an evangelist is "one announcing the good news" (Knox, 1962, p. 356). This could be any person announcing any good news, but usually it refers to a Christian telling others about the person and work of Jesus Christ. The role of evangelist is not well defined in scripture, and there are only three references to evangelists in the New Testament (Acts 2:18; Ephes 5:11; 2 Tim 4:5). Harnack (1904) wrote that any distinction between apostles and evangelists was rarely drawn in the early ages of the church and many church fathers referred to the 12 apostles and the gospel writers as evangelists (e.g., Irenaeus). Although apostles preached the good news, there seems to be a distinction of roles. As with the sparse mention of evangelists in scripture, pastors, the fourth mediatorial leader, has only one mentioned in the New Testament (Ephes 4:11). The role of pastor is not well defined as well. The Greek word for pastor is *poimēn* and literally means shepherd. Shepherding evokes a mental image from the Old Testament (e.g., Pslm 23) and would be culturally familiar to the first-century Greco–Roman world. Pastor/shepherd seems to indicate the basic functioning of ministry: love, compassion, care, protection, and provision (Bayes, 2010). Eusebius (circa A.D. 260-339) gave us insight into the operation of the evangelist and the pastor:

> For indeed most of the disciples of that time, animated by the divine word with more ardent love for philosophy, had already fulfilled the command of the Savior, and had distributed their goods to the needy. Then started out upon long journeys they performed the office of evangelists, being filled with the desire to preach Christ to those who had not yet heard the word of faith, and to deliver them the divine gospels.

> And when they had only laid the foundations of the faith in foreign places, they appointed others as pastors, and entrusted them with the

> nurture of those that had recently been brought in, while they themselves went on again to other countries and nations, with the grace and the co-operation of God. (*Church History*, 3.37.2-3)

This insight into the roles of first-century evangelists and pastors reveals that the mediatorial role of the evangelist is delivering the gospel message to unbelievers and the role of the pastor is to care for the needs of the new converts.

The final mediatorial leader is the teacher. Harnack (1904) wrote that teachers were respected with very high esteem in Judaism as indicated by Jesus' rebuke of them, "The teachers of the law and the Pharisees sit on Moses' seat. So you must obey them and do everything they tell you. But do not do what they do for they do not practice what they preach" (Matt 23:1b-3). Rabbis held a high position with those of the Pharisees. Teachers in the first-century church no doubt enjoyed a similar respect, especially of following the example of Christ or of Paul. If the mediatorial role of the evangelist is to preach and persuade non-Christians to become Christians and the role of the pastor is caring for new converts, then the mediatorial roles of teachers would be to teach new converts the gospel in fuller detail.

Role theory concerns one of the most important characteristics of social behavior—the fact that human beings behave in ways that are different and predictable depending on their respective social identities and the situation (Biddle, 1986). Our analysis of specific social categories revealed how Paul drew the boundaries between the in-group (the body of believers) and the out-group (Jewish and Gentile unbelievers). Common cultural topics revealed the leadership roles that mediate the state of the immature Christian or unbeliever and the desired state of maturity and unity in the body. Role theory helps us see how the leadership roles can help to get individuals from the out-group to the in-group.

There is some confusion and incongruity in role theories, but Biddle's (1986) terminology is used. Role theory began as a theatrical metaphor that concerns itself with concepts such as patterned and characteristic social behavior, identities that are assumed by social participants, and scripts for behavior that are understood and adhered to by all participants. Role theories are organized around the notion that individuals occupy a variety of social roles or positions, each of which specifies certain normative behaviors and attitudes (Jackson, 1998). Role theory fell out of use after the mid-20th century, but the concept of role remains a basic tool for sociological understanding. Because there is so much diversity and confusion as to terms and definitions posited by role theorists, only two role theory concepts are employed; role and expectation. In functional role theory, roles are conceived as the shared, normative expectations that prescribe and explain these behaviors. Actors in the social system have presumably been taught these norms and may be counted upon to conform to norms for their own conduct and to sanction others for conformity to norms applying to the latter (Biddle, 1986).

A loose application of role theory to Ephesians 4:1-16 reveals that Paul listed five roles that aid in bringing the body to unity and maturity. Theoretically, each role of an apostle, prophet, evangelist, pastor, or teacher would be specific to the individual, and his or her behavior would be normative. Although roles may overlap one another, an individual may exchange one role for another, or at times an individual may occupy a role on a temporary base, an individual will better meet his or her expectations when the role is clearly defined. To meet expectations (or "stay on script" to continue the theatrical metaphor), each actor should know what the other actors are doing and trust them to do it. The apostle depends on the prophet to hear from God and deliver the message, the evangelist must depend upon the pastor to care for new converts, and the pastor depends upon the teacher to educate them. Each actor must know his or her role and the script (expectations).

(c) Final Categories

Cultural location concerns the manner in which people present their propositions, reasons, and arguments both to themselves and to other people through the rhetoric they use (V. K. Robbins, 1996a). Discovering the cultural location (in contrast to the social location) of readers or writers reveals their dispositions, prepositions, and values, which influence the writing and reading of a text. To aid in finding the cultural location of a text, V. K. Robbins (1996b) developed a typology of culture through study of the sociology of culture. His typology separates people into a dominant culture, subculture, counterculture (alternate), contra-culture (oppositional), or liminal (outlier) culture. Paul's exhortation to the saints in Asia is clearly separatist rhetoric, indicating a separate culture—a subculture. A subculture rhetoric imitates the dominate culture and claims to enact them better than the members of the dominant society. The most prominent feature of a conceptual subculture is their basic assumptions of life, the world, and nature. Subcultures differ from one another according to the prominence of one of three characteristics: (a) a network of communication and loyalty, (b) a conceptual system, and (c) an ethnic heritage and identity. Each of these was evident in the first-century church.

One characteristic of a subculture, according to V. K. Robbins (1996a), is a network of communication and loyalty. Christianity exists not merely as a power or principle in this world but also as an institutional and organized form, which is intended to preserve and protect it (Schaff, 1996). Though the church is a spiritual entity, it is also visible with apostles, teachers, leaders, structure, sacred rites, and (for better or worse) traditions. The church had everything it needed for an organization to operate and flourish. The church had zealous leaders, members, a message, and a divine commission. Although a subculture to the Roman Empire, Christianity was established and expanded by taking advantage of the structure and relative peace that Rome provided. From Rome, a network of highways extended to bring the most distant provinces into intimate connection with the great city. Sheldon (1988) wrote that probably Europe at the beginning of this century enjoyed no better means of communication by land than were provided in the major part of the Roman Empire. Rome's land routes were second only to their sea routes. Every great city in the Roman Empire was connected by either a land or sea route. It is no accident that a significant body of believers was established in every major city in Asia.

Paul is the first missionary of record and was the vanguard for the spread of Christianity setting the pace and missionary example. Paul's primary mission was to the Gentiles. Considering that the Jew had a prior claim to the gospel and that synagogues throughout the empire were pioneer stations for

Christian missions, Paul naturally addressed himself to the Jews and proselytes (Schaff, 1996). However, Paul almost always found that the proselytes were more open to the gospel than his own brethren. This missionary method produced the nucleus of new congregations and provided a natural bridge for preaching to the gentiles. Paul's new churches were generally composed of a mix of Jew and Gentile believers. Paul's influence over the church remained high, even over the churches that he did not personally establish. Church leaders also took advantage of the ease of communication the Roman Empire provided. Documents (sermons or letters) from the disciples (Peter, Paul, James, and John) were circulated to the churches in Asia for exhortation, teaching, and correction.

A second characteristic of a subculture is a conceptual system. Christianity is not merely a system of beliefs and doctrines but life. Christianity does not begin with religious views and notions, though it includes these, but it comes as new life as regeneration, conversion, and sanctification (Schaff, 1996). Persecution of Christians in the first century hindered the establishment of written dogma, however the apostolic letters, the gospels, and book of Acts were (and are still) the foundation of Christian belief. Although not dating to the first century and having been adapted through the years to adjust for theological clarity, the Apostle's creed is the best summary of early Christian belief:

> I believe in God the Father, Almighty, Maker of heaven and earth; And in Jesus Christ, his only begotten Son, our Lord; Who was conceived by the Holy Ghost, born of the Virgin Mary; Suffered under Pontius Pilate; was crucified, dead and buried; He descended into hell; The third day he rose again from the dead; He ascended into heaven, and sits at the right hand of God the Father Almighty; From thence he shall come to judge the quick and the dead; I believe in the Holy Ghost; I believe in the holy catholic church; the communion of saints; The forgiveness of sins; The resurrection of the body; And the life everlasting. Amen.

This so-called Apostle's creed is the earliest Christian creed and covers the basic beliefs of the first-century church. It has remarkably held up for almost two millennia and offers every Christian group, from Paul until today, a starting point for dialogue. This creed provides the nucleus of the Christian conceptual system.

A third characteristic of a subculture is ethnic heritage and identity. Christians are not centered on an ethnic identity, geographic center, or political system—Christians are centered on the person and work of Jesus Christ. Christ is the center of their lives and their message. The ancient epistle of Mathetes to Diognetus (A.D. 130) sums up the spiritual heritage and identity of Christians:

> Christians are distinguished from other men neither by country, nor language, nor the customs which they observe. For they neither inhabit cities of their own, nor employ a peculiar form of speech, nor lead a life which is marked out by any singularity. The course of conduct which they follow has not been devised by any speculation or deliberation of inquisitive men; nor do they, like some, proclaim themselves the advocates of any merely human doctrines. But, inhabiting Greek as well as barbarian cities, according as the lot of each of them has determined, and following the customs of the natives in respect to clothing, food, and the rest of their ordinary conduct, they display to us their wonderful and confessedly striking method of life. They dwell in their own countries, but simply as sojourners. As citizens, they share in all things with others, and yet endure all things as if foreigners. Every foreign land is to them as their native country, and every land of their birth as a land of strangers.

This epistle gives a good description of the Christian of the first century (before the establishment of the Roman Church). Identity for first-century Christians is not geographical or racial; their identity comes from the shared belief of and devotion to Jesus Christ. If the geographical center for the Jew is Jerusalem, and the geographical center for the Roman is Rome, then the geographical center for the first-century Christian is heaven where Christ is seated on his throne.

(d) Summary of Cultural and Social Texture Analysis

The specific, common, and final categories of cultural and social texture analysis reveal a conversionist reaction or rhetoric toward the world. Paul drew a distinction between two groups—unbelievers and believers. These two groups are referred to as in-groups and out-groups in social identity theory. Social identity theory states that a sense of identity and belonging is revealed within a social group. Categorizing or deciding which group to associate with, identifying with that particular group, and comparing that group to other groups brings a defined identity, cohesion, and clarity to the group. Also revealed were the five mediatorial roles with a leadership capacity—the apostle, prophet, evangelist, pastor, and teacher. These leaders are given to the church for the maturing of the members with unity within the body as a primary goal. These roles mediate Paul's desired states of believers to their current state, working toward the unity of the body. Authority was also revealed to be explicit in the ascended Lord (and ultimately in the Trinity). The Christian subculture was also revealed with a unique network of communication taking advantage of Roman infrastructure. Christians also share in a common conceptual system and in a common identity—the Christian subculture.

Section 1.23 *Sacred Texture Analysis*

As themes emerge through the analysis of inner texture and cultural and social texture, the sacred texture is examined. Sacred texture reveals human and divine relations in the text. Those who study the New Testament are interested in finding insights into how human life relates to the divine. The purpose of sacred texture analysis is to locate the ways a text speaks about God or realms of religious life. V. K. Robbins (1996a) suggested a method of analysis that will guide the interpreter in a programmatic search for sacred aspects of a text (whether or not the text is scripture). V. K. Robbin's guide includes aspects of texture that includes references to deity, holy persons, and religious community. Sacred textural analysis gives insight into what the text is saying about how believers are intended to relate to the divine, to each other, to opponents, and how to live holy lives (Snodderly, 2008) and emerges through a study of the other textures (Moon, 2004). The current study's purpose for examining sacred texture is to discover aspects concerning the relationship of Christ's ascension to Christian leadership.

(a) Deity

Identifying God's presence and describing the nature of God provides a starting point for analyzing and interpreting the sacred texture of a text (V. K. Robbins, 1996a). Inner texture analysis reveals deity in the text through repetitive words and phrases (see Table 11). The reference to "one God and Father," the repeated reference to the Spirit, and the repetitive references to Christ indicate the presence of all three members of the Trinity (*perichoretic* partners). Verses 4-5 particularly reveal the Trinity (one Spirit, one Lord, one God).

Table 11: Deity

Verse	Repetitive word
3	unity of the Spirit
4	one Spirit
5	one Lord
6	one God and Father
7	Christ's gift
8	He [Christ] ascended
	He [Christ] led
	He [Christ] gave
9	He [Christ] ascended
	He [Christ] also had descended
10	He [Christ] who descended
	Is Himself [Christ]
	also He [Christ] who ascended
11	and He [Christ] gave
15	Him who is the head, even Christ

If this portion of scripture was a narrative, the main character would be Jesus Christ. The text is centered on him; however, Paul stressed unity not only within the Godhead, but also with God's church. Verses 8-10 are a reference to Christ's incarnation and exaltation. The defining doctrine of Christology is the incarnation—God coming to earth in the form of man. The incarnation is

Paul's point in the Philippians hymn:

> Have this attitude in yourselves which was also in Christ Jesus, who, although He existed in the form of God, did not regard equality with God a thing to be grasped, but emptied Himself, taking the form of a bond-servant, and being made in the likeness of men. Being found in appearance as a man, He humbled Himself by becoming obedient to the point of death, even death on a cross. For this reason also, God highly exalted Him, and bestowed on Him the name which is above every name, so that at the name of Jesus every knee will bow, of those on earth and under the earth and that every tongue will confess that Jesus Christ is Lord, to the glory of the Father. (Phil 2:5-11)

Martin (1997) wrote that this passage allows us to see it as setting Christ before us as the example that guides the Christian in his or her conduct toward others. However, Martin stated that the exaltation and authority of the Lord is the basis of Paul's paraenetic appeal in Philippians and that the lordship of Christ is the hymn's central thought. The same is true in Ephesians 4. While the incarnation can be seen in the "descend" references, Paul's greater purpose is in showing the lordship and authority of Christ. It is also the reason for Paul's use of Psalm 68:18, which references a victorious king receiving gifts (see previous discussions regarding Psalms 68) and his argument for Christ's authority and ability to give the gifts of apostle, prophet, evangelist, pastor, and teacher to the church.

The first-century writings (not including the New Testament canon) are characterized by a certain meagerness and a want of definiteness, and there was no clear concept of the Trinity (Berkhof, 1937), but the belief in the Trinity is affirmed in their writings (Enns, 1989). In the first two centuries A.D., there was little conscious attempt to formulate theological and philosophical issues like the Trinity. We do find the use of the triadic formula (Father, Son, and Holy Spirit) but little attempt to explain it. The doctrine of the Trinity was finally given a definite form at the Council of Constantinople (A.D. 381) in a statement in which the church made explicit the beliefs previously held implicit (Erickson, 1998). It took almost 300 years to formulate Paul's teaching about the Trinity into doctrinal form. The ancient concept of the *perichoresis* describing the Trinity refers to the mutual indwelling (oneness) without confusion (or with distinction). According to Cunningham (1998), both concepts are necessary to describe the Trinity. It has been a difficult task for theologians to give equal space to "oneness" and "difference." Cunningham suggested that most theologians have chosen to travel down one road and offer a "tip of the hat" to the other to avoid the criticism that they have overemphasized singularity and neglected difference or overemphasized difference and neglected singularity. Our pericope reveals both the oneness (vv. 4-6) of the godhead and the distinction of Christ (vv. 7-11).

Two attributes of Christ are revealed in Ephesian 4:1-16. The first is Christ's exalted status to the right hand of God (implicit in Ephes 4 but stated explicitly in Ephes 1). Being ascended far above all the heavens (v. 10) clearly establishes Christ as equal to the Father in all authority and power. The second is, because of the authority and power that Christ yields, he has the power to give gifts to the church. Also implicit in the giving is the empowering or the enabling of the apostle, prophet, evangelist, pastor, and teacher to fulfill their calling and function to bring unity and maturity to the body of believers. Thus, the deity our pericope reveals is Christ—second *perichoretic* partner—and the relationship of deity to man is Lord and benefactor.

(b) Holy Persons

Regularly, texts feature one or more people who have a special relation to God or to divine powers—holy persons. V. K. Robbins (1996a) stated that Jesus is the holy person par excellence, but I argue Jesus should be viewed as deity more than a holy person in this text. Christian doctrine views Jesus as 100% human and 100% God. References to Jesus as Son of Man in the gospels are to stress the human aspect of Christ's nature and identification with humanity. Paul, in Ephesians 4:1-16, stressed the divine aspect of Christ's nature to show his ability and authority to bestow gifts upon people. This portion of scripture does, however, include holy persons in the person of Paul the apostle and in the five gifted leaders listed in verse 11.

Paul introduced himself in Ephesians 1:1 as an "apostle of Christ Jesus by the will of God." Having already introduced himself in Chapter 1, Paul again referred to himself using the first-person pronoun "I" and described himself this time as "the prisoner of the Lord." Paul's reference to himself as an apostle by the will of God connects himself to God and establishes his authority as God's messenger or "sent one" to deliver God's message to the churches. Witherington (2007) suggested that Paul's reference to his imprisonment and chains suggests that the audience needs to realize the seriousness and possible consequences of behaving in a Christian manner in a non-Christian world and to also stir the deeper emotions of the audience so they will be more ready to receive the wisdom imparted.

Paul was an example for the first-century Christian. Castelli (1991) posited that *mimesis* (example) was an aspect of Paul's apostolic authority. Paul referred to *mimesis* five times in his letters in the context of urging the audience to follow his example for Christian behavior. This example is usually in conjunction with the example of Christ (see Table 12).

Table 12: Paul's Example (*Mimesis*)

Verse	Reference to Pauline *Mimesis*
1 Thess 1:6	You also became imitators of us and the Lord, having received the word in much tribulation with joy of the Holy Spirit.
1 Thess 2:14	For you, brethren, became imitators of the churches of God in Christ Jesus that are in Judea.
Phil 3:17	Brethren, join in following my example, and observe those who walk according to the pattern you have in us.
1 Cor 4:16	Therefore, I exhort you, be imitators of me.
1 Cor 11:1	Be imitators of me, just as I also am of Christ.

The notion of mimesis is common in antiquity (Castelli, 1991). A survey of ancient discourses reveals some generalizations about the idea of imitation that Paul inherited from the Greco–Roman culture (Castelli, 1991): (a) mimesis is always articulated as a hierarchical relationship, whereby the "copy" is but a derivation of the "model" and cannot aspire to the privileged status of the model, (b) mimesis presupposes a valorization of sameness over difference—unity and harmony are associated with sameness while differences are attributed characteristics of diffusion, disorder, and discord—and (c) the notion of the authority of the model plays a fundamental role in the mimetic relationship. A holy person (one separated unto God for a particular purpose) is naturally set up to be an example for early Christians.

In addition to Paul, the gifted people referred to in verse 11—the apostle, prophet, evangelist, pastor, and teacher—are also holy persons. These persons are called and gifted to perform specific functions in and for the body of Christ. The word *holy* comes from the Greek adjective *hagios* that means set apart to or by God, consecrated, or holy. Used as a noun, *hagios* is translated Saint and refers to Christians. A *holy person* is a saint or a Christian who has been separated by God from the world. Apostles, prophets, evangelists, pastors, and teachers are first saints, but they have been equipped by God with a special set of skills and given the authority to accomplish God's purposes. In the context of Ephesians, this purpose is to bring the church to maturity and unity.

(c) Religious Community

The gospel is not a purely personal matter, it has a social dimension—it is a communal affair (Banks, 1994). A relationship with God assumes a relationship with other Christians that, in Paul's language, are the "church" or the "body of Christ." The community of God is revealed in the inner texture repetitive use of "body" images. This is a theme for the entire book of Ephesians and the "body" or "body of Christ" is the focus of our text (4:1-16). The body imagery is unique to Paul (Minear, 2004). Modern interpreters should keep in mind that 21st-century understanding of the body is further advanced than Paul's understanding, and they should avoid anachronistic interpretations. Table 13 lists all of the references to body in Ephesians.

Table 13: References to Body in Ephesians

Verse	Reference
1:23	which is His body, the fullness of Him who fills all in all.
2:16	and might reconcile them both in one body to God through the cross, by it having put to death the enemy.
3:6	to be specific, that the Gentiles are fellow heirs and fellow members of the body, and fellow partakers of the promise in Christ Jesus through the gospel.
4:4	There is one body and one Spirit, just also you were called in one hope of your calling;
4:12	for the equipping of the saints for the work of service, to the building up of the body of Christ;
4:15	but speaking the truth in love, we are to grow up in all aspects into Him who is the head, even Christ
4:16	from whom the whole body, being fit and held together by what every joint supplies, according to the proper working of each individual part, causes the growth of the body for the building up of itself in love.
5:23	For the husband is the head of the wife, as Christ also is the head of the Church, He Himself being Savior of the body.
5:29-30	for no one ever hated his own flesh, but nourishes and cherishes it, just as Christ also does the church because we are members of His body.

Paul's conception of the church as a body expresses fundamental ideas important to the identity and function of the church. The body and members illustrate the unity and diversity of the church (especially seen in Paul's description of the church as a body in 1 Cor. 12). Many scholars have acknowledged that the primary theme of Ephesians 4 is unity (Lincoln, 1990; Lloyd-Jones, 1980; Witherington, 2007). In the whole section of Ephesians 4:1-16, the Christian community is seen as a living organism. The body grows as the individual parts each contribute to the developing maturity and growth of the whole, the ultimate goal being the fullness of Christ himself. The distinction of the five leadership gifts in verse 11 shows that diversity among the members does not hinder unity; on the contrary, diversity of the members aids the unity of the body. The body metaphor reveals a second important concept that is essential for the understanding of the church—headship. Christ has been revealed as the head of the church. Ultimate power and authority is attributed to God the Father in verse 6, but Christ is specifically named the head over the whole body in verse 15.

Body may be Paul's most descriptive label for the church, but his most common term for the church is *ekklēsia*. Although the English word *church* is not used in Ephesians 4:1-16, it is used throughout the rest of the book and requires mentioning. *Ekklēsia* is a difficult word to translate because it is a common Greek word for assembly that is used in more than one way by the apostolic writers. The exact meaning must be interpreted by the context in which it is found and the overall thinking of the writer (Giles, 1995). The Greek root suggests a "calling out" or "setting apart" of a particular group, indicating a kind of distinction between members of the particular assembly and the wider culture (Cunningham, 1998). Assembly is the general translation for *ekklēsia*, but in Paul, the background of the word is the Old Testament (LXX) use of the *ekklēsia* as the people of God. Implicit in the word is the claim that the church stands in direct continuity with the Old Testament people of God (Ladd, 1974). Paul used the two terms, body and *ekklēsia*, in Ephesians 5:22-28 (especially v. 23) to urge husbands to love their wives with the same love that God has toward his church, picturing the relationship between God and his church.

Ephesians 4:1-16 says more specifically about the church than any other part of Ephesians. It also reveals how some of the members of the community function and help the body to grow. Verse 12 reveals the purpose of the five leadership functions with three prepositional phrases: (a) for the equipping (completing or perfecting) of the saints, (b) for the work of service, and (c) to the building up of (edifying) the body of Christ. There has been much discussion around the interpretation of verse 12. The Revised Standard Version translates the three prepositional phrases as if the designated leaders were given by Christ for the equipping of the saints, work of service, and building up of the body of Christ. This translation makes these three matters the sole responsibility of the leaders listed in verse 11 (Giles, 1995; see Figure 5).

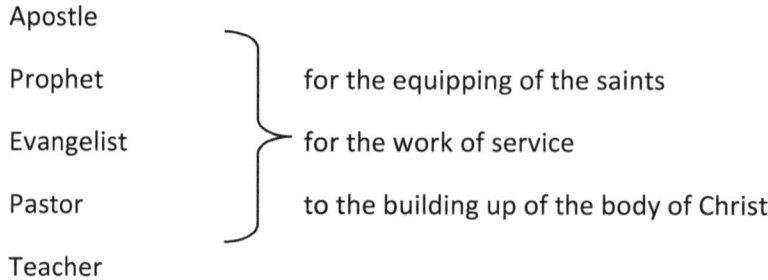

Figure 5: Ephesians 4:12 (functions of the leaders).

In this option, the leaders listed in verse 11 bear all of the responsibility for the ultimate goal of building up the body of Christ. The New Revised Standard Version, on the other hand, considers the second and third prepositional phrases dependent upon the first (see Figure 6).

Figure 6: Ephesians 4:12 (functions of the saints).

In the second option, the leaders of the church listed in verse 11 have only the task of equipping the saints so that they in turn can fulfill the work of service and the building up of the body of Christ. Both translations are possible. In recent times, the latter has been preferred because it highlights the ministry of the whole church (Giles, 1995). The issue has also been raised whether the apostle, prophet, evangelist, pastor, and teacher should be interpreted as offices or as individuals with a specific function. Bayes (2010) concluded that there may be some evidence for the existence of an office of prophet and teacher in the first-century church, but there is little evidence for the offices of apostle, evangelist, and pastor. The conclusion is that the functions (not offices) of apostle, prophet, evangelist, pastor, and teacher were given to edify and build the church. The logical interpretation is that these gifted leaders equip other believers so they might use their gifts to bring the body of Christ to maturity and unity. Each member of the Christian community has a vital role in the development and health of the community.

A sense of community has been defined as a feeling that members have of belonging, a feeling that members matter to one another and to the group, and a shared faith that members' needs will be met through their commitment to be together (McMillan & Chavis, 1986). This definition has four elements that seem to be present in a mature Christian community: membership (or a sense of belonging or connection to the group), influence and participation (the feeling that you matter to the group and make the group better), integration and fulfillment of needs (reciprocal relationships where individual needs are shared and met), and shared emotional connection (identifying with the community and the feeling that experiences and situations in life are commonly understood by the group). Paul's body metaphor for the functioning of the church allows believers to achieve a sense of community and have an active role in the development of the community.

(d) Ethics

Ethics concerns the responsibility of humans to think and act in special ways in both ordinary and extraordinary circumstances (V. K. Robbins, 1996a). Ethical refers to behavior considered right or wrong according to our own beliefs—no matter the culture or society. Ethical failure usually falls into one of three areas: deceiving, stealing, or harming (R. A. Howard & Korver, 2008). Each is forbidden in the Decalogue and Paul associates this aberrant behavior with Gentile or un-Christian behavior. The general purpose of Ephesians is to remind Christians of their identity and to encourage them to pursue the values and behaviors that characterize them. Ephesians has several interrelated themes: the power of God over all other principalities, powers, and authorities; the unity of Jew and Gentile into one body in Christ; and the appeal for maturity and holy living. In Ephesians 4:1, Paul implored the saints to walk worthy of their calling. Paul later described the Gentile life as a life of "sensuality for the practice of every kind of impurity with greediness" (4:19) and urged the saints to "put on the new self, which is in the likeness of

God has been created in righteousness and holiness in truth" (4:24) and listed some behaviors to avoid (stealing, unwholesome speech, bitterness, anger, and malice) and replaced them with good behaviors (hard work, speak edifying words, kindness, tenderness, and forgiveness). Paul described the Christian's past state and God's desired states for the church in ethical terms.

(e) Summary of Sacred Texture

Sacred texture analysis leads the interpreter to examine relationships between the human and divine in a text. The relationship of human and divine in Ephesians 4:1-16 is described in terms of power and authority. God (in Trinitarian form), having all power and authority gives gifts (i.e., people separated by calling and gifted for a special function) by the ascended and seated Christ (the second *perichoretic* partner) to mediate the process of ministry to bring Christians to maturity and of building up of the body of Christ (the Christian church).

Section 1.24   Summary of Relevant Findings

V. K. Robbins' (1996a, 1996b) method of Socio-rhetorical analysis was applied to Ephesians 4:1-16 to address the research question: What is the empowering relationship between the ascended Christ and the leadership ministries? Specifically, the inner texture, cultural and social texture, and sacred texture of the text were analyzed. The findings reveal multiple aspects to the relationship between the exalted Christ and leaders. Inner texture analyzes the words of the text for emerging themes, arguments, and relevant information. The repetitive words and phrases and the opening–middle–ending of the inner texture reveals several themes in the text: calling, unity, authority, and maturity. Each theme was present in Paul's argument for the saints to live right. Inner texture analysis can be summed up: Christ gave the gifts of apostle, prophet, evangelists, pastor, and teacher to help the saints walk worthy of their calling and become mature as believes and live in unity.

Cultural and social texture analysis in particular reveals information relevant to the research question. Specific topics show that the text points toward a conversionist attitude toward the world. Paul drew a distinction between believers and Gentiles as two distinct groups and exhorted the saints to be mature and live in unity with the body. Common cultural topics analysis reveals that the exalted Christ gave gifted individuals (apostle, prophet, evangelist, pastor, and teacher), with authority directly from God, as a mediator between the past sinful state of the saint and the desired state of maturity and unity in the body. Final cultural topics revealed a subculture with a unique network of communication. Paul's pioneering missionary method and communication through circular epistles took advantage of the Roman infrastructure. The Christian community had a common conceptual system that united the churches. They also shared in a common identity with the person of Christ whom they exemplified.

Sacred texture analysis is particularly important for the examination of human and divine relationships. This analysis reveals the presence of each member of the Trinity, yet the text focuses upon Jesus Christ as deity and ultimate authority. Holy persons were present in Paul and the five gifted leaders listed in Ephesians 4:11. These holy persons were revealed to have been given for the specific purpose of equipping the saints, ministering to the body, and building up the community of believers that are identified, not by race or place, but in Christ.

A summary of the information reveals several points leading toward a model of divine empowerment:

1. Divine empowerment is participation with the Trinity in the context of calling and membership in a common community.
2. Divine empowerment focuses on desired behavior and relationships.
3. Divinely empowered agents mediate the old or present state of being and the desired state of maturity and unity of the saints. Mediators have at least five possible functions:
    a. Mediators are authorized by God as envoys.
    b. Mediators speak for God.
    c. Mediators speak about God.
    d. Mediators show the care and love of God.
    e. Mediators inspire and instruct the saints.

Chapter 5 – Discussion

There has been increased interest in leadership empowerment in an organizational setting over the past two decades (Honold, 1997). Theorists and writers have conceptualized empowerment from several perspectives. Some are interested in giving groups and individuals social equality and control over their lives. These are concerned with enabling disenfranchised members to overcome domination. For them, empowerment is akin to liberation. Others conceptualize empowerment by equipping subordinates with information, resources, and support and to be given assignments to complete. Still others empower by building the confidence and efficacy in employees while giving them meaning and a sense of influence. Research has shown validity in each of these concepts of empowerment. However, researchers have not adequately explored the spiritual or divine aspect of organizational empowerment in spite of the increased interest in workplace spirituality.

The current study addressed the divine aspect of leadership by examining the relationship between God and leadership roles in the first-century church. The research question for this study asked: What is the empowering relationship between the ascended Christ and the leadership ministries in Ephesians 4:1-16? Ephesians 4:1-16 was chosen to be examined because of the importance of Paul's epistles to the development of the church and because it specifically associates deity (the ascended Christ) with leadership functions. Through Socio-rhetorical analysis of the text, it was found that leaders participate with God; they are divinely empowered and authorized to mediate the relationship between men and between man and God, helping them to mature and live in unity.

This chapter summarizes the finding of the Socio-rhetorical analysis of Ephesians 4:1-16. The components for a model of divine empowerment are proposed. A model for empowerment is suggested that includes components from all four theoretical empowerment views. Individual components can be linked together and applied in a fashion that will fit the organization. Finally, the proposed concatenated model of empowerment is considered in light of the major contemporary leadership theories.

Section 1.25   Summary of Findings

Divine empowerment for leaders comes through calling, membership, and participation. The call in Ephesians comes from an explicit source—the God of the Bible. A call has been defined as a profound impression from God that establishes parameters for your life and can be altered only by a subsequent, superseding impression from God (Iorg, 2008). In the nonreligious context of workplace spirituality, calling has been defined as the experience of transcendence or how one makes a difference through service to others and, in doing so, derives meaning and purpose in life (Fry, 2003). This experience of transcendence, according to this concept, is by choice where individuals acknowledge a creator, supreme being, higher power, a god of love, or Allah, Jehovah, Buddha, or any other transcendent being (Fry, Matherly, & Ouimet, 2010). Central to the many Christian interpretations of calling is the idea that there is something that God has called me to do with my life, and my life has meaning and purpose at least in part because I am fulfilling my calling (Placher, 2005). This meaning and purpose is what proponents of workplace spirituality refer to as transcendence. Paul often reminded the churches of their calling: called to be saints (Rom 1:7), being sanctified by their calling (1 Cor 1:2), and to be faithful to God who called them (1 Cor 1:9). For Paul, calling is an act of God that initiates membership into the body of Christ by those who hear and act upon the calling. Calling then initiates participation with God.

Paul was clear in Ephesians 4:4 that there is only one body, one community of believers whose membership is attained by embracing the gospel (Banks, 1994), specifically membership through the "blood of Christ" (Ephes 2:13). Paul distinguished between the Gentiles (whom he equated with sin and lostness) and saints. Individuals tend to categorize themselves and identify with groups based upon common variables. To be a part of the body of Christ, they are categorized by their belief in the good news of Jesus Christ. This is what they identify with and by which comparisons are drawn with other groups. Members of the body of Christ are also identified by common behaviors. In the first three chapters of Paul's Ephesian sermon, he identified the boundaries of the body to which the saints belong. The last three chapters of Ephesians identify behaviors and attitudes that are common to the body. There are two basic concepts that make up "membership." First is the means by which individuals are categorized and identified for inclusion to a certain group. Second are the feeling and the advantages of belonging to a group. Fry (2003) wrote that membership encompasses the cultural and social structures we are immersed in and through which we seek to be understood and appreciated. Membership has been defined as the feeling of belonging or of sharing a sense of personal relatedness—a feeling that one has invested part of oneself to become a member and has a right to be a member (McMillan & Chavis, 1986). Membership is the first step to the process of developing a sense of community and conveys upon people a set of rights and responsibilities that are always characterized by belonging to the community (Bess, Fisher, Sonn, & Bishop, 2002). There may be a conceptual link between sense of community and empowerment. A sense of community may give community members the sense of control and social support necessary for development (Miers & Fisher, 2002). Membership or identifying with a particular group (in-groups) provides a sense of being understood and accepted. Membership promotes unity and cohesion within the group and strengthens relationships.

Ephesians 4:1-16 suggests participation between God and man in the process of unifying the community of believers and the development of individual members into mature saints. A major theme, if not the main theme, of the book of Ephesians is unity, and unity is the dominant theme of 4:1-16. Paul was clear that unity is a vital aspect of God's desired behavior for the body, explicitly instructing the saints to "keep the unity of the Spirit" (v. 3) until we all "come to the unity of the faith" (v. 13). The believer's example for unity is the divine Trinity that is revealed in verses 4-6. The terms *perichoresis* and polyphony allow for participation between God and man by "joining in the dance" and "joining in harmonically" with God's actions for the accomplishing of his will. Paul expressed God's instructions to the churches in Asia to live in unity as mature saints. Paul strengthened this argument by revealing that God has facilitated this process by giving equipped and empowered leaders to aid in the process of building maturity and unity. This is the very example of *perichoresis* and polyphony—participation with the divine.

Analysis of our text reveals the distinction of authority in the relationship between deity and leaders. Divine authority is implicit in Christ's giving leaders to the church (apostle, prophet, evangelist, pastor, and teacher). The divine authority that accompanies the function of apostle and prophet as legates of God was known in first-century Judea, and we can safely assume that the same divine authority was extended to the evangelist, pastor, and teacher as well. Authority is a central feature of the structure of formal organizations and is derived from implicit or explicit contracts concerning the individual's position or knowledge (Bass, 2008). The modern concept of authority (especially in organizations) is almost entirely based upon implicit sources (Schütz, 2007). This contemporary view of authority exists within social organizations and is constantly being endorsed and supported by the leaders and their followers. This implicit source of authority exists because of shared goals and for the benefit of the organization. In the past, sources of authority were more explicit. Historically, authority had a divine origin. In ancient times, dynastic rulers and Roman emperors felt they had a divine right to rule (Durant, 1971). Authority was a family inheritance, but it was divinely given. The source of authority must be more than merely implicit (Schütz, 2007). Paul clearly stated that Christ is seated in "heavenly places above all rule and authority and power and dominion, and every name" (Ephes 1:21) and reiterated this fact in Ephesians 4:8-10, directly connecting this ultimate authority and power to the gift of leaders in verse 11 showing a direct and explicit source of authority for these leaders.

In Ephesians 4:1-16, Paul revealed God's concern for the churches in Asia for individual maturity and unity in the body. Therefore, God gave the gifts of apostle, prophet, evangelist, pastor, and teacher for equipping the members, serving, and strengthening the body. These leaders or leadership functions were given to the body for the ultimate purpose of building up believers until they are united and developed. They mediate the unifying and maturing process in at least five ways. Generalizing the functions of the apostle, prophet, evangelist, pastor, and teacher may reveal how they would function in organizations and churches today. The day-to-day function of the apostle is difficult to discern. What is known about apostles in the New Testament and the cultural equivalent of ambassadors or envoys is that they were authorized to take a message to another group of people. While working in the capacity of apostle, they acted with the full authority of their sender to the extent that they accurately represented the sender's message (Keener, 1993). Apostles in the first century were sent out to take a specific message to another sovereign body. Apostleship assumes a relationship with and knowledge of the sending sovereign. Apostles then were given by Christ, according to Ephesians 4:11, to represent God as the author of the directive of unifying the body and becoming mature.

The role of the apostle and prophet are similar—both speak for God—but apostle seems to have an overseeing function that prophets do not have (Keener, 1993). Prophets speak forth God's message by divine inspiration. Keener (1993) noted that some Old Testament prophets were commissioned with special authority to oversee prophetic awakenings (e.g., Elisha or Jeremiah) or to judge Israel (e.g., Deborah or Samuel). The function of an evangelist (which is unique to the New Testament and early church) is also a speaking function. Whereas the apostle and prophet speak for God, the evangelist speaks about God. Specifically, the evangelist tells about the person and work of Christ Jesus primarily to those who do not already have knowledge or a relationship with him.

While the pastor and teacher may be one role, they are two separate functions—shepherding and teaching. Pastor is only found once in the New Testament, yet the function of a shepherd is well known. Shepherding is a metaphor, and metaphors assume some cultural competence (Laniak, 2006). Laniak (2007) indicated that there are three critical functions of shepherds: providing, protecting, and guiding. Teaching presumes the transfer of knowledge from one individual to another. In the biblical sense, teaching is the process of educating the people of God about God and the things of God. The roles of shepherd and teacher are much more personal than the roles of apostle, prophet, and evangelist. The function of the shepherd then is to show the love and care of God in tangible ways, and the function of the teacher is to instruct about God and to inspire people to live godly lives. Each leader enters the divine dance with God by fulfilling the roles that God has designated for them.

Leaders are empowered by participating with God through calling and membership (identification with God and other saints). Being authorized directly by God, they in turn empower others in their mediatorial roles that connect them to God and to the body of saints. Simply stated, leaders are empowered when they participate with God for the purpose of facilitating individual maturity and unifying relationships. Leadership empowerment comes by participating with God through a divine call and identification with the group for the purpose of building up of the body. Empowered leaders then are authorized by God to mediate these relationships. The focus of divine empowerment is on relationships and individual development. Figure 7 shows the relationship of the components of divine empowerment and does not depict a process of empowerment.

Figure 7: Components of divine empowerment.

Section 1.26   Toward an Integrated Theory of Empowerment

Empowerment theory lacks a single unifying model capable of integrating the multiple levels of activity and complex relations that characterize the empowerment process. Existing empowerment theories are based upon differing perspectives from job structure, intrinsic task motivation, and environmental fit to perceptions and commitment (T. L. Robbins et al., 2002). Empowerment is not an easily defined construct because it is an ongoing process, taking place in a dynamic environment, involving many elements that operate on differing levels of analysis. The three most common perspectives of empowerment are the critical social, structural, and psychological. Several researchers have suggested integrated empowerment models. These integrated models usually incorporate only components of structural empowerment and psychological empowerment (Cho, 2008; Laschsinger, Gilbert, et al., 2010). T. L. Robbins et al. (2002) included other variables such as organizational context and individual differences into their complicated model. Although most attempts at an integrated empowerment model only incorporate components of structural and psychological empowerment, a few have incorporated aspects of critical social empowerment into the discussion (Bradbury-Jones et al., 2008; Casey et al., 2010). The current research suggests the addition of a spiritual or divine aspect to empowerment.

While describing power, Haugaard (2010) resisted the quest for a single meaning of power and offered a plural view of power based on family resemblance. According to Haugaard, there are a cluster of concepts—each of which qualify as power whose differing perspectives are not mutually exclusive. The same family resemblance approach to explaining power should also be applied to explaining empowerment. Given the various theoretical concepts of empowerment (social, structural, psychological, and divine), the relationships of each can be represented by a Venn diagram with four interlocking circles representing the relationship between each theoretical view of empowerment (see Figure 8).

Figure 8: Relationships of empowerment theories.

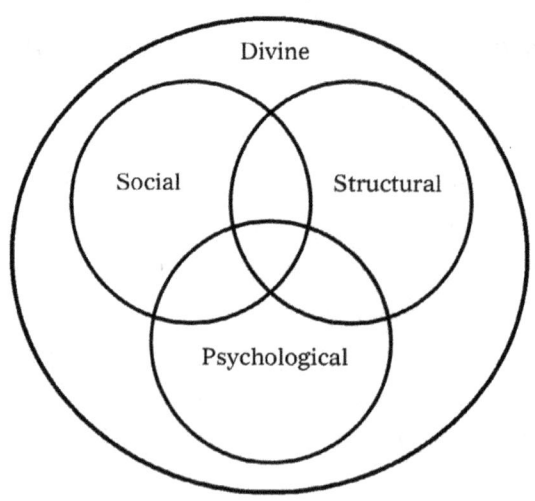

There are differences and commonalities in each theoretical perspective as indicated by the Venn diagram. Each empowerment theory focuses upon different aspects of organizational life. A family resemblance approach allows for each empowering aspect to function in different but complementary ways and be defined individually and not forced into a unified theory of empowerment. A family approach to empowerment has four members: social, structural, psychological, and divine. Social empowerment is concerned with social standing, individual independence, and justice. Social empowerment focuses upon the status of the subordinate in relationship to the power holders and the other members of the group. Structural empowerment focuses upon distribution of power and control of vital organizational resources necessary for task completion and organizational advancement. Psychological empowerment focuses upon cognitive and psychological experiences and intrinsic motivations. Divine empowerment, as conceived by this research, focuses upon participation with God through divinely appointed roles for accomplishing personal growth and group harmony. A suggested application of existing empowerment theories is to allow each mode of empowerment to address different aspects of empowerment sequentially. A close look at how each conceptual model functionally empowers helps to link these models.

(a) Divine Empowerment

This research showed that leaders are divinely empowered and authorized to participate with God by mediating the relationships between God and man and among men for the purpose of building maturity and unity. (The term divine is used here instead of spiritual to distinguish it from similar concepts in spiritual leadership and to associate empowerment as a work of the Trinity and not just the Holy Spirit.) The focus of divine empowerment is primarily on relationships and spiritual development. Five components of divine empowerment that influence unity and maturity have been identified: participation, calling, membership, authorization and mediating roles (see Figure 7).

Perichoresis has been used to describe the possibility of leaders participating with God in accomplishing God's mission. Fiddes (2000) explained how *perichoresis* illustrates the possibility of man's participation with God. Theologians of the fourth and fifth centuries thought of God as the fountainhead of the communion of the divine persons in the Godhead. The Father sent forth the Son, and then the Spirit came through the Son, so that the Father is the cause of the communion. The persons are in each other and permeate each other, and the source of this mutual penetration is the Father's ecstatic love.

> There is a kind of "progressive" dance in which participants move outside the inner circle of dancers to make contact with others, and then come back in again, bringing other dancers with them. So the dance goes out from the Father and back in again to the Father. The Father sends out the Son through whom the Spirit proceeds as the life-giver in creation, and in the Spirit created persons return in worship through the Son to the Father. (Fiddes, 2000, p. 75)

The image of the dancers draws man into participation with the movements of mission and of worship within the dance. This illustration demonstrates not only the unity in the Godhead but also the need for unity between God and man and among men. This illustration also allows for diversity among the dancers. Even among the members of the Trinity, there are distinctions between the divine persons. There is also diversity among men and a greater need for unity.

Participation comes in the context of calling and membership. Calling is a profound impression from God that establishes parameters for your life (Iorg, 2008). There are two aspects common to a call. The first common element of calling, Christian or secular, is the idea of being connected with a divine power regardless of the name or title of the higher power. This study, however, showed that the ultimate source of calling is the Trinity. The second common element of calling is the notion of making a difference, deriving meaning and purpose in life (Fry, 2003; Placher, 2005). Membership or identifying with a particular group is important to the concept of participation. According to social identity theory, membership includes categorizing people by commonalities, identifying with the group by adopting additional characteristics of the group, and comparing your group with others (Ashforth & Mael, 1989). Membership is the feeling of belonging or of sharing a sense of personal relatedness (McMillan & Chavis, 1986) and results in the feelings of being understood and appreciated (Fry, 2003).

Divine empowerment has five interrelated elements: a divine call, participation with God, identification with a group, direct authorization from God, and functioning in a mediatorial role. These five elements work together for the purpose of building unity among God and the church and for maturing the community of believers.

(b) Social Empowerment

Social empowerment is in the early stages of development (Casey et al., 2010). Critical social theory is concerned with enabling disenfranchised members to overcome domination and is based on the premise that certain groups in society are in a subordinated position. Organizations are flatter now than any time in history; however, every organization will have a hierarchical power structure. Those with greater authority and power will always be at the top and subordinates below. Social empowerment addresses social issues such as oppression, freedom, fairness, equity, equality, and social standing. Casey et al. (2010) found that critical social empowerment was a predictor of psychological empowerment and job satisfaction among a group of nurses whose position was culturally subordinated. This study measured participation in decision making and if they were viewed as professionals (the feeling of significance and acceptance). The findings showed that nurses who had more feelings of respect and were given more participation in decisions that affect themselves and the organization had higher feelings of psychological empowerment and job satisfaction. This study found that empowerment was conceptualized in terms of freedom to make decision with authority and to have choices.

Because social issues are an organizational reality, social empowerment should not be ignored. Oppression is the experience of repeated, widespread, systemic injustice (Deutsch, 2006). Equity theory and justice theory give some insight into social empowerment. Equity theory predicts a sense of being treated unfairly when we see others we consider similar to ourselves in effort, performance, status, experience, and so forth being treated beneficially while we are not treated the same (Bass, 2008). When people feel treated fairly, they are more likely to be motivated; and the sense of being unfairly treated is more prone to feelings of dissatisfaction and demotivation. The way that people measure this sense of fairness is at the heart of equity theory. Distributive justice is the fairness with which rewards and resources are distributed to members of a group or organization, consistent with their contributions, in comparison with others. Rewards and resources can be distributed equitably or equally. Equity principle asserts that people should receive benefits in proportion to their contribution, while equality principle states that all members of a group should share its benefits equally (Deutsch, 2006). Equity is most prominent in organizations in which economic productivity is the primary goal, and equality is dominant when social harmony, cohesiveness, or fostering enjoyable social relations is the primary emphasis. Therefore, the ways in which an organization distributes resources will vary depending upon the goals of the organization. In addition to assessing distributive justice, people judge the fairness of the procedures that determine outcomes. Procedural justice refers to the perceived fairness of the organization's processes and procedures used to make resource and allocation decisions (Ivancevich et al., 2008).

Some social empowerment research states that groups and individuals seek control and mastery over the social, economic, and political aspects of their lives (Jennings et al., 2006). This conceptualization of social empowerment envisions empowerment as having some control over their situation in life. Being given a role in decision making that affect the subordinates' immediate situation or the goals of the organization has been found to have an empowering affect (Bradbury-Jones, 2008). In a qualitative study of two focus groups of nurses with signs of being an oppressed group, Fulton (1997) found they conceptualized empowerment in terms of freedom to make decisions with authority and to have choices.

Further research in social empowerment is needed. However, this review of the limited social empowerment research revealed four items that indicate social empowerment: (a) participation in decision making leading to feelings of control and empowerment, (b) the sense of being treated fairly by superiors and organizational processes, (c) equitable or equal distribution of rewards and organizational resources, and (d) the feeling of significance and mattering to the organization as opposed to feelings of subordination or oppression.

(c) Structural Empowerment

Structural empowerment has been labeled as a relational construct that describes the perceived power or control that a leader has over others (Conger & Kanungo, 1988). It focuses on sharing power in organizations through participation and involvement at all levels. Structural empowerment has been theoretically defined as access to organizational structures in the work environment through lines of communication, support, information, and resources, which offer workers opportunities to share in decision making, assist in control of resources, and grow in their jobs (O'Brien, 2011). Four components of structural empowerment have been identified. This model has been tested extensively with favorable results. The first component shared by management is information. Information means having the knowledge of policies, goals, data, technical knowledge, and organizational required to be effective. The second component is support and consists of feedback, guidance, advice, and assistance from superiors and peers. The third component is access to resources, which is the ability of individuals to access materials, funds, supplies, time, manpower, and equipment required to successfully complete a task. The final component is having the opportunity for advancement and growth that entails access to challenges, rewards, and professional development. Workers are thought to be empowered by giving access to these resources.

(d) Psychological Empowerment

Structural empowerment is the perception of the presence or absence of empowering conditions in the workplace, and psychological empowerment is the employee's psychological interpretation or relation to these conditions

(Laschinger, Finegan, et al., 2004). Empowerment is not something that management does to employees but a mindset that employees have about their role in the organization. The first to conceptualize psychological empowerment was Conger and Kanungo (1988) who defined psychological empowerment as a process of enhancing feelings of self-efficacy through identifying conditions that foster powerlessness and removing them with organizational practices and efficacy information. Thomas and Velthouse (1990) further developed the concept of psychological empowerment in terms of cognitive variables or task assessments that determine motivation. They defined empowerment as increased intrinsic task motivation manifested in a set of four cognitions reflecting an individual's orientation to his or her work role: (a) meaning, (b) competence (self-efficacy), (c) self-determination, and (d) impact. Meaning or meaningfulness is the fit of the work role and the individual's beliefs and values, competence is an individual's belief in his or her capacity to accomplish work assignments, self-determination is a sense of choice governing his or her actions, and impact refers to the sense of being able to influence organizational activities and outcomes (Spreitzer, 1996). These four intrinsic needs give individuals a sense of power; thus, as they advanced in each of these cognitions, they have the increasing sense of empowerment. Management empowers employees by facilitating the process of developing and supporting these cognitions. This empowerment model has been extensively tested as well.

(e) Concatenated Empowerment Model

Several researchers have proposed integrated models of empowerment for organizational leadership (Cho, 2008; Laschinger, Gilbert, et al., 2010; T. L. Robbins et al., 2002). There is a need to incorporate empowering components from each theoretical family: social, structural, psychological, and divine perspectives. See Table 14 for components of each family.

Table 14: Family Resemblance Empowerment Theories

Social	Structural	Psychological	Divine
Participation	Opportunity	Meaning	Calling
Fair treatment	Information	Competence	Participation
Equity/Equality	Support	Self-determination	Membership
Significance	Resources	Impact	Authority
			Mediating role

A model that includes each family of empowerment is suggested (see Figure 9). This model does not recommend a particular order for the empowering families to be applied. The suggested application of this model is to allow each family to be linked sequentially according to the individual or group empowerment needs. Concatenation is the linking of various elements into a logical and usable form. Empowering actions can be linked together to address feelings of unempowerment. Every organization is different and will choose to empower their members in different ways and to different levels. Concatenation will allow organizational leaders to link and implement families of empowerment in ways that will fit their organizational needs. Feelings of empowerment as a result of structural empowering actions may not translate to similar feelings of social empowerment, and feelings of social empowerment may not translate to feelings of psychological empowerment. Because each empowerment family focuses on different aspects of empowerment and requires different empowering actions, sequential application of each empowerment aspect will likely see better results. Separating empowering actions according to the family of empowerment will help to keep from confusing the feelings of empowerment from one family of empowerment to another.

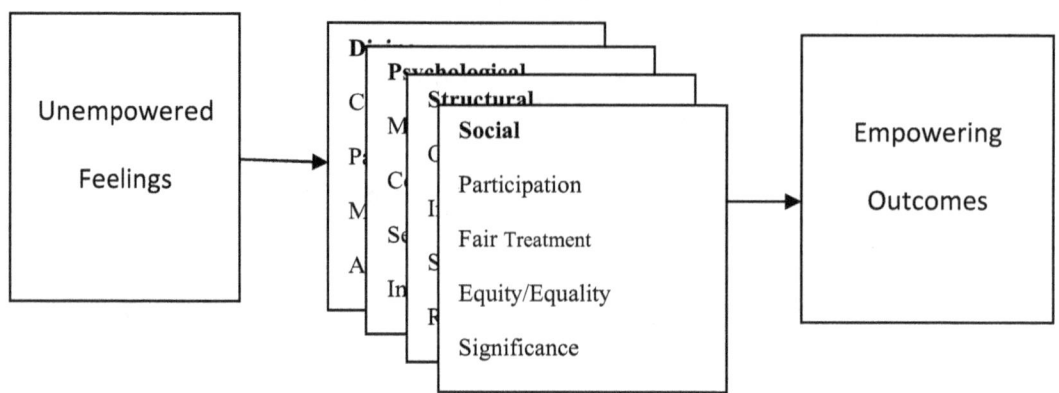

Figure 9: Suggested concatenated empowerment model.

Individual application of a concatenated empowerment model first identifies individual feelings of unempowerment and then identifies the feelings as social, structural, psychological, divine, or a combination of them. Leaders can then decide how the unempowered feeling will be best remedied—through actions of social empowerment, structural empowerment, psychological empowerment, or divine empowerment (or a combination of several). Empowering actions then can be taken and subsequent feedback obtained to insure feelings of unempowerment are being addressed. For organizational empowerment, the concatenated empowerment model can be used to systematically build an empowering organizational culture by incorporating empowering practices by management in each of the empowerment families.

This model allows for variables and a dynamic organizational environment depending upon organizational goals and leadership structures by linking the empowering components in a manner that fits the organization. Public organizations will be managed differently and have different goals than for-profit corporations. Variables that might affect enacting empowering efforts are the level of employee skill, development, and knowledge, organizational structure, leadership style, work environment, and so on. An advanced employee may not need psychological empowerment initially as much as he or she needs structural empowerment. One group of employees may need to be psychologically empowered while another group needs to be structurally empowered. An organization in impoverished areas may need to be socially empowered first to build trust and organizational commitment. Entry-level employees may need to connect with their divine calling and find their roles in forming community. Numerous current leadership theories include aspects of empowerment. Therefore, awareness of the various aspects of empowerment is necessary for today's organizations.

Section 1.27 Implications for Leadership Theory

There is little doubt that achieving empowerment is a major emphasis of organizational development (Austin & Bartunek, 2006), but there is little consensus on how empowerment is achieved. Most leadership research and theories over the past 50 years have emphasized the characteristics of the leader (Yukl, 2010). However, a shift from focusing primarily upon the characteristics of the leader to characteristics of followers, leader–follower relationships, and the situation took place and produced a number of follower-sensitive theories. In recent years, there have been several leadership theories that emphasize empowering their followers. Of these, transformational leadership, servant leadership, authentic leadership, and spiritual leadership include elements of empowerment or lend themselves well to empowerment. Each of these theories has a different focus, but they each emphasize the importance of their followers. A brief examination of each theory and how it approaches follower empowerment will show how the application of a concatenated empowerment model will help aid in follower empowerment.

(a) Transformational Leadership

There has been an explosion of interest in leadership, and the theory of transformational leadership has rapidly become the approach of choice for much of the research and application (Bass & Riggio, 2006). Burns (1978) introduced the concept of transforming leadership. Based on Burn's concept and House's 1976 theory of charismatic leadership, Bernard Bass and his colleagues developed the model of transformational leadership (Bass & Riggio, 2006) that focuses on empowering followers. Transformational leaders stimulate and inspire followers to both achieve extraordinary outcomes and develop their own leadership capacity. They help followers grow and develop into leaders by responding to their needs by empowering them and by aligning the objectives and goals of the individual followers, the leaders, the group, and the organization. Transformational leaders do more with colleagues and followers than set up simple exchanges or agreements, they behave in ways to achieve superior results by employing one or more transformational components of idealized influence, inspirational motivation, intellectual stimulation, or individualized consideration (Bass & Avolio, 1994; Bass & Riggio, 2006).

These "four I's" have empowering characteristics. First, idealized influence (II) is the way that leaders behave that results in their being role models for their followers because they are admired, respected, and trusted. Followers identify with the leaders because they consider the needs of followers above their own, they share risks with followers, they can be counted on to do the right thing, they demonstrate high standards of ethical and moral conduct, and they avoid using power for personal gain. The second component is inspirational motivation (IM). Transformational leaders behave in ways that motivate and inspire followers by providing meaning and challenge, arousing team spirit, displaying enthusiasm and optimism, involving followers in envisioning attractive future states, creating clearly communicated expectations, and by demonstrating commitment to goals and shared vision. The third I is intellectual stimulation (IS). Transformational leaders stimulate followers' efforts to be innovative and creative. Followers are encouraged to be creative, followers are included in solving problems, they are encouraged to take new approaches, and their input is not publically criticized. The final component is individualized consideration (IC). Transformational leaders give special and individual attention to followers' needs for achievement and growth by acting as a coach and/or mentor (Bass & Avolio, 1994).

"At the heart of transformational leadership is the development of followers, with much of this occurring through effective empowering of followers by leaders" (Bass & Riggio, 2006, p. 193). The challenge for transformational leaders is to instill a sense of power in others by changing their internal beliefs about themselves (Yammarino, 1994). Transformational leaders can influence internal beliefs by providing positive emotional support, giving words of encouragement and positive persuasion, modeling observable effective behavior, and assigning opportunities for successful task completion. Empowering leadership means providing autonomy to one's followers (Bass & Riggio, 2006). For transformational leadership, ultimate empowerment is sharing and distributing power through delegation. Leaders become the ultimate developers of others; turning tasks over to them; allowing them to take ownership and responsibility for their jobs; and providing them with choices, opportunities, and feedback.

This description of transformational leadership includes elements of structural, psychological, and social empowerment. Structurally, transformational leaders give followers opportunities for advancement and growth; they support followers with guidance, advice, and feedback; and they equip subordinates with any information and resources needed to be successful. Also contained within this description of transformational leadership are the four cognitions of psychological empowerment that a transforming leader fosters in their followers. Transformational leaders help followers find meaning in their work; they inspire competence and self-efficacy by encouraging their work and development; and they promote self-determination, share decision-making capacities, and help establish individual impact by delegating responsibilities to them. A transforming leader shows individualized consideration by giving special attention to their followers and their needs and takes on the role of mentor and coach. This close treatment of subordinates fosters feelings of trust and fair treatment. Whereas transformational leadership is concerned with emotions, values, ethics, standards, and long-term goals and includes assessing followers' motives, satisfying their needs, and treating them as full human beings (Northouse, 2007), followers of transformational leader will be socially empowered. Transformational leaders provide opportunities for follower participation in decision-making and promote autonomy. They foster feelings of significance by showing individual concern and providing opportunities for participation and development, strive to treat all followers fairly, and distribute rewards and resources equitably or equally.

Although divinity might not be intentionally excluded, reference to transcendence is not a part of the transformational leadership theory dialogue. Transformational leadership may allow for a sense of transcendence or the more explicit presence of divinity; however, the literature on transformational leadership (except for transformational leadership in a faith-based context) does not include any discussion of a higher power. A discussion about predictors and correlates of transformational leadership such as personality, self-concept, openness to experience, hardiness, locus of control, personal traits, and cognitive/social/ emotional intelligence (Bass & Riggio, 2006) is void of any view of transcendence or divinity. Therefore, as the theory exists today, it is lacking in divine empowerment.

(b) Servant Leadership

Servant leadership was first conceived by Robert Greenleaf who saw the need for a new leadership model that puts serving others—including employees, customers, and community—as the number one priority (Spears, 1995). The primary difference between transformational leadership and servant leadership is the focus of the leader. Transformational leaders' focus is directed toward the organization, and his behavior builds follower commitment toward organizational goals, while the servant leaders' focus is on the followers, and the achievement of organizational objectives is a subordinate outcome (Stone, Russell, & Patterson, 2004). Servant leadership emphasizes increased service to others, a holistic approach to work, a sense of community, and shared decision-making power (Spears & Lawrence, 2002). Ten characteristics of servant leadership have been identified from careful study of Greenleaf's writings: (a) a deep commitment to listening intently to others; (b) striving to understand and empathize with others; (c) healing broken spirits and emotional hurts of self and others; (d) awareness, especially self-awareness; (e) reliance on persuasion rather than on authoritarian power; (f) ability to look at a problem from a conceptualizing perspective; (g) the ability to foresee the likely outcomes of a situation; (h) stewardship or holding institutions in trust for the greater good of society; (i) the responsibility to do everything within his power to nurture the personal, professional, and spiritual growth of followers; and (j) seeking to identify some means for building community among those who work within a given organization. The best test for servant leadership is to ask, do those served grow as persons? Do they become healthier, wiser, freer, more autonomous, and more likely to become servants themselves (Spears, 1995)?

Central to servant leadership is power and its use (Skowkeir, 2002). It is essential to actively and intentionally distribute organizational power in order to meet the best test for servant leadership. Skowkeir (2002) posited that the best test and business goals are not mutually exclusive and made a business case for servant leadership in corporations. He suggested that the four key components of business (profitability, quality and reliability improvement, reducing response and cycle time, and innovative responses to customers and market) can be managed effectively by addressing these business components concurrently through power sharing. Capacity is the extent to which an organization can concurrently manage these business components, and the distribution of power directly impacts capacity. By examining organizational methods and intentions, the servant leader can assess the value of distributing organizational power. Servant leadership, as conceived by Greenleaf and colleagues, has inherent empowering qualities such as power sharing and meeting followers' needs, but as a theory it is limited in application.

Patterson's (2003) model of leader–follower interaction helps explain servant leadership more than other previous models or conceptualizations of servant leaders (Winston, 2003). Patterson's theory of servant leadership is based upon virtue theory, which addresses the idea of doing the right things with a focus on moral character. Patterson's explorations into the attitudes, beliefs, and behaviors of leaders led her to see seven virtuous constructs in her leader–follower model: (a) *agapao* love, (b) humility, (c) altruism, (d) vision, (e) trust, (f) empowerment, and (g) service. This model is an improvement over the works of Greenleaf (2003) and Spears (1995) and explains the how of servant leadership (Winston, 2003). Figure 10 details how the servant leadership constructs work together, beginning with *agapao* love and ending in service.

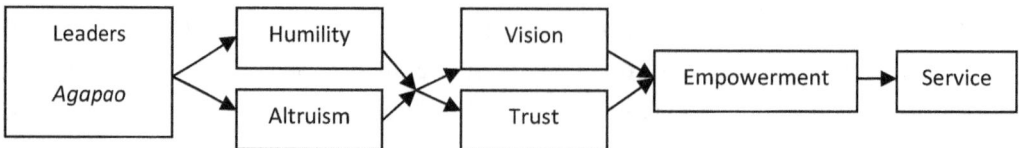

Figure 10: Patterson's (2003) servant leader model. Reprinted from *Servant Leadership: A Theoretical Model* (p. 7), by K. Patterson, 2003, paper presented at the Servant Leadership Research Roundtable, Regent University, Virginia Beach, VA. Retrieved from www.regent.edu/acad/global/publications/sl_proceedings/2003/patterson_servant_leadership.pdf

Greenleaf has been called the father of the empowerment movement because empowerment is one of the most important characteristics of servant leadership (Patterson, 2003). Empowerment is an explicit component in Patterson's (2003) servant leadership model. Patterson defined empowerment as entrusting power to others, really giving it away, and listed several empowering actions: effective listening, making people feel significant, putting an emphasis on teamwork, valuing of love and equality, and teaching and developing people; emphasizing service, a holistic approach to work, personal development, and decision making; helping to clarify expectations, goals, and responsibilities; letting people do their jobs by enabling them to learn, grow, and progress; allowing for self-direction and freedom to fail; and giving up control and letting the followers take charge as needed. These empowering actions correspond directly to components of social, structural, and psychological empowerment. The goals of servant leadership and divine empowerment are complementary. Greenleaf's (2003) expressed goal for servant leadership is for those being served to become servants and the goal of Patterson's servant leadership model is service. They correspond well to the focus of divine empowerment—individual maturity and group unity. Both are focused on others and the well-being of others and not upon organizational outcomes.

Servant leadership corresponds well to components of divine empowerment, but the largest gap between servant leadership and divine empowerment is the expressed presence (or absence) of deity. Divine empowerment explicitly links leaders to God and to each other. Servant leadership as conceived by

Greenleaf, Patterson, and others is not overtly Christian or even religious, but their ideals spring from the Judeo–Christian ethic and worldview. Wilkes (1996) pointed out that Robert Greenleaf and J. Oswald Sanders (Christian preacher and author) called for the same quality in a leader: a servant's heart. Patterson's seven virtues (leader *agapao*, humility, altruism, follower-focused vision, trust, empowerment, and service) are each expounded upon in the Bible. The anchor or cornerstone of Patterson's model, the leaders' *agapeo*, is taken directly from the Bible (Winston, 2002). While Greenleaf's concept of servant leadership is compatible with Christian thought and practice, it is not specifically grounded in God or gods. Patterson's model is not expressly Christian; however, the language is Christian and divine empowerment can be linked to Patterson's model.

(c) Authentic Leadership

Authentic leaders genuinely desire to serve others through their leadership. They are more interested in empowering the people they lead to make a difference than they are in power, money, or prestige for themselves (George, 2003). The concept of authenticity has roots in Greek philosophy—"To thine own self be true" (Avolio & Gardner, 2005). In 1999, Bass and Steidlmeier (1999) first conceptualized the authentic transformational leader, which emerged as the growing theoretical field of authentic leadership theory. Bass and Steidlmeier introduced issues of authenticity among leaders. However, they did not set out to develop authentic leadership theory; they intended only a defense of the moral basis for transformational leadership. Avolio (2010) explained his personal interest in authentic leadership. Avolio, while exploring data on transformational leadership development, noticed that in many organizations as leaders moved up the level of leadership, the mean values for the transformational scale increased. The organizations promote individuals on the basis of performance, but somehow they end up being transformational—a seeming paradox to Avolio. He concluded that three possibilities explained this paradox: (a) as a leader advances, life experience and wisdom develops the leaders into a moral leader focused on transforming followers; (b) there were flaws in the measurement of transformational leadership; or (c) a combination of the two (his final conclusion). Avolio also credited serendipity in helping to conceptualize authentic leadership when he teamed up with Fred Luthans who was working with what he called positive organizational behavior. Their collaboration, influenced by their previous work, defined authentic leadership as "a process that draws from both positive psychological capacities and a highly developed organizational context, which results in both greater self-awareness and self-regulated positive behavior on the part of leaders and associates, fostering positive self-development" (Luthans & Avolio, 2003, p. 243).

Building on Luthans and Avolio's (2003) and Ilies, Morgeson, and Mahrgang's (2005) conceptualizations of authentic leadership, Walumbwa, Avolio, Gardner, Wernsing, and Peterson (2008) developed the Authentic Leadership Questionnaire that measures four components: (a) self-awareness, (b) relational transparency, (c) balanced processing, and (d) internalized moral perspective. They initially viewed authentic leadership as being composed of five distinct but related components: self-awareness, relational transparency, internalized regulation, balanced processing of information, and positive moral perspective. However, for interests of theoretical parsimony, internalized regulation and positive moral perspective merged into internalized moral perspective because they are conceptually equivalent—they both involve exhibiting behavior that is consistent with one's internal values and standards.

Self-awareness refers to demonstrating an understanding of how one derives and makes meaning of the world and how that meaning-making process impacts the way one views oneself over time. It also refers to showing an understanding of one's strengths and weaknesses and the multifaceted nature of the self that includes gaining insight into self through exposure to others and being aware of one's impact on other people (Kernis, 2003). Relational transparency refers to presenting one's authentic self—as opposed to a fake or distorted self—to others. Such behavior promotes trust through disclosures that involve openly sharing information and expressions of one's true thoughts and feelings while trying to minimize displays of inappropriate emotions (Kernis, 2003). Relational transparency involves presenting one's genuine as opposed to fake self through selective self-disclosure to create bonds based on intimacy and trust with close others and encouraging them to do the same (Gardner, Avolio, Luthans, May, & Walumbwa, 2005). Balanced processing refers to leaders who show that they objectively analyze all relevant data before coming to a decision. Authentic leaders are driven by self-verification motives to make accurate and balanced self-assessments and act upon these assessments to pursue core beliefs and end values without getting sidetracked by ego-defense motives such as self-enhancement and self-protection (Gardner et al., 2005). Internalized moral perspective refers to an internalized and integrated form of self-regulation. It is guided by internal moral standards and values versus group, organizational, and societal pressures; it results in expressed decision making and behavior that is consistent with these internalized values (Gardner et al., 2005). Although others have conceptualized authentic leadership, the theory set forth by Avolio and colleagues is by far the most widely used and accepted.

Authentic leadership theory is primarily a normative theory that describes an ideal leader for organizations that integrates ideas of effective leadership with concerns for ethical leadership (Yukl, 2010). In contrast, transformational leadership concentrates upon the influence leaders have upon the follower. Authentic leaders are described as leading by example as they demonstrate transparent decision making, confidence, resilience, hope, and consistency between their words and actions, and followers come to identify with these leaders and their values (Gardner et al., 2005). Therefore, authentic leaders empower followers by setting the example and by building an empowering organizational climate with their actions. Avolio and Gardner (2005) proposed, "Environments that provide open access to information, resources, support, and equal opportunity for everyone to learn and develop will empower and enable leaders and their associates to accomplish their work more effectively" (p. 327). Authentic leaders can create an empowering climate by providing open access to information, resources, support, and opportunity to learn and develop and by treating followers in a fair and positive manner (Gardner et al., 2005). As with transformational leadership, authentic leadership theory promotes social, structural, and psychological empowering behavior, but it also misses a divine connection. Since the roots of authentic leadership theory come from transformational leadership theory, they are functionally similar, but the focus of authentic leadership is the ethical and moral nature of the leader and their example.

(d) Spiritual Leadership

Spirituality in the workplace is seen as one of the most important trends in the 21st century and is gaining increased attention both from corporate America and academicians as a legitimate field of study (Parboteeah & Cullen, 2010). Fry (2003) argued that previous leadership theories have focused in varying degrees on one or more aspects of the physical, mental, or emotional elements of human interaction in organizations and have neglected the spiritual component. Therefore, Fry developed a theory of spiritual leadership. He defined spiritual leadership as comprising the values, attitudes, and behaviors that are necessary to intrinsically motivate themselves and others so that they have a sense of spiritual survival through calling and membership. Spiritual leadership entails the creation of a vision where organizational members experience a sense of calling where their life has meaning and makes a difference and the establishing of a social or organizational culture based on altruistic love where the leaders and followers have genuine care, concern, and appreciation for the group that produces a sense of membership and where they feel understood and appreciated. Operationally, spiritual leadership draws from the inner life or spiritual practice to develop the values, attitudes, and behaviors that are necessary to motivate one's self and others so they have a sense of spiritual well-being. The purpose of spiritual leadership is to tap into the fundamental needs of both leader and follower for spiritual well-being through calling and membership; to create vision and value congruence across the individual, empowered team, and organizational levels; and to foster higher levels of employee well-being, organizational commitment, financial performance, and social responsibility (Fry & Cohen, 2009).

Spiritual leadership is described as an intrinsic motivational model that incorporates vision, hope/faith, and altruistic love, theories of workplace spirituality and spiritual survival, and organizational outcomes of commitment and productivity. Fry's (2003) spiritual leadership model is primarily a motivational construct and, therefore, empowers primarily by motivating followers. Fry and Cohen (2009) compared spiritual leaders to J. Collins' (2001) Level 5 leaders who transcend self-interest through a paradoxical mix of humility and professional will. They establish organizational culture by creating an environment of inclusion, personal responsibility, and open and honest communication among employees so that they feel empowered to raise and make decisions. Spiritual leadership focuses upon psychologically empowering their followers by instilling vision, helping followers discover their calling and meaning in life, and showing that they are understood and appreciated. Followers are also socially empowered by fair and honest treatment and personal and professional development. Followers are structurally empowered by showing interest in their participation in organizational decisions.

Spiritual leadership correlates greater to divine empowerment than transformational, servant, or authentic leadership because of Fry's (2003) inclusion of a higher power; yet he stopped short of calling this higher power God. Fry and Slocum (2007) noted a difference in religion (that is concerned with a system of beliefs, ritual prayers, rites and ceremonies, and related formulized practices and ideas) and spirituality (that is concerned with qualities of the human spirit including positive psychological concepts, such as love, compassion, tolerance, forgiveness, contentment, personal responsibility, and a sense of harmony with one's environment). However, Fry's model divinely empowers in that it specifically connects the individual to a higher power and allows for individual thoughts about whom or what this power is—including the Christian God. It seems the hesitancy regarding the use of spiritual is over organized religion and not over a specific deity. Fry referred to this sense of transcendence as having a calling through one's work, and membership (community or social connection) as the need to be understood and appreciated (Fry, Matherly, et al., 2010). Our model of divine empowerment also includes calling through membership but goes further in naming the source as God. Spiritual leadership leaves the choice of a divine power up to the individual, whereas the source of divine empowerment is the Trinity.

(e) Summary

This summary of transformational leadership, servant leadership, authentic leadership, and spiritual leadership revealed some similarities and differences on how they function and their approaches to empowerment. They are similar in that they each put high value upon follower development and empowerment, they stress high moral and ethical practice and behavior, and all model moral and ethical character; they all influence the organizational culture and climate, and they all put followers before organizational goals (either exclusively or to make them more productive). There are also notable differences. They have different methods of accomplishing organizational goals; they have different ways of empowering followers; and each acknowledge transcendence, higher power, or God differently (explicitly, implicitly, or not at all; see Table 15). The diversity of these leadership models is an indicator for the need of a unified method of empowerment. The use of a concatenated model of empowerment can assure that leaders are achieving their full empowering potential.

Table 15: Differences Between Leadership Theories

Theory	*Transformational*	*Servant*	*Authentic*	*Spiritual*
Transcendence	Void of mention	Implied	Void of mention	Higher power
Focus	Focus is on the relationship of leader/follower	Focus is on serving the follower	Focus is on modeling moral and ethical behavior	Focus is on motivating followers
Empowerment	Social, structural, and psychological empowerment	Social, structural, and psychological empowerment	They empower by example and by developing empowering culture	Social, structural, psychological, and divine empowerment
Goals	Organizational outcomes	Serving followers	Personal effective and ethical leadership	Organizational commitment and productivity

Section 1.28 Implications for Ecclesial Leadership

Empowerment is an important topic for the church. However, it is a concept that has numerous connotations, depending upon the theological context of the person or group using the term. Spiritual empowerment for the Pentecostal or Charismatic has different implications from those of a Reformed tradition. Empowerment in organizational leadership means something quite different from empowerment in a Christian context. However, Christian leaders have begun using constructs from organizational empowerment as components in church transformation and leadership development models (Elliston, 1992; Ford, 1991; Herrington et al., 2000), and some have combined the organizational construct of empowerment with Holy Spirit empowerment with some success (Campbell, 2005). There has been a need for a model of divine empowerment that can be integrated with theories of organizational empowerment. This proposed model of divine empowerment (see Figure 7) combined with a concatenated empowerment model (see Figure 9) will fill this gap. This divine empowerment model was developed from the examination of Ephesians 4:1-16 where leadership roles are directly connected to God. This empowerment model has five interrelated components: (a) calling is a profound impression from God that establishes parameters for your life; (b) participation is joining the divine dance with the Trinity to participate in God's plan; (c) membership is the feeling of belonging to a group and a sense of relatedness and purpose; (d) authority is power conferred by a superior being—in this case it is power from the seated Christ; and (e) mediatorial roles of leading, speaking for God, speaking about God, showing God's love and care, or instructing and inspiring the saints.

Section 1.29 Limitations of This Study

Pentecostal and Charismatic readers may feel that the role of the Holy Spirit in leader empowerment has been minimized. However, the purpose of this study was to focus on the role of Christ and the Trinity in leadership empowerment. While the role of the Spirit is integral to divine empowerment, a fuller exploration into the Spirit's role in empowering leaders is beyond the scope of this study.

The analysis of Ephesians 4:1-16 was extensive but not exhaustive. There are several limitations to this study. The most obvious limitation of this study was that it only analyzed 16 verses in the book of Ephesians. This study sought to discover the relationship between the ascension of Christ and leader empowerment in Ephesians 4:1-16. Whereas this pericope was chosen because of the direct link between the ascension and leadership roles, there are other texts that show links between the exalted Christ or God and leadership that may shed further light upon this question. Additionally, this study required some examination of other texts in Ephesians as they directly weighed upon the findings, but it was done briefly and only to the extent that it was necessary to gain understanding. A full analysis of Ephesians would have added greatly but was beyond the scope of this study.

Another limitation of this study was in the method of analysis itself. This study utilized Socio-rhetorical analysis as developed by V. K. Robbins (1996a, 1996b). This research only analyzed the inner texture, social and cultural texture, and sacred textures. It would be nearly impossible to exhaust Socio-rhetorical analysis. While many social and cultural aspects relevant to the research question were examined, there may be more social or cultural features still in need of investigation that may impact directly upon the relationships this study examined. Additionally, the ideological texture was not considered.

Section 1.30   *Future Research*

The limitations of this study also revealed areas that need further investigation. The first suggestion for additional study is the analysis of the other ascension texts in scripture. The analysis of these ascension scriptures may bring greater understanding to our research question. There are several other texts that explicitly or implicitly connect Christ's ascension, exaltation, or authority to leadership or divine mandate. This study considered only one of the lists of gifts in relationship to leadership. Additional analysis of the gifts listed in 1 Corinthians 12 and 14 and Romans 12 promises to inform our understanding of the relationship between the members of the Trinity and leadership empowerment.

This study considered intertexture only to the extent it was necessary to understand the rhetorical aspects of Ephesians 4:1-16. A more in-depth analysis of intertexture may reveal more insights to this study. This study also did not analyze the ideological texture. Future research into the ideological texture may be the most important next step in the final analysis of the text. Leadership empowerment has to do with the use of power. A full analysis of the ideology of power (as suggested by V. K. Robbins, 1996a, 1996b) will bring fuller understanding of divine empowerment.

Fuller examination of the proposed divine leadership models is warranted. Socio-rhetorical analysis of Ephesians 4:1-16 revealed five aspects to divine empowerment (i.e., calling, participation, membership, authority, and mediating roles). These aspects along with the suggested empowerment models should be examined closer for generalizability. Additionally, a fuller application of the proposed concatenated empowerment model should be expounded upon and tested.

Cosmology and *perichoresis* in relation to leadership should be looked into fuller. Ephesians presents a unique view of cosmology. The cosmological aspect of the ascended Christ promises to have direct implications upon leadership. The cosmology of God in general and Christ specifically as it relates to leadership should be examined. Additionally, the use of *perichoresis* (divine dance) was used to describe the possibility of men participating with God. Whereas there has been renewed interest in the doctrine of the Trinity (Cunningham, 1998) and the Trinity has been examined in relationship to pastoral practice (Fiddes, 2000; Pembroke, 2006), additional study into the Trinity and leadership is needed with additional attention to the role of the Holy Spirit and leadership.

References

Aamodt, M. G. (2010). *Industrial/organizational psychology: An applied approach*. Belmont, CA: Wadsworth.

Ailon, G. (2006). What B would otherwise do: A critique of conceptualizations of power in organizational theory. *Organization 13*(6), 771-800. doi:10:1177/1350508406068404

Allen, A. (1998). Rethinking power. *Hypatia, 13*(1), 21-40. Retrieved from http://www.jstor.org/stable/3810605

Anderson, C., Spataro, S. E., & Flynn, F. J. (2008). Personality and organizational culture as determinants of influence. *Journal of Applied Psychology, 93*(3), 702-710. doi:10.1037/0021-9010.93.3.702

Anderson, G. L. (2005). Baptism in the Holy Spirit, initial evidence, and a new model. *Enrichment, 10*(1), 70-78.

Appelbaum, S. H., & Honeggar, K. (1998). Empowerment: A contrasting overview of organizations in general and nursing in particular—An examination of organizational factors, managerial behaviors, job design, and structural power. *Empowerment in Organizations, 6*(2), 29-50. doi:10.1108/14634449810210715

Argyris, C. (1998). Empowerment: The emperor's new clothes. *Harvard Business Review*, 98-105. Retrieved from http://hbr.org/product/empowerment-the-emperor-s-new-clothes/an/98302-PDF-ENG

Aristotle. (1960). *The rhetoric of Aristotle* (L. Cooper, Trans.). Englewood Cliffs, NJ: Prentice Hall.

Arnold, C. E. (2010). Ephesians. In C. E. Arnold (Ed.), *Zondervan exegetical commentary on the New Testament* (Kindle ed.). Grand Rapids, MI: Zondervan.

Ashforth, B. E., & Mael, F. (1989). Social identity theory and the organization. *Academy of Management Review, 14*(1), 20-39. doi: 10.2307/258189

Austin, J. R., & Bartunek, J. M. (2006). Theories and practices of organizational development. In J. V. Gallos (Ed.), *Organizational development: A Jossey-Bass reader* (Kindle ed., pp. 89-132). San Francisco, CA: John Wiley & Sons.

Avolio, B. (2010). Pursuing authentic leadership development. In N. Nohria, & R. Khurana (Eds.), *Handbook of leadership practices* (Kindle ed., pp. 721-750). Boston, MA: Harvard Business press.

Avolio, B. J., & Gardner, W. L. (2005). Authentic leadership development: Getting to the positive forms of leadership. *The Leadership Quarterly, 16*(3), 315-823. doi:10.1016/j.leaqua.2005.03.001

Avolio, B. J., Zhu, W., Koh, W., & Bhatia, P. (2004). Transformational leadership and organizational commitment: Mediating role of psychological empowerment and moderating role of structural distance. *Journal of Organizational Behavior, 25*, 951-968. doi:10.1002/job.283

Ayers, M. (2006). Toward a theology of leadership. *Journal of Biblical Perspectives in Leadership, 1*(1), 3-27. Retrieved from http://www.regent.edu/acad/global/publications/jbpl/Ayers_JBPL_V1No1.pdf

Babson, S. (1995). Lean production and labor: Empowerment and exploitation. In S. Babson (Ed.), *Lean work: Empowerment and exploitation in the global auto industry* (pp. 1-37). Detroit, MI: Wayne State University Press.

Bacharach, S. B., & Lawler, E. J. (1980). *Power and politics in organizations.* San Francisco, CA: Jossey-Bass.

Bachrach, P., & Baratz, M. S. (1962). Two faces of power. *The American Political Science Review, 56*(4), 947-952. doi:10.2307/1952796

Bălan, S. (2010). M. Foucault's view on power relations. *Cogito Multidisciplinary Journal, 2*(2). Retrieved from http://cogito.ucdc.ro/arhiva.html

Ballenger, I. E. (1997). Ephesians 4:1-16. *Interpretation, 51*(3), 292-295. doi:10.1177/002096439605100309

Bancroft, E. H. (1946). *Christian theology: Systematic and Biblical* (Rev. ed.). Grand Rapids, MI: Zondervan.

Bandura, A. (1977). Self-efficacy: Toward a unifying theory of behavioral change. *Psychological Review, 84*, 191-215. doi:10.1037/0033-295X.84.2.191

Banks, R. J. (1994). *Paul's idea of community.* Peabody, MA: Hendrickson.

Barbalet, J. M. (1985). Power and resistance. *The British Journal of Sociology, 36*(4), 531-548. doi:10.2307/590330

Barentsen, J. (2011). *Emerging leadership in the Pauline mission: A social identity perspective on local leadership development in Corinth and Ephesus*. Eugene, OR: PICKWICK.

Barnett, M., & Duval, R. (2005). Power in international politics. *International Organization, 59*(1), 39-75. doi:10.1017/S0020818305050010

Bartram, T., & Casimir, G. (2006). The relationship between leadership and follower in-role performance and satisfaction with the leader: The mediating effects of empowerment and trust in the leader. *Leadership & Organization Development Journal, 28*(1), 4-19. doi:10.1108/01437730710718218

Baruch, Y. (1998). Applying empowerment: Organizational model. *Career Development, 3*(2), 82-87. doi:10.1108/13620439810207608

Bass, B. M. (2008). *The Bass handbook of leadership: Theory, research, and managerial applications* (4th ed.). New York: Free Press.

Bass, B. M., & Avolio, B. J. (1994). Introduction. In B. M. Bass, & B. J. Avolio (Eds.), *Improving organizational effectiveness through transformational leadership* (pp. 1-9). Thousand Oaks, CA: SAGE.

Bass, B. M., & Riggio, R. E. (2006). *Transformational leadership*. Mahwah, NJ: Lawrence Erlbaum Associates.

Bass, B. M., & Steidlmeier, P. (1999). Ethics, character, and authentic transformational leadership behavior. *The Leadership Quarterly, 10*(2), 191-217. doi:10.1016/S1048(99)00016-8

Bay, U. U. H. (2007). *The politics of empowerment in Australian critical social work* (Doctoral dissertation, RMIT University). Retrieved from http://researchbank.rmit.edu.au/eserv/rmit:9502/Bay.pdf

Bayes, J. D. (2010). Five-fold ministry: A social and cultural texture analysis of Ephesians 4:11-16. *Journal of Biblical Perspectives in Leadership, 3*(1), 113-122. http://www.regent.edu/acad/global/publications/jbpl/vol3no1/Bayes_JBPLV3I1_pgs113-122.pdf

Bekker, C. J. (2006). *The Philippians hymn (2:5-11) as an early mimetic Christological model of Christian leadership in Roman Philippi.* Paper presented at the Servant Leadership Research Roundtable, Regent University, Virginia Beach, VA. Retrieved from http://www.regent.edu/ acad/global-old/publications/sl_proceedings/2006/bekker.pdf

Bekker, C. J. (2009). Towards a theoretical model of Christian leadership. *Journal of Biblical Perspectives in Leadership, 2*(2), 142-152. Retrieved from http://www.regent.edu/acad/global/publications/jbpl/vol2no2/Bekker_JBPLV2N2_Final.pdf

Bennis, W., & Nanus, B. (2003). *Leaders: Strategies for taking charge* (2nd ed.). New York, NY: Harper Collins e-books.

Berkhof, L. (1937). *The history of Christian doctrine.* Grand Rapids, MI: Baker Book House.

Berkhof, L. (1938). *Systematic theology* (Kindle ed.). Retrieved from http://archive.org/details/SystematicTheology

Bess, K. D., Fisher, A. T., Sonn, C. C., & Biship, B. J. (2002). Psychological sense of community. In A. T. Fisher, C. C. Sonn, & B. J. Bishop (Eds.), *Psychological sense of community: Research, applications and implications* (pp. 3-22). New York, NY: Kluwer Academic/Plenum.

Biddle, B. J. (1986). Recent developments in role theory. *Annuals review of study, 12*, 67-92. doi:10.1146/annurev.soc.12.1.67

Blanchard, K., & Hodges, P. (2005). *Lead like Jesus* (Kindle ed.). Nashville, TN: Thomas Nelson.

Boice, J. M. (1996). *Psalms* (Vol. 2). Grand Rapids, MI: Baker Books.

Bottoms, S. I. (2011). *Restoring the centrality of the Spirit's empowerment for carrying out the Great Commission: A course to equip Christians at Journey Church in the process of evangelism* (Doctoral dissertation). Available from ProQuest Dissertations and Theses database. (UMI No. 3481528)

Bradbury-Jones, C., Sambrook, S., & Irvine, F. (2008). Power and empowerment: A fourth theoretical approach. *Journal of Advanced Nursing, 62*, 258-266. doi:10.1111/j.1365-2648.2008.04598.x

Bromiley, G. W. (1979). Authority. In W. G. Bromiley (Ed.), *International Standard Bible Encyclopedia* (Vol. 1, pp. 365-371). Grand Rapids, MI: William B. Eerdmans.

Broyles, C. G. (1999). Psalms. In R. L. Hubbard, & R. K. Johnston (Eds.), *New international biblical commentary* (Vol. II). Peabody, MA: Hendrickson.

Bruce, F. F. (2012). *The epistle to the Ephesians* (Kindle ed.). Claverton Down, Bath, UK: Creative Communications Ltd.

Brumback, C. (1955). *Accent on the ascension*. Springfield, MO: Gospel Publishing House.

Buchanan, J. R. (2009). *The benefits of analysis for expository preaching* (Doctoral dissertation). Available from ProQuest Dissertations and Theses database. (UMI No. 3352775)

Burns, J. M. (1978). *Leadership*. New York, NY: Perennial.

Buswell, J. O. (1962). *A systematic theology of the Christian religion* (Vol. II). Grand Rapids, MI: Zondervan Publishing House.

Buturovic, A. (1996). Spiritual empowerment through spiritual submission. *Canadian Women Studies, 17*(1), 53-56. Retrieved from http://www.synergiescanada.org/journals/ont/cws/484/8909

Calvin, J. (1548). *Commentary on Galatians and Ephesians*. Retrieved from Christian Classic Ethereal Library website: http://www.ccel.org/ccel/calvin/calcom41.html

Campbell, L. R. (2005). *Empowering indigenous leaders for the Alaska context of ministry* (Doctoral dissertation). Available from ProQuest Dissertations and Theses database. (UMI No. 3164688)

Casey, M., Saunders, J., & O'Hara, T. (2010). Impact of critical social empowerment and job satisfaction in nursing and midwifery settings. *Journal of Nursing Management, 18*, 24-34. doi:10.1111/j.1365-2834.2009.01040.x

Castelli, E. A. (1991). *Imitating Paul: A discourse of power*. Louisville, KY: Westminster/John Knox Press.

Çavuş, M. F., & Demir, Y. (2010). The impacts of structural and psychological empowerment on burnout: A research on staff nurses in Turkish state hospitals. *Canadian Social Science, 6*(4), 63-72. Retrieved from http://cscanada.net/index.php/css/article/download/1102/1121

Cerillo, A. (1991). Pentecostals and the city. In M. W. Dempster, B. D. Klaus, & D. Peterson (Eds.), *Called & empowered: Global mission in Pentecostal perspective* (pp. 98-119). Peabody, MA: Hendrickson.

Chang, L., & Liu, C. (2008). Employee empowerment, innovative behavior and job productivity of public health nurses: A cross-sectional questionnaire survey. *International Journal of Nursing Studies, 45*, 1442-1448. doi:10.1016/j.ijnurstu.2007.12.006

Chang, L., Shih, C., & Lin, S. (2009). The mediating role of psychological empowerment on job satisfaction and organizational commitment for school health nurses: A cross-sectional questionnaire survey. *International Journal of Nursing Studies, 47*, 427-433. doi:10.1016/j.ijnurstu.2009.09.007

Cho, T. (2008). *An integrative model of empowerment and individual performance under conditions of organizational individualism and collectivism in public organizations* (Doctoral dissertation). Available from ProQuest Dissertations and Theses database. (UMI No. 3312240)

Christman, R. (2007). *Servant leadership and power in positional-led organizations*. Paper presented at the Servant Leadership Research Roundtable, Regent University, Virginia Beach, VA. Retrieved from http://regent.edu/acad/ global/publications/sl_proceedings/2007/christman.pdf

Ciulla, J. (2004). Leadership and the problem of bogus empowerment. In J. Ciulla (Ed.), *Ethics, the heart of leadership* (2nd ed., pp. 59-82). Westport, CT: PRAEGER.

Clarke, A. D. (2008). *A Pauline theology of church leadership*. New York, NY: t&t clark.

Coleman, H. J. (1996). Why employee empowerment is not just a fad. *Leadership & Organizational Development, 17*(4), 29-36. doi:10.1108/01437739610120574

Coll, R. (1986). Power, powerlessness, and empowerment. *Religious Education, 81*(3), 412-423. doi:10.1080/0034408600810307

Collins, D. (1999). Born to fail? Empowerment, ambiguity and set overlap. *Personal Review, 28*(3), 208-221. doi:10.1108/00483489910264598

Collins, J. (2001). *Good to great.* New York, NY: Collins Business.

Conger, J. A., & Kanungo, R. N. (1988). The empowerment process: Integrating theory and practice. *Academy of Management Review, 13*(3), 471-482. doi:10.2307/258093

Conybeare, W. J., & Howson, J. S. (1980). *The life and epistles of St. Paul.* Grand Rapids, MI: Wm. B. Eerdmans.

Cooper, L. (1960). *The rhetoric of Aristotle.* Englewood, NJ: Prentice Hall.

Creswell, J. W. (2009). *Research design: Qualitative, quantitative, and mixed methods approach* (2nd ed.). Thousand Oaks, CA: Sage.

Crewe, D. (2010). Power: The supposed definitions revisited. *Journal of Theoretical and Philosophical Criminology, 2*(2), 22-68. Retrieved from http://connection.ebscohost.com/c/articles/57332693/power-supposed-definitions-revisited

Crowther, S. S. (2012). *An examination of leadership principles in 1 Peter in comparison to authentic and kenotic models of leadership* (Doctoral dissertation) Available from ProQuest Dissertations and Theses database. (UMI No. 3515407)

Cunningham, D. S. (1998). *These three are one: The practice of Trinitarian theology.* Malden, MA: Blackwell.

Dahl, R. A. (1957). The concept of power. *Behavioral Science, 2*(3), 201-215. doi:10.1002/bs.3830020303

DeSilva, D. A. (2000). *Honor, patronage, kinship & purity.* Downers Grove, IL: IVP Academic.

DeSilva, D. A. (2004). *An introduction to the New Testament: Contexts, methods, & ministry formation.* Downers Grove, IL: IVP Academic.

Deutsch, M. (2006). Justice and conflict. In M. Deutsch, P. T. Coleman, & E. C. Marcus (Eds.), *The handbook of conflict resolution* (2nd ed., pp. 43-68). San Francisco, CA: Jossey-Bass.

Dewettinck, K., & Van Ameijde, M. (2011). Linking leadership empowerment behavior to employee attitudes and behavioral intentions: Testing the mediating role of psychological empowerment. *Personnel Review, 40*(3), 248-305. doi:10.1108/00483481111118621

Dodd, B. J. (2003). *Empowered church leaders*. Downers Grove, IL: InterVarsity Press.

Domhoff, G. W. (2005). *Basics of studying power*. Retrieved from http://www2.ucsc.edu/whorulesamerica/methods/studying_power.html

Dorman, D. A. (1985). The purpose of empowerment in the Christian life. *Pneuma: The Journal of the Society for Pentecostal Studies, 7*(2), 147-165. doi:10.1163/157007485x00111

Dorries, D. W. (2006). *Spirit-filled Christology: Merging theology and power*. San Diego, CA: Aventine Press.

Dowding, K. (2006). Three-dimensional power: A discussion of Steven Lukes' power: A radical view. *Political Studies Review, 4*, 163-145. doi:10.1111/j.1478-9299.2006.000100.x

Duffield, G. P., & Van Cleave, N. M. (1987). *Foundations of Pentecostal theology*. Los Angeles, CA: L.I.F.E. Bible College.

Dulles, A. R. (2002). *Models of the church*. New York, NY: Doubleday.

Durant, W. (1971). Caesar and Christ. In *The story of civilization* (Vol. 3). New York, NY: MJF Books.

Edersheim, A. (1890). *The life and times of Jesus the Messiah*. Retrieved from Christian Classic Ethereal Library website: http://www.ccel.org/ccel/edersheim/lifetimes

Edwards, P., & Collinson, M. (2002). Empowerment and managerial labor strategies: Pragmatism regained. *Work and Occupation, 29*, 272-299. doi:10.1177/0730888402029003002

Ellis, E. E. (1989). *Pauline theology: Ministry and society*. Grand Rapids, MI: William B. Eerdmans.

Elliston, E. J. (1992). *Home grown leaders*. Pasadena, CA: William Carey Library.

Elyon, D., & Au, K. Y. (1999). Exploring empowerment cross-cultural differences along the power distance dimensions. *International Relations, 23*(3), 373-385. doi:10.1016/S0147-1767(99)00002-4

Enns, P. (1989). *The Moody handbook of theology*. Chicago, IL: Moody Press.

Erickson, M. J. (1998). *Christian theology* (2nd ed.). Grand Rapids, MI: Baker Academic.

Evans, C. S. (2006). Introduction: Understanding Jesus the Christ as human and divine. In C. S. Evans (Ed.), *Exploring kenotic Christology: The self-emptying of God* (pp. 1-24). Vancouver, British Columbia: Regent College Publishing.

Fairhead, J., & Griffin, R. (2000). *The power potential of the less-powerful within network development and dissolution. A political sense making process (PSP) model of rapid network development and dissolution.* Proceedings of the 16th Annual IMP Converence, Bath, England. Retrieved from http://impgroup.org/uploads/papers/295.pdf

Fairholm, G. W. (1998). *Perspectives on leadership: From the science of management to its spiritual heart* (Kindle ed.). Westport, CT: PRAEGER.

Farrow, D. (1999). *Ascension and ecclesia*. Grand Rapids, MI: William B. Eerdmans.

Farrow, D. (2011). *Ascension theology*. New York, NY: t&tclark.

Faulkner, J., & Laschinger, H. (2008). The effects of structural and psychological empowerment on perceived respect in acute care nurses. *Journal of Nursing Management, 16*, 214-221. doi:10.1111/j.1365-2834.2007.00781.x

Fee, G. D. (1983). *New Testament exegesis: A handbook for students and pastors*. Philadelphia, PA: The Westminster Press.

Fee, G. D. (1994). *God's empowering presence: The Holy Spirit in the letters of Paul*. Peabody, MA: Hendrickson.

Fee, G. D. (1996). *Paul, the Spirit, and the people of God*. Grand Rapids, MI: Baker Academic.

Fee, G. D. (2006). The New Testament and kenosis Christology. In C. S. Evans (Ed.), *Exploring kenotic Christology: The self-emptying of God* (pp. 25-44). Vancouver, British Columbia: Regent College Publishing.

Fee, G. D. (2007). *Pauline Christology: An exegetical-theological study*. Peabody, MA: Hendrickson.

Fee, G. D., & Stewart, D. (1982). *How to read the Bible for all its worth: A guide to understanding the Bible*. Grand Rapids, MI: Zondervan Publishing House.

Fettke, S. M. (2011). *God's empowered people: A Pentecostal theology of the laity*. Eugene, OR: Wipf & Stock.

Fiddes, P. S. (2000). *Participating in God: A pastoral doctrine of the Trinity*. Louiseville, KY: Westminster John Knox Press.

Fields, D. L. (2002). *Taking the measure of work: A guide to validated scales for organizational research and diagnosis*. Thousand Oaks, CA: SAGE.

Ford, L. (1991). *Transforming leadership: Jesus' way of creating vision, shaping values & empowering change* (Kindle ed.). Downers Grove, IL: InterVarsity Press.

Foucault, M. (1982). The subject and power. *Critical Inquiry, 8*(4), 777-795. doi:10.1086/448181

Foulkes, F. (1983). The epistle of Paul to the Ephesians. In R. V. G. Tasker (Ed.), *The Tyndale New Testament commentaries* (Vol. 10). Grand Rapids, MI: William B. Eerdmans.

Freeman, H. E. (1968). *An introduction to the Old Testament prophets*. Chicago, IL: Moody Press.

French, J. R. P. (1956). A formal theory of social power. *Psychological Review, 63*(3), 181-194. doi:10.1037/h0046123

French, J. R. P., & Raven, B. (2001). The basis of social power. In W. E. Natemeyer, & J. T. McMahon (Eds.), *Classics of organizational behavior* (3rd ed., pp. 253-267). Long Grove, IL: Waveland Press.

Fritzmyer, J. A. (1984). The ascension of Christ and Pentecost. *Theological Studies, 45*, 409-440. Retrieved from http://www.ts.mu.edu/readers/content/pdf/45/45.3/45.3.1.pdf

Fry, L. W. (2003). Toward a theory of spiritual leadership. *The Leadership Quarterly, 14*, 693-727. doi:10.1016/j.leaqua.2003.09.001

Fry, L. W. (2005). Introduction: Toward a paradigm of spiritual leadership. *The Leadership Quarterly, 16*(Special Issue), 619-622. doi:10.1016/j.leaqua.2005.07.001

Fry, L. W. (2006). *Spiritual leadership and organizational performance: An exploratory study*. Paper presented at the Academy of Management, Atlanta, GA. Retrieved from http://precisionmi.com/Leadership.htm

Fry, L. W. (2008). Maximizing the triple bottom line through spiritual leadership. *Organizational Dynamics, 37*(1), 86-96. doi:10.1016.j.orgdyn.2007.11.004

Fry, L. W., & Cohen, M. P. (2009). Spiritual leadership as a paradigm for organizational transformation and recovery from extended work hour cultures. *Journal of Business Ethics, 84*, 265-278. doi:10.1007/s10551-008-9695-2

Fry, L. W., Matherly, L. L., & Ouimet, J. R. (2010). The spiritual leadership balanced scorecard business model: The case of Cordon Blue-Tomasso Corporation. *Journal of Management, Spirituality & Religion, 7*(4), 283-314. doi: 10.1080/14766086.2010.524983

Fry, L. W., & Slocum, J. W. (2007). Maximizing the triple bottom line through spiritual leadership. *Organizational Dynamics, 37*(1), 86-96. doi:10.1016/j.orgdyn.2007.11.004

Fulton, Y. (1997). Nurses' view on empowerment: A critical social theory perspective. *Journal of Advanced Nursing, 26*, 529-536. doi:10.1046/j.1365-2648.1997.t01-13-00999.x

Gardner, W. L., Avolio, B. J., Luthans, F., May, D. R., & Walumbwa, F. O. (2005). "Can you see the real me?" A self-based model of authentic leaders and follower development. *The Leadership Quarterly, 16*(3), 343-372. doi:10.1016/j.leaqua.2005.03.003

Garrett, J. L. (1990). *Systematic theology: Biblical, historical, and evangelical* (Vol. 1). Grand Rapids, MI: William B. Eerdmans.

Gaventa, J. (2003). *Power after Lukes: An overview of theories of power since Lukes and their application to development*. Retrieved from http://www.powercube.net/wp-content/uploads/2009/11/power_after_lukes.pdf

Gaventa, J. (2006). Finding the space for change: A power analysis. *IDS Bulletin, 37*(6), 23-33. doi:10.1111/j.1759-5436.2006.tb00320.x

George, B. (2003). *Authentic leadership: Rediscovering the secrets to creating lasting values* (Kindle ed.). San Francisco, CA: Jossey-Bass.

Giacalone, R. A., & Jurkiewicz, C. L. (2010). The science of workplace spirituality. In R. A. Giacalone, & C. L. Jurkiewicz (Eds.), *Handbook of workplace spirituality and organizational performance* (2nd ed., pp. 3-26). New York, NY: M. E. Sharp.

Gibbon, E. (1845). *The history of the decline and fall of the Roman Empire.* Retrieved from Christian Classic Ethereal Library website: www.ccel.org/ccel/gibbon/decline

Giles, K. (1995). *What on earth is the church? An exploration in New Testament theology.* Downers Grove, IL: InterVarsity Press.

Gjertstad, E. (2005). *Ethics and power in governance: Avoiding totalitarianism, dogmatism and relativism.* Retrieved from http://ebookbrowse.com/eevastiina-gjerstad-pdf-d117223406

Gombis, T. G. (2005). Cosmic Lordship and divine gift-giving: Psalms 68 in Ephesians 4. *Novum Testamentum, 47*(4), 367-380. doi:10.1163/156853605774482081

Gowler, B. D. (2010). interpretation: Textures of a text and its reception. *Journal for the study of the New Testament, 33*(2), 191-206. doi:10.1177/0142064X10385857

Greenleaf, R. K. (2003). The servant as leader. In H. Beazley, J. Begg, & L. C. Spears (Eds.), *The servant-leader within* (pp. 29-74). New York, NY: Paulist Press.

Grudem, W. (1994). *Systematic theology: An introduction to biblical doctrine.* Grand Rapids, MI: Zondervan.

Gundry, R. H. (2010). *Commentary on Ephesians* (Kindle ed.). Grand Rapids, MI: Baker Academic.

Guynes, D. R. (1986). *The gospel of the ascension.* Kuala Lumpur, Malaysia: Calvary Church Press.

Hammet, E. H. (2005). *Spiritual leadership in a secular age*. St. Louis, MO: Chalice Press.

Hardy, C., & Clegg, S. R. (1999). Some dare call it power. In S. R. Clegg & C. Hardy (Eds.), *Studying organization: Theory and method* (pp. 368-387). London, England: SAGE.

Hardy, C., & Leiba-O'Sullivan, S. (1998). The power behind empowerment: Implications for research and practice. *Human Relations, 51*(4), 451-483. doi:10.1177/0018726798051000402

Harnack, A. (1904). *The mission and expansion of Christianity in the first century*. Retrieved from Christian Classics Ethereal Library website: www.ccel.org/ccel/harnack/mission

Harris, K. J., Wheeler, A. R., & Kacmar, K. M. (2009). Leader–member exchange and empowerment: Direct and interactive effects on job satisfaction, turnover intentions, and performance. *The Leadership Quarterly, 20*, 371-382. doi:10.1016/j.leaqua.2009.03.006

Harris, W. H. (1994). The ascent and descent of Christ in Ephesians 4:9-10. *Bibliotheca Sacra, 151*, 198-214. Retrieved from http://www.galaxie.com/article/bsac151-602-05

Haroutunian, J. (1956). The doctrine of the ascension: A study of the New Testament teaching. *Interpretation, 10*, 270-281. Retrieved from http://dx.doi.org/10.1177/002096435601000302

Haugaard, M. (2010). Power: A "family resemblance" concept. *European Journal of Cultural Studies, 13*(4), 419-438. doi:10.1177/1367549410377152

Hemphill, K. (1992). *Mirror, mirror on the wall: Discovering your true self through spiritual gifts*. Nashville, TN: Broadman Press.

Herrington, J., Bonen, M., & Furr, J. H. (2000). *Leading congregational change*. San Francisco, CA: Jossey-Bass.

Hersey, P., Blanchard, K. H., & Natemeyer, W. E. (2001). Situational leadership and power. In W. E. Natemeyer & J. T. McMahon (Eds.), *Classics of organizational behavior* (3rd ed., pp. 321-329). Long Grove, IL: Waveland Press.

Hinson, M. C. (2007). *The descent of Christ in Ephesians 4:9: Its impact upon the use of the Apostle's Creed* (Senior Thesis, Liberty

University). Retrieved from http://digitalcommons.liberty.edu/cgi/viewcontent.cgi?article=1017 &context=honors

Hobbes, T. (1651). *Leviathan* (Kindle ed.). Retrieved from Amazon.com.

Hocutt, M. A., & Stone, T. H. (1998). The impact of employee empowerment on the quality of a service recovery effort. *Journal of Quality Management, 3*(1), 117-132. doi:10.1016/S1084-8568(99)80107-2

Hodge, C. (1940). *Systematic theology* (Vol. 1). Grand Rapids, MI: Wm. B. Eerdmans.

Holdcroft, L. T. (1999). *The Holy Spirit: A Pentecostal interpretation*. Abbotsford, Canada: CeeTeC.

Holler, M. J. (2007). *Niccollò Machiavelli on power*. Beiträge zur Wirtschaftsforschung (Contributions to Economic Research) [Working paper No. 149]. Retrieved from http://dx.doi.org/10.2139/ssrn.956093

Honold, L. (1997). A review of the literature on employee empowerment. *Empowerment in Organizations, 5*(4), 202-212. doi:10.1108/14634449710195471

Horsthuis, J. (2011). Participants with God: A perichoretic theology of leadership. *Journal of Religious Leadership, 10*(1), 71-107. Retrieved from http://arl-jrl.org/Volumes/Horsthuis11.pdf

Howard, A. (1998). The empowering leader: Unrealized opportunities. In G. Hickman (Ed.), *Leading organizations: Perspectives for a new era* (pp. 202-213). Thousand Oaks, CA: SAGE.

Howard, R. A., & Korver, C. D. (2008). *Ethics for the real world*. Boston, MA: Harvard Business Press.

Howell, D. N. (2003). *Servants of the servant: A biblical theology of leadership*. Eugene, OR: Wipf & Stock.

Huey, F. B., & Corely, B. (1983). *A student's dictionary for biblical and theological studies*. Grand Rapids, MI: Academic Books.

Hui, M. K., Au, K., & Fock, H. (2004). Empowerment effects across cultures. *Journal of International Business Studies, 35*, 14-60. doi:10.1057/palgrave.jibs.8400067

Humborstad, S. I. W., & Perry, C. (2011). Employee empowerment, job satisfaction and organizational commitment: An in-depth empirical investigation. *Chinese Management Studies, 5*(3), 325-344. doi:10.1108/17506141111163390

Ilies, R., Morgeson, F. P., & Nahrgang, J. D. (2005). Authentic leadership and eudaemonic well-being: Understanding leader–follower outcomes. *The Leadership Quarterly, 16*(3), 373-394. doi:10.1016/j.leaqua.2005.03.002

Iorg, J. (2008). *Is God calling me?* (Kindle ed.). Nashville, TN: B & H.

Ivancevich, J. M., Konopaske, R., & Matteson, M.T. (2008). *Organizational behavior and management*. New York, NY: McGraw-Hill Irwin.

Jackson, J. (1998). Contemporary criticisms of role theory. *Journal of Occupational Science, 5*(2), 49-55. doi:10.1080/14427591.1998.9686433

Jennings, L. B., Parra-Medina, D. M., Messias, D. K. H., & McLoughlin, K. (2006). Toward a critical–social theory of youth empowerment. *Journal of Community Practice, 14*(1/2), 31-55. doi:10.1300/J125v14n01_03

Kanter, R. M. (1979). Power failure in management circuits. *Harvard Business Review, 57*(4), 1-13. Retrieved from http://ils.unc.edu/daniel/131/ cco4/Kanter.pdf

Kanter, R. M. (1993). *Men and women of the corporation* (Kindle ed.). New York, NY: Basic Books.

Kärkkäinen, V. (2002a). *Pneumatology* (Kindle ed.). Grand Rapids, MI: Baker Academic.

Kärkkäinen, V. (2002b). *Toward a pneumatological theology*. New York, NY: University Press of America.

Kearins, K. (1996). Power in organizational analysis: Delineating and contrasting a Foucauldian perspective. *Electronic Journal of Radical Organizational Theory, 2*(2), 1-25. Retrieved from http://www.mngt.waikato.ac.nz/ejrot/Vol2_2/Kearins.pdf

Keener, C. S. (1993). *The IVP Bible background commentary*. Downers Grove, IL: InterVarsity Press.

Keener, C. S. (1996). *3 crucial questions about the Holy Spirit.* Grand Rapids, MI: Baker Books.

Keener, C. S. (1997). *The Spirit in the Gospels and Acts: Divine purity and power.* Grand Rapids, MI: Baker Academic.

Keener, C. S. (2001). *Gift & giver: The Holy Spirit for today* (Kindle ed.). Grand Rapids, MI: Baker Academic.

Keener, C. S. (2007). Why does Luke use tongues as a sign of the Spirit's empowerment? *Journal of Pentecostal Theology, 15*(2), 177-184. doi:10.1177/0966736907076336

Keener, C. S. (2009). Power of Pentecost: Luke's missiology in Acts 1-2. *Asian Journal of Pentecostal Studies, 12*(2), 47-73. Retrieved from http://apts.edu/aeimages//File/AJPS_PDF/09-_1_Craig_S._Keener_2.pdf

Keltner, D., Gruenfeld, D. H., & Anderson, C. (2003). *Power, approach, and inhibition.* Psychology Review, *11*(02), 265-284. doi:10.1037/0033-295X.110.2.265

Kernis, M. H. (2003). Toward a conceptualization of optimal self-esteem. *Psychological Inquiry, 14*(1), 203-211. doi:10.1207/S15327965PLI1401_01

Kets de Vries, M. F. R. (1991). Whatever happened to the philosopher–king? The leader's addiction to power. *Journal of Management Studies, 28*(4), 339-350. doi:10.1111/j.1467-6486.1991.tb00285.x

Khan, M. T., Saboor, A., Khan, N. A., & Ali, I. (2011). Connotation of employees' empowerment emerging challenges. *European Journal of Social Sciences, 22*(4), 556-564. Retrieved from http://www.eurojournals.com/EJSS_22_4_10.pdf

Kirkman, B. L., & Rosen, B. (1999). Beyond self-management: Antecedents and consequences of team empowerment. *Academy of Management Journal 42*(1), 58-74. doi:10.2307/256874

Klaus, B. D., & Triplett, L. O. (1991). National leadership in Pentecostal missions. In M. W. Dempster, B. D. Klaus, & D. Peterson (Eds.), *Called & empowered: Global mission in Pentecostal perspective* (pp. 225-241). Peabody, MA: Hendrickson.

Knox, D. B. (1962). Evangelist. In J. D. Douglas (Ed.), *New Bible dictionary* (2nd ed., pp. 356-357). Leicestor, England: Inter-Varsity Press.

Koberg, C. S., Boss, R. W., Senjem, J. C., & Goodman, E. A. (1999). Antecedents and outcomes of empowerment. *Group Organization Management, 24*(1), 71-91. doi:10.1177/1059601199241005

Koch, G. R. (1998). Spiritual empowerment: A metaphor for counseling. *Counseling & Values, 43*(1), 19-27. doi:10.1002/j.2161-007X.1998.tb00957.x

Korac-Kakabadse, N., Kouzmin, A., & Kakabadse, A. (2002). Spirituality and praxis. *Journal of Management Psychology, 17*(3), 165-182. doi:10.1108/02683940210423079

Kotter, J. P. (1996). *Leading change.* Boston, MA: Harvard Business School Press.

Kouzes, J. M., & Posner, B. Z. (2004). *Christian reflections on the leadership challenge* (Kindle ed.). San Francisco, CA: Jossey-Bass.

Kuokkanen, L., & Leino-Kilpi, H. (2000). Power and empowerment in nursing: Three theoretical approaches. *Journal of Advanced Nursing, 31*(1), 235-241. doi:10.1046/j.1365-2648.2000.01241.x

Ladd, G. E. (1974). *A theology of the New Testament* (Rev. ed.). Grand Rapids, MI: William B. Eerdmans.

Land, S. J. (2010). *Pentecostal spirituality: A passion for the kingdom.* Cleveland, TN: CPT Press.

Landes, L. (1994). The myth and misdirection of employee empowerment. *Training, 31*(3), 116. Retrieved from http://business.highbeam.com/137618/ article-1G1-15294726/myth-and-misdirection-employee-empowerment

Laniak, T. S. (2006). *Shepherds after my own heart: Pastoral traditions and leadership in the Bible.* Downers Grove, IL: InterVarsity Press.

Laniak, T. S. (2007). *While shepherds watch their flocks: Rediscovering biblical leadership.* Shepherd Leader Productions.

Laschinger, H. K. S., Finegan, J. E., Shamian, J., & Wilk, J. E. (2004). A longitudinal analysis of the impact of workplace empowerment on work satisfaction. *Journal of Organizational Behaviors, 25*, 527-545. doi:10.5465/APBPP.2002.7516663

Laschinger, H. K. S., Gilbert, S., Smith, L. M., & Leslie, K. (2010). Towards a comprehensive theory of nurse/patient empowerment: Applying Kanter's empowerment theory to patient care. *Journal of Nursing Management, 18*, 4-13. doi:10.1111/j.1365-2834.2009.01046.x

Laschinger, H. K. S., Leiter, M., Day, A., & Gilin, D. (2009). Workplace empowerment, incivility, and burnout: Impact on staff nurse recruitment and retention outcomes. *Journal of Management, 17*, 302-311. doi:10.1111/j.1365-2834.2009.00999.x

Lee, M., & Koh, J. (2001). Is empowerment really a new concept? *The International Journal of Human Resource Management, 12*(4), 684-695. doi:10.1080/09586190110037344

Lee, S. S. (2008). *Relationships among leadership empowerment, job satisfaction, and employee loyalty in university dining student workers* (Doctoral dissertation). Available from ProQuest Dissertations and Theses database. (UMI No. 3307092)

Lin, D. (1994). Spiritual gifts. In S. M. Horton (Ed.), *Systematic theology* (pp. 457-488). Springfield, MO: Logion Press.

Lincoln, A. T. (1990). Ephesians. In D. A. Hubbard, & G. W. Barker (Eds.), *Word Biblical commentary* (Vol. 42). Dallas, TX: Word Book.

Litman-Adizes, T., Raven, B. H., & Fontaine, G. (1978). Consequences of social power and causal attribution for compliance as seen by power holder and target. *Personality and Social Psychology Bulletin, 4*, 260-264. doi:10.1177/014616727800400218

Lloyd-Jones, D. M. (1980). *Christian unity: An exposition of Ephesians 4:1-16*. Grand Rapids, MI: Baker Books.

Lukes, S. (1975). *Power: A radical view*. London, England: McMillian Education.

Lusch, R. F., & Brown, J. R. (1982). A modified model of power in the marketing channel. *Journal of Marketing Research, 19*(3), 312-232. doi:10.2307/3151565

Luthans, F., & Avolio, B. J. (2003). Authentic leadership: A positive development approach. In K. S. Cameron, J. E. Dutton, & R. E. Quinn (Eds.), *Positive organizational scholarship* (Kindle ed., pp. 241-261). San Francisco, CA: Barrett-Koehler.

Macchia, F. (2006). *Baptized in the Spirit* (Kindle ed.). Grand Rapids, MI: Zondervan.

Macchia, F. D. (2008). Baptized in the Spirit: Reflections in response to my reviewers. *Journal of Pentecostal Theology, 16*, 14-20. doi:10.1163/174552508x294170

Machiavelli, N. (2012). *The prince* (W. K. Marriott, Trans., Kindle ed.). New York, NY: Doubleday.

Makau-Olwendo, A. (2009). Influencing the laity's theologizing for spiritual empowerment: An African perspective. *Common Ground Journal, 7*(1), 113-126. Retrieved from www.commongroundjournal.org/volnum/v07n01.pdf

Martin, R. P. (1997). *A hymn of Christ*. Downers Grove, IL: InterVarsity Press.

McCormick, D. W. (1994). Spirituality and management. *Journal of Psychology, 9*(6), 5-8. doi:10.1108/02683949410070142

McDermot, K., Laschinger, H. K. S., & Shamain, J. (1996). Work empowerment and organizational commitment. *Nursing Management, 27*(5), 44-47. doi:10.1097/00006247-199605000-00010

McGrath, A. E. (1994). *Christian theology: An introduction*. Oxford, UK: Blackwell.

McMillan, D. W., & Chavis, D. M. (1986). Sense of community: A definition and theory. *Journal of Community Psychology, 14*, 6-23. doi:10.1002/1520-6629(198601)14:1<6::AID-JCOP2290140103>3.0.CO;2-I

McRoberts, K. D. (1994). The Holy Trinity. In S. M. Horton (Ed.), *Systematic theology* (pp. 145-177). Springfield, MO: Logion Press.

Menon, S. T. (2001). Employee empowerment: An integrative psychological approach. *Applied Psychology: An International Review, 50*(1), 153-183. doi:10.1111/1464/0597.00052

Menzies, R. P. (2004). *Empowered for witness: The Spirit in Luke-Acts*. New York NY: t&tclark.

Metzger, B. M. (1971). *A textual commentary on the Greek New Testament* (3rd ed.). Stuttgart, Germany: United Bible Society.

Michel, K. A., Miles, D. A., Miller, J., Gibson, C. G., Holloway, J. B., & Gilligan, C. (2012). *Divine empowerment: A transformational study of Christian leadership development* (Kindle ed.). Retrieved from Amazon.com

Miers, R., & Fisher, A. T. (2002). Being church and community. In A. T. Fisher, C. C. Sonn, & B. J. Bishop (Eds.), *Psychological sense of community: Research, applications, and implications* (pp. 141-160). New York, NY: Kluwer Academic/Plenum.

Miller, D. R. (2005). *Empowered for global missions: A missionary look at the book of Acts.* USA: Life Publishers International. Retrieved from http://www.decadeofpentecost.org/ebooks/Empowered.pdf

Miller, D. R. (2008). *In step with the Spirit: Studies in the Spirit-filled walk.* Springfield, MO: AIA. Retrieved from http://www.decadeofpentecost.org/ebooks/InStep.pdf

Miller, D. R. (2009). *Experiencing the Spirit: A study on the work of the Holy Spirit in the life of the believer.* Springfield, MO: AIA. Retrieved from http://www.decadeofpentecost.org/ebooks/Experiencing_the_Spirit_Revised%20Edition.pdf

Minear, P. S. (2004). *Images of the church in the New Testament.* Louisville, KY: Westminster/John Knox Press.

Mintzberg, H. (2005). The power game and the players. In J. M. Shafritz, J. S. Ott, & Y. S. Jang (Eds.), *Classics of organizational theory* (6th ed., pp. 334-341). Belmont, CA: Wadsworth.

Moon, J. (2004). *Paul's discourse for the Corinthians' edification* (Doctoral dissertation, University of Stellenbosch). Retrieved from http://hdl.handle.net/10019.1/16066

Newman, S. (2005). *Power and politics in poststructuralist thought: New Theories of the political* (ebook ed.). New York, NY: Routledge. Retrieved from http://ebookbrowse.com/newman-power-and-politics-in-poststructuralist-thought-new-theories-of-the-political-pdf-d109229153

Niewold, J. W. (2006). *Incarnational leadership: Towards a distinctly Christian theory of leadership* (Doctoral dissertation) Available from ProQuest Dissertations and Theses database. (UMI No. 3243512)

Ning, S., Zhang, H., Libo, W., & Qiujie, L. (2009). The impact of nurse empowerment on job satisfaction. *Journal of Advanced Nursing, 65*(12), 2642-2648. doi:10.1111/j.1365-2648.2009.05133.x

Northouse, P. G. (2007). *Leadership: Theory and practice* (4th ed.). Thousand Oaks, CA: SAGE.

Nye, J. S. (2010). Power and leadership. In N. Nohria & R. Khurana (Eds.), *Handbook of leadership and practice* (Kindle ed., pp. 305-332), Boston, MA: Harvard Business School.

O'Brien, J. L. (2010). *Structural empowerment, psychological empowerment and burnout in registered staff nurses working in outpatient dialysis centers* (Doctoral dissertation). Available from ProQuest Dissertations and Theses database. (UMI No. 3408877)

O'Brien, J. L. (2011). Relationships among structural empowerment, psychological empowerment, and burnout in registered staff nurses working in outpatient dialysis centers. *Nephrology Nursing Journal, 38.* Retrieved from http://www.prolibraries.com/anna/?select=new_sessionlist&conferenceID=42&f_2=147

Offerman, L. (2010). Empowerment. In G. R. Hickman (Ed.). *Leading organizations: Perspectives in a new era* (2nd ed., pp. 191-194). Los Angeles, CA: SAGE.

Osborne, G. R. (2006). *The hermeneutical spiral: A comprehensive introduction to Biblical interpretation* (Rev. ed.). Downers Grove, IL: IVP Academic.

Ostroff, C. (1992). The relationship between satisfaction, attitudes, and performance: An organizational level analysis. *Journal of Applied Psychology, 77*(6), 963-974. doi:10.1037//0021-9010.77.6.963

Parboteeah, K. P., & Cullen, J. B. (2010). Ethical climates and spirituality. In R. A. Giacalone, & C. L. Jurkiewicz (Eds.), *Handbook of workplace spirituality and organizational performance* (2nd ed., pp. 99-113). New York, NY: M. E. Sharp.

Pate, L. D. (1991). Pentecostal mission from the two-thirds world. In M. W. Dempster, B. D. Klaus, & D. Peterson (Eds.), *Called & empowered: Global mission in Pentecostal perspective* (pp. 242-258). Peabody, MA: Hendrickson.

Patton, M. Q. (2002). *Qualitative research & evaluation methods* (3rd ed.). Thousand Oaks, CA: Sage.

Patterson, K. (2003). *Servant leadership: A theoretical model.* Paper presented at the Servant Leadership Research Roundtable, Regent University, Virginia Beach, VA. Retrieved from www.regent.edu/acad/global/publications/ sl_proceedings/2003/patterson_servant_leadership.pdf

Patzia, A. G. (1990). Ephesians, Colossians, Philemon. In W. W. Gasque (Ed.), *New International Biblical commentary* (Vol. 10). Peabody, MA: Hendrickson.

Pelit, E., Öztürk, Y., & Arslantürk, Y. (2011). The effects of employee empowerment on employee job satisfaction: A study on hotels in Turkey. *International Journal of Contemporary Hospitality, 23*(6), 784-802. doi:10.1108/09596111111153475

Pembroke, N. (2006). *Renewing pastoral practice: Trinitarian perspectives on pastoral care and counseling.* Burlington, VT: Ashgate.

Petrucci, T. (2011). Divine empowerment of leaders in early Christianity. *Emerging Leadership Journeys, 4*(1), 58-69. Retrieved from http://www.regent. edu/acad/global/publications/elj/vol4iss1/Petrucci_V4I1_pp58-69.pdf

Pfeffer, J. (2005). Understanding the role of power in decision-making. In J. M. Shafritz, J. S. Ott, & Y. S. Jang (Eds.), *Classics of organizational theory* (6th ed., pp. 289-303). Belmont, CA: Wadsworth.

Placher, W. C. (2005). *Callings* (Kindle ed.). Grand Rapids, MI: William B. Eerdmans.

Poole, E. (2008). Organizational spirituality: A literature review. *Journal of Business Ethics, 84*, 577-588. doi:10.1007/s10551-008-9726-z

Prime, D., & Begg, A. (2004). *Pastor: Understanding our calling and work* (Kindle ed.). Chicago, IL: Moody.

Psoinos, A., & Smithson, S. (2002). Employee empowerment in manufacturing: A study of organizations in the UK. *New Technology, 17*(2), 132-148. doi:10.1111/1468-005X.00099

Pyakuryal, K. (2001). Weberian model of social stratification—A viewpoint. *Occasional papers in Sociology and Anthropology, 7*, 14-25. Retrieved from http://www.nepjol.info.php/OPSA/article/view/1108

Ramsay, W. M. (1904). *The seven letters to the seven churches in Asia.* Retrieved from Christian Classics Ethereal Library website: www.ccel.org/ramsay/letters.html

Raven, B. H. (1999). Kurt Lewin address: Influence, power, religion, and the mechanisms of social control. *Journal of Social Issues, 55*(1), 161-186. doi:10.1111/0022-4537.00111

Read, J. H. (1991). Thomas Hobbes: Power in the state of nature, power in civil society. *Polity, 23*(4), 505-525. doi:10.2307/3235060

Reymond, R. L. (1991). Incarnation. In W. A. Elwell (Ed.), *The concise Evangelical dictionary of theology* (p. 243). Grand Rapids, MI: Baker Book House.

Robbins, T. L., Crino, M. D., & Fredendall, L. D. (2002). An integrative model of the empowerment process. *Human Resources Management Review, 12*, 419-443. doi:10.1016/S1053-4822(02)00068-2

Robbins, V. K. (n.d.). *interpretation.* Retrieved from http://www.religion.emory.edu/faculty/robbins/SRI/index.html

Robbins, V. K. (1996a). *Exploring the texture of texts: A guide to interpretation.* Harrisburg, PA: Trinity Press International.

Robbins, V. K. (1996b). *The tapestry of early Christian literature: Rhetoric, society, and ideology.* New York, NY: Routledge.

Robbins, V. K. (1999). *interpretation from its beginnings to the present.* Retrieved from www.religion.emory.edu/faculty/robbins/Pdfs/SNTSPretSocRhetfromBeginning.pdf

Robbins, V. K. (2004). *Beginnings and developments in interpretation.* Retrieved from www.religion.emory.edu/faculty/robbins/Pdfs/SRIBegDevRRA.pdf

Ryan, D. (2006). *Max Weber: "Class, status, and party."* Retrieved from http://www.ac.wwu.edu/~jimi/363/webercsp.pdf

Ryken, L. (1987). *Words of life: A literary introduction to the New Testament*. Grand Rapids, MI: Baker Book House.

Ryrie, C. C. (1999). *Basic theology*. Chicago, IL: Moody Press.

Sadan, E. (2004). *Empowerment and community planning* (ebook). Retrieved from http://mpow.org

Salancik, G. R., & Pfeffer. J. (2001). Who gets power—And how they hold on to it? In W. E. Natemeyer, & J. T. McMahon (Eds.), *Classics of organizational behavior* (3rd ed., pp. 303-320). Long Grove, IL: Waveland Press.

Schaff, P. (1996). Apostolic Christianity. In *History of the Christian church* (Vol. 1, 3rd ed.). Peabody, MA: Hendrickson.

Schreiner, I. R. (1990). *Interpreting the Pauline epistles*. Grand Rapids, MI: Baker Book House.

Schütz, J. H. (2007). *Paul and the anatomy of apostolic authority*. Louisville, KY: Westminster John Knox Press.

Seibert, S. E., Silver, S. R., & Randolph, W. A. (2004). Taking empowerment to the next level: A multiple-level model of empowerment, performance, and satisfaction. *Academy of Management Journal, 47*(3), 332-349. doi:10.2307/20159585

Self, C. L. S. (2009). *Love and organizational leadership: An intertexture analysis of 1 Corinthians 13* (Doctoral dissertation). Available from ProQuest Dissertations and Theses database. (UMI No. 3377775)

Shedd, W. G. T. (1888). *Dogmatic theology* (Vol. 1). Retrieved from http://www.archive.org/details/dogmatictheolog01shedgoog

Sheldon, H. C. (1988). The early church. In *History of the Christian church* (Vol. 1). Peabody, MA: Hendrickson.

Showkeir, J. D. (2002). The business case for servant-leadership. In L. C. Spears, & M. Lawrence (Eds.), *Focus on leadership: Servant-leadership for the 21st century* (pp. 153-166). New York, NY: John Wiley & Sons.

Smith, G. V. (1975). Paul's use of Psalms 68:18 in Ephesians 4:8. *Journal of the Evangelical Theological Society, 18*(3), 181-189.

Smith, G. V. (1986). Prophet. In G. W. Bromiley (Ed.), *The new international standard Bible encyclopedia* (Vol. 3, pp. 986-1004). Grand Rapids, MI: William B. Eerdmans.

Smith, V., & Smith, Y. S. (2003). *An analysis of power in Christian leadership.* Proceedings of the Christian Business Faculty Association Conference, Virginia Beach, VA. Retrieved from www.cbfa.org/Smith.pdf

Smith, W. (n.d.). *Smith's Bible dictionary.* Retrieved from Christian Classics Ethereal Library website: www.ccel.org/ccel/smith_w/bibledict

Snodderly, M. E. (2008). *A investigation of the Johannine understanding of the "works of the devil" in 1 John 3:8.* Retrieved from http://uir.unisa.ac.za/handle/10500/2843

Spears, L. C. (1995). Introduction: Servant-leadership and the Greenleaf legacy. In L. C. Spears (Ed.), *Reflections on leadership* (pp. 1-15). New York, NY: John Wiley & Sons.

Spears, L. C., & Lawrence, M. (2002). Introduction: Tracing the past, present, and future of servant-leadership. In L. C. Spears, & M. Lawrence (Eds.), *Focus on leadership: Servant-leadership for the 21st century* (pp. 1-16). New York, NY: John Wiley & Sons.

Spreitzer, G. M. (1995). Psychological empowerment in the workplace: Dimensions, measurement and validation. *Academy of Management Journal, 38*(5), 1442-1465. doi:10.2307/256865

Spreitzer, G. M. (1996). Social structural characteristics of psychological empowerment. *Academy of Management, 39*(2), 483-504. doi:10.2307/256789

Spreitzer, G. M. (2008). Taking stock: A review of more than twenty years of research on empowerment at work. In J. Barling & C. L. Cooper (Eds.), *The SAGE handbook of organizational behavior* (Vol. 1-2, pp. 54-72). London, England: SAGE. Retrieved from http://knowledge.sagepub.com/view/ hdbk_orgbehavior1/n4.xml

Stern, D. H. (1992). *Jewish New Testament commentary.* Clarksville, MD: Jewish New Testament Publications.

Stetzer, E., & Rainer, T. S. (2010). *Transformational church.* Nashville, TN: B&H.

Stone, A. G., Russell, R. F., & Patterson, K. (2003). Transformational leadership versus servant leadership: A difference in leader focus. *The Leadership & Organizational Development Journal, 25*(4), 349-361. doi:10:1108/01437730410538671

Strong, A. H. (1889). *Systematic theology*. Retrieved from http://archive.org/details/systematictheolo00str

Stronstad, R. (1984). *The charismatic theology of St. Luke*. Peabody, MA: Hendrickson.

Sun, L., Zhang, Z., Qi, J., & Chen, Z. X. (2010). Empowerment and creativity: A cross-level investigation. *The Leadership Quarterly, 23*, 55-65. doi:10.1016/j.leaqua.2011.11.005

Tajfel, H., & Turner, J. C. (1985). The social identity theory of ingroup behavior. In S. Worchel & W. G. Austin (Eds.), *Psychology of intergroup relations* (2nd ed., pp. 7-24). Chicago, IL: Nelson-Hall.

Taylor, F. W. (2011). The principles of scientific management. In W. E. Natemeyer & J. T. McMahon (Eds.), *Classics of organizational behavior* (3rd ed., pp. 3-18). Long Grove, IL: Waveland Press.

Taylor, R. A. (1991). The use of Psalm 68:18 in Ephesians 4:8 in light of the ancient versions. *Bibliotheca Sacra, 148*, 319-336.

Thielman, F. S. (2007). Ephesians. In G. K. Beal, & D. A. Carson (Eds.), *Commentary on the New Testament use of the Old Testament* (pp. 813-833). Grand Rapids, MI: Baker Academic.

Thiessen, H. C. (1979). *Lectures in systematic theology*. Grand Rapids, MI: William B. Eerdmans.

Thomas, K. W., & Velthouse, B. A. (1990). Cognitive elements of empowerment: An "interpretive" model of intrinsic task motivation. *Academy of Management Review, 15*(4), 666-681. doi:10.5465/AMR.1990.4310926

Toon, P. (1984). *The ascension of our Lord*. New York, NY: Thomas Nelson.

Unger, M. (1998). Prophets. In *Unger's Bible dictionary*. Chicago, IL: Moody.

Wachob, W. H. (1993). "The rich in faith" and "poor in spirit": The function of a saying of Jesus in the epistle of James. *Dissertation Abstract International-A, 54*(08), 3074.

Wagner, C. P. (1979). *Your spiritual gifts can help your church grow.* Ventura, CA: Regal Books.

Wagner, J. I. J., Cummings, G., Smith, D. L., Olsen, J., Anderson, L., & Warren, S. (2010). The relationship between structural empowerment and psychological empowerment for nurses: A systematic review. *Journal of Nursing Empowerment, 18,* 448-462. doi:10.1111/j.1365-2834.2010.01088.x

Walumbwa, F. O., Avolio, B. J., Garder, W. L., Wernsing, T. S., & Peterson, S. J. (2008). Authentic leadership: Development and validation of a theory-based measure. *Journal of Management, 34*(1), 89-126. doi:10.1177/0149206307308913

Walvoord, J. F. (1964). The present universal Lordship of Christ. *Bibliotheca Sacra,* 99-106. Retrieved from http://www.walvoord.com/article198

Warrington, K. (2008). *Pentecostal theology: A theology of empowerment.* New York, NY: t&tclark.

Weissberg, R. (1999). *The politics of empowerment* (Kindle ed.). Westport, CT: Praeger.

Westcott, B. F., Y Hort, F. J. A. (1988). *Introduction to the New Testament in the original Greek.* Peabody, MA: Hendrickson.

Wilkes, C. G. (1996). *Jesus on leadership: Becoming a servant leader.* Nashville, TN: LifeWay Press.

Wilkes, C. G. (1998). *Jesus on leadership.* Carol Stream, IL: Tyndale House.

Wilkinson, A. (1998). Empowerment: Theory and practice. *Personnel Review, 27*(1), 40-56. doi:10.1108/00483489810368549

Willer, D., Lovaglia, M. J., & Markousky, B. (1997). Power and influence: A theoretical bridge. *Social Focus, 76*(2), 571-603. doi:10.2307/2580725

Williams, J. R. (1996). *Renewal theology: Systematic theology from a Charismatic perspective.* Grand Rapids, MI: Zondervan Publishing House.

Wilson, A. (2007). Christ ascended for us—"The ascension: What is it and why does it matter?" *Evangel, 25*(2), 48-52. Retrieved from http://www.biblicalstudies.org.uk/pdf/evangel/25-2_wilson.pdf.

Wilson, B., & Laschinger, H. K. S. (1994). Staff nurses perspectives of job empowerment and organizational commitment: A test of Kanter's theory of structural power in organizations. *Journal of Nursing Administration, 24*(45), 39-47. doi:10.1097/00005110-199404010-00007

Wilson, E. J. (2008). Hard power, soft power, smart power. *The ANNALS of the American of Political and Social Science, 616,* 110-124. doi:10.1177/0002716207312618

Winston, B. (2002). *Be a leader for God's sake.* Virginia Beach, VA: Regent University Press, School of Leadership.

Winston, B. (2003). *Extending Patterson's servant leadership model: Explaining how leaders and followers interact in a circular model.* Paper presented at the Servant Leadership Research Roundtable, Virgina Beach, VA. Retrieved from http://www.regent.edu/acad/global/publications/sl_proceedings/winston_extending_patterson.pdf

Witherington, B. (1998). *The Acts of the Apostles: A commentary.* Grand Rapids, MI: William B. Eerdmans.

Witherington, B. (2007). *The letters to Philemon, the Colossians, and the Ephesians: A commentary on the captivity epistles.* Grand Rapids, MI: William B. Eerdmans.

Witherington, B. (2009). *What's in the Word: Rethinking the character of the New Testament* (Kindle ed.). Waco, TX: Balor University Press.

Wood, S. A. (1978). Ephesians. In F. E. Gaebeien, & J. D. Douglas (Eds.), *The expositor's Bible commentary* (Vol. 11, pp. 5-92). Grand Rapids, MI: Zondervan Publishing House.

Yammarino, F. J. (1994). Indirect leadership: Transformational leadership at a distance. In B. M. Bass, & B. J. Avolio (Eds.), *Improving organizational effectiveness through transformational leadership* (pp. 26-47). Thousand Oaks, CA: SAGE.

Yong, A. (2006). Discerning the Spirit. *Christian Century, 123*(5), 31-33. Retrieved from http://www.christiancentury.org/article/2006-03/discerning-spirit

Yukl, G. (2010). *Leadership in organizations* (7th ed., Kindle ed.). Upper Saddle River, NJ: Pearson Prentice Hall.

A Model of Divine Empowerment

Table 16: Opening–Middle–Closing Inner Texture

Verse	Calling	Love	Unity	One	Maturity	Body	Authority	Gifting	Ascend	Descend
1	Calling/called									
2		love								
3			Unity of spirit							
4	Called/calling			One...one...one		One body				
5				One...one...one						
6				One...			Who is over all			
7								Grace was given / Christ's gift		
8								Gave gifts to men	He ascended	
9									He ascended	He had also descended
10							Above all heavens	And he gave	He who ascended	He who descended
11										
12					Building up	Body of Christ				
13			Unity of the faith		Mature man					
15		Speaking the truth in love			Grow up in all aspects		Him who is head			
16		Building up...in love	Fitted and held together		Growth of the body & building up	Whole body & of the body				

Appendix A

Ephesians 4:1-16 (English Text)

Ephesians 4:1-16 (New American Standard)

1 Therefore I, the prisoner of the Lord, implore you to walk in a manner worthy of the calling with which you have been called, **2** with all humility and gentleness, with patience, showing tolerance for one another in love, **3** being diligent to preserve the unity of the Spirit in the bond of peace.

4 There is one body and one Spirit, just as also you were called in one hope of your calling; **5** one Lord, one faith, one baptism, **6** one God and Father of all who is over all and through all and in all.

7 But to each one of us grace was given according to the measure of Christ's gift.

8 Therefore it says, "WHEN HE ASCENDED ON HIGH, HE LED CAPTIVE A HOST OF CAPTIVES, AND HE GAVE GIFTS TO MEN."

9 (Now this expression, "He ascended," what does it mean except that He also had descended into the lower parts of the earth?

10 He who descended is Himself also He who ascended far above all the heavens, so that He might fill all things.)

11 And He gave some as apostles, and some as prophets, and some as evangelists, and some as pastors and teachers, **12** for the equipping of the saints for the work of service, to the building up of the body of Christ; **13** until we all attain to the unity of the faith, and of the knowledge of the Son of God, to a mature man, to the measure of the stature which belongs to the fullness of Christ.

14 As a result, we are no longer to be children, tossed here and there by waves and carried about by every wind of doctrine, by the trickery of men, by craftiness in deceitful scheming; **15** but speaking the truth in love, we are to grow up in all aspects into Him who is the head, even Christ, **16** from whom the whole body, being fitted and held together by what every joint supplies, according to the proper working of each individual part, caused the growth of the body for the building up of itself in love.

Appendix B

Ephesians 4:1-16 (English/Greek Text)

Ephesians 4:1-16 (Greek Text)

[Eph.4.1] παρακαλω [I EXHORT] ουν [THEREFORE] υμας [YOU,] εγω [I] ο [THE] δεσμιος [PRISONER] εν [IN "THE"] κυριω [LORD,] αξιως [WORTHILY] περιπατησαι [TO WALK] της [OF THE] κλησεως [CALLING] ης [WHEREWITH] εκληθητε [YE WERE CALLED,]

[Eph.4.2] μετα [WITH] πασης [ALL] ταπεινοφροσυνης [HUMILITY] και [AND] πραοτητος [MEEKNESS,] μετα [WITH] μακροθυμιας [LONGSUFFERING,] ανεχομενοι [BEARING WITH] αλληλων [ONE ANOTHER] εν [IN] αγαπη [LOVE;]

[Eph.4.3] σπουδαζοντες [BEING DILIGENT] τηρειν [TO KEEP] την [THE] ενοτητα [UNITY] του [OF THE] πνευματος [SPIRIT] εν [IN] τω [THE] συνδεσμω της [BOND] ειρηνης [OF PEACE.]

[Eph.4.4] εν [ONE] σωμα [BODY] και [AND] εν [ONE] πνευμα [SPIRIT,] καθως [EVEN AS] και [ALSO] εκληθητε [YE WERE CALLED] εν [IN] μια [ONE] ελπιδι [HOPE] της κλησεως 2821 υμων [OF YOUR CALLING;]

[Eph.4.5] εις [ONE] κυριος [LORD,] μια [ONE] πιστις [FAITH,] εν [ONE] βαπτισμα [BAPTISM;]

[Eph.4.6] εις [ONE] θεος [GOD] και [AND] πατηρ [FATHER] παντων [OF ALL,] ο [WHO "IS"] επι [OVER] παντων [ALL,] και [AND] δια [THROUGH] παντων [ALL,] και [AND] εν [IN] πασιν [ALL] υμιν [YOU.]

[Eph.4.7] ενι δε εκαστω [BUT TO EACH ONE] ημων [OF US] εδοθη η [WAS GIVEN] χαρις [GRACE] κατα [ACCORDING TO] το [THE] μετρον [MEASURE] της [OF THE] δωρεας [GIFT] του [OF THE] χριστου [CHRIST.]

[Eph.4.8] διο [WHEREFORE] λεγει [HE SAYS,] αναβας [HAVING ASCENDED UP] εις [ON] υψος [HIGH] ηχμαλωτευσεν [HE LED CAPTIVE] αιχμαλωσιαν [CAPTIVITY,] και [AND] εδωκεν [GAVE] δοματα τοις [GIFTS] ανθρωποις [TO MEN.]

[Eph.4.9] το δε [BUT THAT] ανεβη [HE ASCENDED,] τι [WHAT] εστιν [IS IT] ει μη [BUT] οτι [THAT] και [ALSO] κατεβη [HE DESCENDED] πρωτον [FIRST] εις [INTO] τα [THE] κατωτερα [LOWER] μερη [PARTS] της [OF THE] γης [EARTH?]

[Eph.4.10] ο [HE THAT] καταβας [DESCENDED] αυτος [THE SAME] εστιν [IS] και [ALSO] ο [WHO] αναβας [ASCENDED] υπερανω [ABOVE] παντων [ALL] των [THE] ουρανων [HEAVENS,] ινα [THAT] πληρωση [HE MIGHT FILL] τα 3588 παντα [ALL THINGS;]

[Eph.4.11] και [AND] αυτος [HE] εδωκεν [GAVE] τους μεν [SOME] αποστολους [APOSTLES,] τους δε [AND SOME] προφητας [PROPHETS,] τους δε [AND SOME] ευαγγελιστας [EVANGELISTS,] τους δε [AND SOME] ποιμενας [SHEPHERDS] και [AND] διδασκαλους [TEACHERS,]

[Eph.4.12] προς [WITH A VIEW TO] τον [THE] καταρτισμον [PERFECTING] των [OF THE] αγιων [SAINTS;] εις [FOR] εργον [WORK] διακονιας [OF "THE" SERVICE,] εις [FOR] οικοδομην [BUILDING UP] του [OF THE] σωματος [BODY] του [OF THE] χριστου [CHRIST;]

[Eph.4.13] μεχρι [UNTIL] καταντησωμεν οι [WE MAY ARRIVE] παντες [ALL] εις [AT] την [THE] ενοτητα [UNITY] της [OF THE] πιστεως [FAITH] και [AND] της [OF THE] επιγνωσεως [KNOWLEDGE] του [OF THE] υιου του [SON] θεου [OF GOD,] εις [AT] ανδρα [A MAN] τελειον [FULL GROWN] εις [AT "THE"] μετρον [MEASURE] ηλικιας [OF "THE" STATURE] του [OF THE] πληρωματος [FULNESS] του [OF THE] χριστου [CHRIST;]

[Eph.4.14] ινα [THAT] μηκετι [NO LONGER] ωμεν [WE MAY BE] νηπιοι [INFANTS,] κλυδωνιζομενοι [BEING TOSSED] και [AND] περιφερομενοι [CARRIED ABOUT] παντι [BY EVERY] ανεμω [WIND] της [OF THE] διδασκαλιας [TEACHING] εν [IN] τη [THE] κυβεια των [SLEIGHT] ανθρωπων [OF MEN,] εν [IN] πανουργια [CRAFTINESS] προς [WITH A VIEW TO] την [THE] μεθοδειαν της [SYSTEMATIZING] πλανης [OF ERROR;]

[Eph.4.15] αληθευοντες δε [BUT HOLDING THE TRUTH] εν [IN] αγαπη [LOVE] αυξησωμεν [WE MAY GROW UP] εις [INTO] αυτον [HIM] τα παντα [IN ALL THINGS,] ος [WHO] εστιν [IS] η [THE] κεφαλη [HEAD,] ο [THE] χριστος [CHRIST :]

[Eph.4.16] εξ [FROM] ου [WHOM] παν [ALL] το [THE] σωμα [BODY,] συναρμολογουμενον [FITTED TOGETHER] και [AND] συμβιβαζομενον

[COMPACTED] δια [BY] πασης [EVERY] αφης της [JOINT] επιχορηγιας [OF SUPPLY] κατ [ACCORDING TO "THE"] ενεργειαν [WORKING] εν [IN " ITS "] μετρω [MEASURE] ενος εκαστου [OF EACH ONE] μερους [PART,] την [THE] αυξησιν [INCREASE] του [OF THE] σωματος [BODY] ποιειται [MAKES FOR ITSELF] εις [TO] οικοδομην ["THE" BUILDING UP] εαυτου [OF ITSELF] εν [IN] αγαπη [LOVE.]

ABOUT THE AUTHOR

Dr. Jimmy D. Bayes has over twenty-five years working in corporations, nonprofit organizations, and churches. He has started or helped start four nonprofit organizations and is part owner of a training company.

Training and education has always been his focus and he has an earned Ph.D. in Organizational Leadership from Regent University. He currently conducts training in entrepreneurship, employee training, and organizational development as well as coaching and consulting.

Dr. Bayes lives in Bryan, Texas with his family.

www.ingramcontent.com/pod-product-compliance
Lightning Source LLC
Chambersburg PA
CBHW080540170426
43195CB00016B/2626